Praise for

Introducing Christian Ethics

"A masterpiece! One of our best Christian ethicists synthesizes a lifetime of careful reflection in this superb survey of Christian ethics. In this brilliant combination of scholarly theory and practical wisdom, Gushee combines personal experience and theoretical analysis. Above all, Gushee seeks to be faithful to the biblical Jesus. A must read."
—**Ronald J. Sider, founder of Evangelicals for Social Action, Distinguished Professor Emeritus of Theology, Holistic Ministry and Public Policy, Palmer Seminary at Eastern University**

"The effort to find the right text to help guide students through their introduction to the field of Christian ethics can be arduous. David Gushee, former president of the Society of Christian Ethics and the American Academy of Religion, provides a ready solution to that problem in this accessible, yet extremely thorough, overview of the field. In its pages, Gushee is exhaustive and creative as he demonstrates extreme acuity and dexterity that can only come from decades of serious engagement with the field. He offers a comprehensive overview of Christian moral theories and an engagement with topics that help students to value the meaning and use of authoritative sources for Christian moral life. These collected classroom lectures provide readers of all levels with insight. This is a tremendous addition to the study of Christian ethics."
—**Reggie L. Williams, Ph.D., Professor of Christian Ethics, McCormick Theological Seminary**

"David Gushee not only has outdone himself, but also has raised the bar for the field of Christian social ethics. *Introducing Christian Ethics* is a standard bearer that should serve as required reading for all core courses in theological ethics, a reflective guide for every scholar in the field, and a path forward for thinking people of faith who are searching for ultimate meaning. Different from prior analyses, this text is an intriguing exploration for troubled times that necessitate an even more rigorous, faithful, and impactful approach to ethics. Gushee covers the field in a compellingly cogent and constructive fashion and provides a hopeful vision for all who search for religious significance. The work should be regarded, appreciated and utilized as a true magnum opus in the fullest sense of the term, one from which future generations will harvest the bountiful fruit of Gushee's intellectual labor."
—**Stacey Floyd-Thomas, Associate Professor of Ethics and Society, Vanderbilt University Divinity School**

"An important book by one of the leading voices in Christian ethics in the 21st century. David Gushee demonstrates the unique combination of true scholarship, spiritual mastery, and didactic accessibility. From beginning to end this volume presents a lucid introduction to Christian moral life, offers urgent ethical orientations in the light of the coming of God's Kingdom, and points at fresh and relevant insights into today's moral issues. On top of this, Gushee clearly transmits, and furthers, the legacy of his friend and mentor Glen Stassen, who played a key role in the western church's discussions on violence and non-violence in recent decades, and subsequently its interpretation of the Sermon on the Mount. In short, *Introducing Christian Ethics* may be one of the best moral compasses to consult by students of religion, humanities, theology, philosophy, and anthropology, and by pastors, in the coming years. Christianity balances on the brink of moral meltdown and is in desperate need of spiritual guidance. Gushee's oeuvre, career, and personal journey, evidently make him qualify as 'fidus interpres,' a genuine navigator for the Christian church."
—**Henk Bakker, Full Professor at the Faculty of Religion and Theology, Vrije Universiteit Amsterdam, The Netherlands**

"I've long known David Gushee as a fellow activist, inspired by his faith to advocate for the disinherited and the marginalized. His activism flows from a principled social ethics that is an outcome of his life-long commitment to Christianity. That's how I read *Introducing Christian Ethics*, as a handbook of principled, impassioned activism for how to live a moral life in today's world with its real-life issues and challenges."

—Jennifer Butler, CEO, Faith in Public Life, author of *Who Stole My Bible: Reclaiming Scripture as a Handbook for Resisting Tyranny*

"*Introducing Christian Ethics* is not just a new book, but an urgent prophetic and pastoral call to the American churches right now! White American churches, in particular, are living in captivity to the idols of white Christian nationalism with the real threat of political idolatry replacing Christian ethics. David Gushee is one of the key Christian ethicists of our time, and he is the right person at the right time for this task. He has long been a convenor of ethicists and has always sought to put ethics at the center of our public life. In *Introducing Christian Ethics* David has put together a comprehensive catalogue of the key issues surrounding ethics, applied to faith, and its application to real-world issues. It is a must read for anyone at the intersection of faith and public life."

—Jim Wallis, founder of Sojourners, Chair in Faith and Justice, McCourt School of Public Policy, and Director, Georgetown University Center on Faith and Justice

"*Introducing Christian Ethics* is an inspiring take on Christian life and thought, by an ecumenical scholar with a biblical vision and a passion for justice. Readers will appreciate David Gushee's broad and deep theological knowledge and his acute exploration of social and political challenges. The author's references to his own experiences, and the links to his video presentations, will make the subject matter come alive for students, offering a path into theology that is sure to engage their own questions."

—Lisa Sowle Cahill, J. Donald Monan, S.J. Professor of Theology, Boston College

"This is the book on Christian ethics that many of us have been waiting for. Faced with the challenges of navigating our way in a morally confusing climate, we need some reliable guideposts on the way. And in the light of the 'culture wars' that, sadly, have spilled over into church life, we urgently need to examine again the biblical and theological roots of our faith to determine our ethical stances today."
—**Tony Peck, General Secretary, European Baptist Federation, 2004–2021**

"*Introducing Christian Ethics* is Gushee's comprehensive one-stop manual on what it means to live Christianly. He hits every major ethical issue that Christians are engaging (and debating) with depth, nuance, wisdom, and provocation. I will benefit greatly from this invaluable resource as will any who turn to it for guidance in today's world."
—**Peter Enns, Abram S. Clemens Professor of Biblical Studies at Eastern University and author of *The Bible Tells Me So***

"Readers of this excellent book will welcome the clarity, breadth, and honesty of its author, a well-known post-evangelical Christian ethicist who discusses the moral teaching of Jesus as central to his understanding of ethics … By any standard, this book is a major tome in the field of Christian studies that is destined to replace most similar texts."
—**Peter J. Paris, Elmer G. Homrighausen Professor Emeritus, Christian Social Ethics, Princeton Theological Seminary**

"Built upon the teaching materials that he has used for his long teaching career at a college and a seminary, David Gushee offers a highly accessible, well-informed, and carefully balanced introduction to Christian ethics that is relevant and resourceful for both students and lay Christians. In particular, the ongoing dialogue between Christian ethics and general ethics and the breadth of topics are its distinctive merits. This book deserves the close attention of pastors, professors, and educators who are concerned about the mature moral formation of Christians today."
—**Hak Joon Lee, Lewis B. Smedes Professor of Christian Ethics, Fuller Theological Seminary**

Introducing Christian Ethics

Core Convictions for Christians Today

David P. Gushee

To learn more about this book and its author, please visit
DavidPGushee.com.

Cover design and illustration by Rick Nease
www.RickNeaseArt.com

Published by
Front Edge Publishing
42807 Ford Road, Suite 234
Canton, MI, 48187

Front Edge Publishing books are available for discount bulk purchases for events, corporate use and small groups. Special editions, including books with corporate logos, personalized covers and customized interiors are available for purchase. For more information, contact Front Edge Publishing at info@FrontEdgePublishing.com.

For my beloved grandchildren,
Jonah and Melody

Contents

Foreword

In ancient Rome, a genius was the guiding spirit of a person, family, or place. By the time of Caesar Augustus, who was widely recognized as possessing a particularly powerful genius, the word became associated with divine inspiration. In contemporary usage, genius refers to a person possessing extraordinary innate talents or abilities. However, it is the rare genius that not only exhibits extraordinary ability, but also is able to share that genius with others through great teaching. I have always marveled at the ease with which David Gushee communicates complex ideas in everyday language and I am humbled by the integrity with which he invites his readers along his personal journey.

No one questions Michael Jordan's genius as an athlete—he is regarded as the greatest basketball player of all time—but he never distinguished himself as a coach guiding and forming the next generation of players. In that regard David Gushee's genius far exceeds that of Jordan, for Gushee has distilled a lifetime of learning, thinking, and teaching Christian ethics in universities, seminaries, churches, and other settings into a comprehensive yet very readable book. Drawing on his own extraordinary journey as a practicing Christian and professional ethicist who has engaged all the major moral dilemmas confronting the Christian faith in the postmodern world, *Introducing Christian Ethics* serves as both a practical manual for how one ought to live the Christian life and an encyclopedic introduction to the academic discipline of Christian ethics.

Throughout the text Gushee's considerable genius manages to interject a pastoral focus without sacrificing intellectual rigor, explore contemporary challenges to Christian faith without disregarding the vast resources of the Christian tradition, and give preference to marginalized and silenced voices—those whom Thurman called the "disinherited" of history—without losing sight of the fact that Jesus's good news of liberation extends to both the oppressed *and* their oppressors. In the end, this book is the performative embodiment of Christ-like compassion and prophetic zeal because rather than allow readers to avoid the concrete demands of Jesus's teachings and moral example, the book confronts readers while guiding them through an ultimately edifying process of self-examination.

Rubén Rosario Rodríguez
Professor of Systematic Theology at Saint Louis University

To watch Dr. Gushee reading the
Preface
Follow this link:
https://youtu.be/ZlvNJIs-jWY
Or scan the QR code.

To listen to the audio, follow this link:
https://qrco.de/bcLsAI
Or scan the QR code.

To scan a QR code, download a QR reader from the app store on your device, open the application, follow the directions, and point your device's camera at the code.

Preface

In the Spring term of 2021, during COVID days, I taught my final seminary introduction to Christian ethics course in the United States. My first such course was offered at Southern Baptist Theological Seminary in Fall 1993. I estimate that I offered versions of the introductory course at least 30 times in 28 years, the last half of them at Mercer University's McAfee School of Theology here in Atlanta, Georgia.

I decided in Fall 2020 to write entirely new lectures for this final introductory class. This book is the ultimate result of that effort. I am deeply grateful to all the students who have gone on the seminary ethics journey with me, but I especially wish to express my gratitude to my delightful final class of introductory students at Mercer, with whom these lectures were developed: Angel, Ashley, Jamila, Kristen, Naomi, Rachel, Rochelle, and Talisia.

I am also deeply grateful to the great team at Front Edge Publishing for their enthusiasm in embracing this project and getting it out not only in print, but also in video and audio format for the widest possible use. Warmest thanks go to Jeremy Hall, my dear protégé, co-worker, and friend, who undertook the video and audio production.

The fact that this material is being simultaneously made available in audio, video, ebook, and print formats has affected certain formatting decisions. We want the hearing, viewing, and reading content to be identical. For this reason, I am not using footnotes or endnotes. I demonstrate intellectual indebtedness by naming the author and work within the text, while moving the full reference to the Works Cited section. There are no explanatory notes. This approach requires me to cite only those works that have seriously affected the development of my thinking, which offers insights into my intellectual journey, if nothing else.

All technical terms used in this volume are noted on their first use with the combination of italics and bold, like this: ***technical term***. If the meaning of a technical term is not quoted, I offer a brief sketch within the text.

To help a bit in situating the intellectual lineage of ethics, I give birth and death dates for all deceased scholars mentioned in the book.

A few sections of this book began their life in other venues and have been adapted for use here:

- Chapter 8, on truthfulness, is adapted from a series of essays I published in 2020–21 in my role as senior columnist at Baptist News Global.

- Chapter 9, on the sacredness of life, summarizes material drawn from my 2013 book, *The Sacredness of Human Life*, published by Eerdmans Publishing Company.

- Chapter 12, on forgiveness, adapts and develops concepts in an essay called "The Limitations of Forgiveness," which can be found in *The Art of Forgiveness*, a 2018 collection with Fortress Press edited by Philip Halstead and Myk Habets.

- The quotes from Black novelists that are included in Chapter 15 were first used in my 2018 American Academy of Religion presidential address, entitled "In the Ruins of White Evangelicalism: Interpreting a Compromised Christian Tradition through the Witness of African-American Literature," published in the *Journal of the American Academy of Religion* 87, 1 (March 2019), pp. 1–17.

- Chapter 19, on marriage, summarizes material presented at length in my 2004 work, *Getting Marriage Right*, published by Baker Books.

- Chapter 25 adapts the Glen Stassen/David Gushee Four-Box Diagram, which appears in both the first and second editions of our jointly authored *Kingdom Ethics* (Intervarsity Press, 2003/Eerdmans, 2016). More broadly, *Kingdom Ethics*, especially the second edition, receives sustained attention in this new work.

I am grateful for the cooperation of these publishers in allowing new uses of these materials here.

In *Introducing Christian Ethics*, I take up 25 different subjects within Christian ethics. After the early chapters on scripture, theology, and method, I have arranged the remaining forays by thinking of the order in which moral issues emerge over the course of a lifetime. This is a new approach for me. Being nearly 60 years old and for six years a hands-on grandfather of Jonah and Melody Love, to whom I have dedicated this book, have helped lead me in this direction. Readers and instructors can, of course, take up the material in whatever order they choose.

A note about my intended readership seems relevant. More than in any of my earlier books, I am aiming for a global Christian audience with *Introducing Christian Ethics*. Partly this is because I have had the blessing of gaining a growing international audience in recent years. It is also happily rooted in my 2021 appointment as Chair in Christian Social Ethics at Vrije Universiteit (VU) Amsterdam, in cooperation with the International Baptist Theological Study (IBTS) Centre, one of VU's partner schools.

Even as this book was in development, leaders associated with IBTS Centre began strategizing with me to get this material into churches, colleges, and seminaries in many of the 52 nations with member bodies in the European Baptist Federation. This core IBTS planning group—David McMillan, Mike Pears, and Ingeberg Te Loo—became early readers of the manuscript.

With deep gratitude, I recognize my wife Jeanie and mother-in-law Lynnie for their skillful and time-consuming line-by-line review of the manuscript. The book is infinitely more pleasing to read because of their work. My agent David Morris has also engaged the manuscript carefully and aided greatly in the project's overall development. As always, final responsibility for the text rests with the author.

The legacy of my teacher, friend, and co-author Glen Stassen (1936–2014) looms over this book in a meaningful and complex way. His teaching and scholarship were essential in my development, and some of it, notably the first edition of *Kingdom Ethics*, was a shared venture between us. This new book offers the greatest tribute one can offer to another scholar—sustained critical engagement—some of the time with Glen's solo works, and some of the time with our joint projects.

Finally, the reader will note several references to my father, David Elwood Gushee. He was quite ill when I began this book, and he died before it was completed. Some of our last journey together makes its way into these pages. I honor him as I send this book into the world.

David P. Gushee
Atlanta, Georgia USA
June 2021

To watch Dr. Gushee deliver

Lecture 1: What is (Christian) Ethics?

Follow this link:

https://youtu.be/HYF7S5v6_f4

Or scan the QR code.

To listen to the audio, follow this link:

https://qrco.de/bcLsAI

Or scan the QR code.

To scan a QR code, download a QR reader from the app store on your device, open the application, follow the directions, and point your device's camera at the code.

CHAPTER I

What Is (Christian) Ethics?

1.1 The Historical Lineage of Christian Ethics

Every form of intellectual inquiry has a history. The discipline of Christian ethics is no exception. Here is my brief account of its lineage.

Christian ethics obviously begins with Jesus Christ, his person and work, his moral instruction and example.

Because Jesus is a historical figure, a first-century Galilean Jew, and because his teaching and way of life reveal the clear impact of his people and his context, the history of Christian ethics also can be said to begin with the texts of the Hebrew Bible, developments in Second Temple Judaism, and the challenging circumstances of first-century Jewish life in an occupied homeland.

Because Jewish life, in the homeland and in diaspora, occurred under the thumb of the Roman Empire and was affected by several centuries of Hellenistic influence, and because the early church spread around the Mediterranean world, Greco-Roman culture and moral philosophy also stand at the headwaters of Christian ethics with traces that can be seen in the Bible itself.

Moving forward into the Christian era, two millennia of Christian ethics has followed the contours and reflected the varied influences of Christian ecclesial, theological, and political history. Everything that we know about

Christianity's historical trajectory is relevant to understanding the development of Christian ethics. This is one reason why I tell my students that Christian ethics is intrinsically interdisciplinary. You need biblical studies, theology, philosophy, and church history to really understand it. And that is not to mention the relevant disciplines outside Christian thought.

In my view, the most important dimension of our historical trajectory is the way Christianity became the dominant religion in Europe. Under Rome, and again a millennium later during the colonial era, Europe became the center of political power for a large part of the world. In these circumstances, Christian ethics was transformed from a prophetic-populist Jewish resistance ethic to the moral code of the dominant, and dominating, European gentile civilizations.

However, something unexpected happened. As Christian conquerors spread their distorted version of the faith along with their colonists and their guns, many of the people whom they conquered, enslaved, and dominated embraced Christianity but then developed their own versions of theology and ethics. In one of the supreme ironies of history, these dispossessed peoples, mainly Indigenous, Latin American, African, and Asian, went back to the headwaters of the Christian faith to creatively retrieve the very Jewish-prophetic-populist resistance ethic that Jesus himself embraced and that imperial churches had obscured or reversed.

A geographic metaphor for these fateful developments might look like this. First there was Athens and Jerusalem as the font of Christian theology and ethics. Many of us were taught this version of Christian intellectual heritage. Now add imperial Christian Rome after the fourth century CE to make up a triad of Jerusalem + Athens + Rome. Now go forward a thousand years and add imperial colonizing Europe. Finally, add the surprising twist of subaltern resistance Christianity. The term **subaltern** is a term coined by Italian philosopher Antonio Gramsci (1891–1937) that essentially refers to peoples colonized and dominated by imperial powers. The term intentionally evokes both the "sub" (below) and "alter" (other) dimension of the experience of the colonized.

Christian ethics today comes in various versions reflecting different ways to put together and draw upon this long and complex history. Some versions lean in the direction of Athens and emphasize ancient Greek moral philosophy, with its towering figures of Socrates, Plato, and Aristotle. Others lean in the direction of Jerusalem and mainly work with biblical sources and their multiple trajectories. Some versions move forward a bit to dig deeply into European Christian historical sources, such as the church Fathers. Others focus on one of the Christian traditions birthed during the long era that gave us Roman Catholicism, Eastern Orthodoxy, and various versions of Protestantism. Still others mainly focus on subaltern resistance ethics, with the challenge they offer to every other Christian ethic.

A manageable two-volume set that sketches this history was offered in the early 1990s by Methodist ethicist Philip Wogaman under the titles *Christian Ethics: A Historical Introduction* and *Readings in Christian Ethics*. I taught these books for many years and commend them to you for introductory work. Though the field has continued to develop since that time, it is a good place to engage much of our field's history.

In this book, you will see me attempt various forays that draw from many of these tributaries of Christian ethics. My account of the field for these "last lectures" is certainly that—*my* account. I will do my best to "show my work," as when doing mathematics, to indicate where I am turning within the great tradition of Christian ethics to source the arguments that I develop. No two ethicists do this in the same way.

1.2 Ethics as Critical Reflection on Human Morality

One thing that sets Christian ethics apart from Christian theology is that many of the intellectual problems we ethicists think about are shared with all human beings, not just our fellow Christians. While the average human does not wonder about which atonement theory to embrace, most do think about things like whether lying or violence are ever morally right.

I am suggesting that there is an intrinsic moral dimension to human experience and that Christian ethics joins all human beings in reflecting on that dimension of life.

Following the approach of my doctoral advisor, Lutheran ethicist Larry Rasmussen, in his 1989 co-authored work, with Bruce Birch, *Bible and Ethics in the Christian Life*, I am making a rough distinction between **ethics** and **morality**. Strictly speaking, ethics is the work of critically "investigating morality, assessing it, and making moral recommendations" (p. 39). Morality, in turn, consists of "standards human beings develop and practice concerning their character and behavior toward themselves and others" (*Kingdom Ethics* [*KE*] Glossary, p. 465). A way to remember the distinction is this:

Ethics is the intellectual effort to critically examine human morality. The terms
are not always delineated in this way, but it is helpful to make the distinction.

Notice that my definition of morality is **descriptive**, not **normative**. I
am not saying that humans *should* develop moral standards. I am describing
a fact in the world, one of the most characteristic human behaviors. Humans
do develop and articulate moral standards, all the time.

Just listen when somebody is giving a tongue-lashing to (or about) someone else. You normally hear all kinds of negative **moral judgments** about
the one being criticized. Moral judgments happen when people apply their
working moral standards to somebody's behavior, either applauding or con-
demning actions accordingly.

The intrinsic moral dimension of human experience may seem obvious,
but it has interesting implications. Among them is that humans are the kind
of beings that have the capacity to develop moral standards, and that we
inhabit the kind of world in which we need to do so.

If we were sub-rational beings or purely creatures of instinct, we would
not have the freedom or the capacity to reflect and to emerge with moral
standards (technically called **moral norms**, e.g., definitions of what is morally right and wrong). Plants don't do moral reflection, neither do rocks, nor
presumably, do salmon or salamanders offer moral norms to one another.

Ethics does not invent the human propensity to articulate moral norms.
Instead, ethics is the second-order work of critically describing, assessing,
and proposing alternatives to the moral norms that people have adopted.
Ethics steps back from the maelstrom of human morality to offer critical
thinking about what exactly is going on here.

Some people are not interested in critical reflection about morality. They
simply accept what others tell them is right and wrong, good and bad, moral
and immoral. But what if those others are wrong? Can you think of any
examples of once broadly shared moral norms that we now know were
desperately wrong? I hope so! The work of ethics offers a very important
example of the necessity of critical thinking in human life, because many
times in history prevailing standards of "morality" have proved to be grotesquely immoral.

The term in ethics for the capacity and responsibility of human beings
to make moral choices and to be held accountable for them is **moral
agency**. The presupposition of moral agency is **moral autonomy**, or "moral

self-direction, independence, and self-rule" (*KE* Glossary, p. 464). Moral autonomy and moral agency are central presuppositions of ethics.

We must immediately note that not everyone has sufficient moral autonomy to exercise full moral agency. This would include babies, people in a comatose state, and people with severe mental disabilities. We also must not overlook those individuals and groups whose freedom is so unjustly and severely constrained by oppression that their moral agency has been largely taken away from them. The nature of moral agency in the lives of oppressed people has itself become a key theme in ethics that emerges from subaltern communities.

The work of morality involves choice-making on the part of at least relatively free and rational human beings. When we choose from among moral options, direct ourselves to act accordingly, and agree to be held responsible, we are exercising moral agency.

Think for a moment about the implications of living in the kind of world in which critical reflection on morality is needed. It must be that the proper shape of moral norms is not obvious, self-evident, or agreed. If it were, we would not need to reflect on which moral norms are true, right, or best. This must mean that the world as we find it is at least open to—or even requiring of—our serious ethical reflection. The world turns out to be morally open rather than closed. It requires hard decisions from us. And it is filled with people who utterly disagree with each other.

This could be a counsel of despair. We could stop trying to figure morality out. But, to the contrary, most people do develop heartfelt core moral beliefs. In fact, we do not appear to be able to live without them.

Let's follow James McClendon (1924–2000) and James Smith's 1994 book called *Defusing Religious Relativism* and use the term **convictions** when we are talking about those central beliefs (in our case, moral beliefs) that "cannot be relinquished without making X a significantly different person (or community) than before" (p. 5). Such convictions are life-defining and can be death-defying. They give life meaning and purpose. People will die for them. Sometimes they will also kill for them. Ethics examines that reality along with other dimensions of the moral arena.

1.3 The Big Question(s) of Ethics

One way to deepen our reflection on the moral dimension of human experience is to break it down into the most common questions that people tend to ask. I like to describe this as the One Big Question and then the six not-so-small questions that follow from the One Big Question.

The One Big Question in the moral arena is "How should I/we live?" This can be framed as broadly or as narrowly as one likes. Perhaps on a bleak fall day, over a cup or pipe you might find yourself asking this question in relation to the whole of your life: "How should I live my life?" Prepare for a long day.

Probably most often you and I will be asking this question in relation to a specific issue, concern, or relationship. How should I live in relation to money? In relation to politics? In relation to my mother?

Ethics examines the answers that people give to the question, "How should I (or we) live?" This is the One Big Question, and it has exercised the minds and hearts of pretty much every human being at one time or another.

But it is also possible to break this One Big Question down into several somewhat smaller questions. All of these are morally significant questions. We rarely ask them all, certainly not all at the same time. Whether we find ourselves inclined to ask one or another of these questions provides important clues to the way our moral sensibilities have developed, either from within us or from how we were raised. They also reflect different strands of moral tradition, and the extent to which we are open to critical thinking.

Here are the six not-so-small questions, with a few lines of comment about each. Most will be developed further in the next chapter.

1.3.1 What are the rules?

Human beings very often perceive the existence of moral rules that (ought to) govern our lives. Or if we do not perceive such rules, we seek them out and try to develop them. And of course, we enter a moral world that already exists and is filled with plenty of rules.

We will develop some detailed vocabulary around moral rules in the next chapter, but for now let us just begin by saying that one way to ask the One Big Question—how should I live?—is to break it down to the smaller question, what are the rules that should govern how I live?

The comforting thing about this question is that rules are often clear, direct, and unambiguous. They tell us directly what to do or to refrain from doing. Moral uncertainty is troubling, and in some cases agonizing. Having rules to tell us exactly how we should live removes a great deal of uncertainty. There is a reason why clear, unambiguous moral rules (sometimes called moral laws, or divine commandments) tend to be generated plentifully by religious traditions such as Judaism, Christianity, and Islam.

But, of course, rules also introduce their own problems, such as: What if we cannot agree on what the rules are? What if important moral rules conflict with each other? What if no one has ever made up a moral rule about this situation before?

1.3.2 What are the goals?

These perhaps surprising complexities related to moral rules have helped lead many ethicists to argue that the better question in the moral life is about moral goals. What purposes should I or we seek to achieve in life overall—or in relation to this or that morally significant area of life? Once we determine morally worthy goals to pursue, then the right course of action is that which most clearly advances progress toward those goals.

Some aspects of the moral life seem better addressed by this goals question than by the rules question. Let's say a core goal of your life is to be a loving partner. This sets you on a daily path of trying to discern what being a loving partner requires of you. It's not about adhering to rules, but instead aiming yourself toward this morally substantial goal. Rules alone do not a romance make, that is for sure.

One can easily make the case, as many have, including the ancient Greek philosophers, that rules are subordinate to goals. Take an example from education. For educators, our fundamental goal is to offer quality education to students. Every academic course lists some learning objectives that aim to fulfill this broader goal. The rules that are also listed on a course syllabus exist as means to the end of offering quality education.

When rule-thinking gets out of hand, as it sometimes does, even in academia (!), people can forget the reasons why the rules were there in the first place. But goal-thinkers can sometimes play fast and loose with the rules that provide order and fairness to most human endeavors.

1.3.3 What serves the needs of people and relationships?

This third question, which came into focus through the efforts of modern feminist thinkers beginning with Carol Gilligan's 1982 book *In a Different Voice*, decenters rules and goals and centers the "ethics of care" for people and relationships. The question is what course of action cares best for others and strengthens the relevant relationships involved.

The keen insight embedded in this question is this: Morality is a social concern. Moral questions and challenges arise in relationships. The more important the relationship is to us, the more urgent will be our sense that we need to act in such a way as to care for the people we love and to protect the relationships that we most value.

As I begin this book, I have entered a stage in life in which I have substantial responsibilities of care for my 90-year-old father, who lives in an independent-living community and whose health is fragile. When I wake up each day, one of the questions never far from my mind is this: "What do I need to do today to take care of my father?" And this: "What actions do I need to take that will demonstrate how much I value him and our relationship?"

This is a reminder that the most important moral questions are relational questions. Morality arises in relational contexts. Whatever rules we establish or goals that we set had best help us to care well for others and preserve or enhance important relationships. It is quite striking that this relational and care focus was not central in ethics until modern feminism. This says something rather disturbing about the way many men think, and about the blind spots of a discipline dominated by men until the late 20th century.

One challenge with this third question is determining how, or even whether, to rank-order our relationships such that some receive (for a while, or always) greater and more solicitous care while others receive less. Another concern is whether in attempting to care for people and relationships we might bend or even break important moral rules.

1.3.4 What kind of people should we be?

There is a way of looking at morality that focuses not so much on what we do, or on what the rules are, but on who we are. The term for this is *moral character*, "the qualities that mark or distinguish an individual or a people over time; moral constitution, temperament, and distinctive virtues and vices" (*KE* Glossary, p. 451). One of the great contributions of ancient Greek ethics is the claim that human actions flow from human character, which is where moral effort should therefore focus. This begins us on the trail toward *virtue ethics*—"theories or traditions that emphasize the formation of character and the development of virtue as central to the moral life" (*KE* Glossary, p. 474). Chapter 7 will focus on this subject.

The wisdom of the virtue ethics tradition is immense. Retrieved for Protestant ethics by Stanley Hauerwas in books such as his 1981 *A Community of Character*, and never absent from Catholic and Orthodox ethics, virtue ethics understands that people are not just moment-by-moment decision-makers, but instead have been formed over time and have developed habits, patterns, and characteristics that surface in many different decision-making contexts. Ethicists can write as many moral **action-guides** describing "fitting, right, or good courses of action" as we might like (*KE* Glossary, p. 449), but people will most often do what is in them to do—their actions will reflect their character.

Character ethics has the salutary benefit of focusing not just on decisions or dilemmas but people as they really are, as beings developing over time with a moral momentum shaped by a range of complex factors. But character ethics can be critiqued for sometimes abandoning the effort to offer moral rules or goals in relation to various challenging areas of life, and for overemphasizing the potency of virtuous character to generate good decisions.

1.3.5 What kind of community should we seek to develop?

The fifth not-so-small question turns the focus away from the moral self to the moral community. How do we develop communities of people that are morally sound, good, and just? This is sometimes called **communitarian ethics**, and it also has seen a revival in recent decades through the work of such philosophers as Alasdair MacIntyre, beginning with his influential 1981 book *After Virtue*.

This question focuses on the fact that the development of morality is a social task aimed at the moral well-being of various communities, and not just an individual concern. I am speaking of every kind of social grouping—families, neighborhoods, villages, congregations, schools, political parties, workplaces, civic associations, and nations. Social entities of every type find it necessary to develop moral standards. This might seem strange to us at first, but that's only because many of us have been immersed in a deep cultural individualism that obscures from our view collective moral projects.

But think about it: Most parents at least attempt to teach morality to their children. All schools offer rules, while many offer core moral goals or values. Workplaces give employees thick manuals with the company's vision, values, and rules. Societies communicate some vision of core communal or national moral values and rules.

Those most mistreated in various communities constantly challenge the functioning morality of those groups. Indeed, from the subaltern perspective, the ultimate question of community morality almost always amounts to something more focused, like this: What must we do to demand that this community *stop doing injustice to us*? What steps of liberation might we undertake to create a just community? When understood in this key, communitarian ethics becomes **liberation ethics**, which emerges from below, not from within, a community's power structures. It happens when the main question being asked of the community is when exactly *everyone* will finally get to be free. Various expressions of liberation ethics (and theology) will be noted multiple times in this book.

1.3.6 What behavior is responsible, and responsive, before neighbor and God?

Perhaps you have been surprised not to meet the language of **moral responsibility** until now. For many people, perhaps more in the past than today, the idea that morality involves acting responsibly is central. I want to use this part of the definition of moral responsibility in my book *Kingdom Ethics* (p. 466): "Human beings should act not on the basis of abstract rules but instead by considering the most responsible course of action (e.g., the best *response* to God and people) in a given situation."

What is most interesting about this sixth not-so-small question is the idea that morality is about responsiveness, response-ability—about developing the ability and willingness to *respond* to dilemmas, people, and situations in the best possible manner.

This type of moral thinking, sometimes called **responsibility ethics**, or **response ethics**, developed by the ethicist H. Richard Niebuhr (1894–1962) in his 1963 book *The Responsible Self*, heightens attention to the specific situations in which moral choices arise. The moral question in real life is usually about what kind of response fits best (is most **fitting**) in this exact moment, relating to this person, under these conditions.

If we are religious people, we might also believe that moral challenges come to us, not just from people and situations, but from God. We might believe that our obligation is to find the path that is responsive not just to people but to God. If that is how we look at the world, morality takes on a religious dimension. That leads us to the next and final section of this chapter.

1.4 Christian Ethics, Again

At last, we reach the place in our discussion where we are ready to modify the term "ethics" with the word "Christian," and continue forward from there.

Let me make a few bald assertions that should bear themselves out during this study.

Like a Venn diagram, Christian ethics both overlaps with general human ethics and is distinct from it.

We are fellow human beings with others, and we share with others the intrinsic moral dimension of human experience and the need to think critically about morality.

We are not exempt from any of the complexity of establishing moral standards or the difficulty of living up to the standards that we establish. Despite sometimes overly exalted claims about Christian virtue, we share the human condition and the challenges of the human moral task.

We can learn much from the efforts of ethicists, other communities, and everyday people as they do the work of ethics. We need to humbly join others in what my late Baptist colleague Stan Grenz (1950–2005) called *The Moral Quest* (first published in 2000).

Yet Christians do belong to a faith community to which not everyone belongs. Our committed participation in Christian community can and ought to shape our morality in profound ways.

One of these ways is that we are heirs to the Christian moral tradition that I described at the outset of this chapter. Even though there is plenty of what British theologian-ethicist Samuel Wells memorably described in 2004 as *Improvisation* in Christian ethics, like actors our improv is rooted in a tradition that both sets limits and opens the door to an appropriate originality.

While one can speak of a broad, shared Christian moral tradition, its content is debated. What matters for most everyday Christians are the distinctive moral traditions developed within Christianity's major branches or the thematic distinctives to which we have been exposed or have committed ourselves. We are Baptist or Catholic or Orthodox, liberationist or communitarian or virtue ethicists. And yet all are expressions of the shared Christian tradition, all tributaries of a river that never stops flowing.

Christian ethics is ultimately the effort to know and do God's will as we have met God in Jesus Christ. This means that Christian ethics is ultimately a form of religious and even theological ethics, by contrast with ethics based purely on reason or experience. Traditionally, at least, Christian ethics joins revelation-based religions such as Judaism and Islam in claiming a divine source for at least the most important human moral obligations.

Christian ethics draws on **sources of authority** that to a large extent are internal to the Christian community, which is another distinctive feature. These include the Bible, Christian tradition, church leaders and theologians, and even the spiritual dimensions (and powers) of Christian formation and practice. We will return to this theme in Chapter 3. The complexity of scripture alone provides a sufficient clue as to the challenge of handling the sources that shape Christian ethics. The necessity and the difficulty of reading scripture for ethics will be a constant theme in this book.

Many who read this book will be seminary students. Christian ethics is the work of seminarians in part because of your calling to serve Christ's church in some fashion. As Sondra Wheeler argues in her 2017 book, *The Minister as Moral Theologian*, which we will consider in detail later, Christian ministers bear unique responsibilities within Christian communities to guide God's people to good, right, and fitting moral thinking and action. All Christians are called to be moral. Christian clergy, however, are called not only to be moral but to be moral theologians, e.g., ethicists—to reflect on and shape the morality of Christian communities. It is a high calling indeed.

We are now prepared to dig deeper into the structure of moral theory, a subject in philosophical ethics with relevance in religious and Christian ethics. This will be our next topic.

Discussion Questions:

1. To what extent do you believe that general human morality and then Christian morality will, or should, end up looking similar?

2. Review the distinction between the terms "ethics" and "morality" in this chapter.

3. Can you think of any human beings you know who could not really be described as having moral agency as defined in this discussion?

4. Which of the "six not-so-small questions" of ethics was the most unfamiliar or surprising to you? Which of those questions sounded most familiar to your own approach or background?

5. Can you name a moral conviction that, if you relinquished it, would redefine your identity?

To watch Dr. Gushee deliver

Lecture 2: An Introduction to Moral Theory

Follow this link:

https://youtu.be/tuX8SuQ7eEI

Or scan the QR code.

To listen to the audio, follow this link:

https://qrco.de/bcLtX1

Or scan the QR code.

To scan a QR code, download a QR reader from the app store on your device, open the application, follow the directions, and point your device's camera at the code.

CHAPTER 2

An Introduction to Moral Theory

2.1 Key Technical Vocabulary in Ethics

In this chapter, we are going to consider key technical terms in ethics. The vocabulary you will meet here finds its home in the general human study of ethics—sometimes called *moral philosophy*, because in higher education its study is housed in philosophy departments, and in its origins much of it traces back to ancient Greek philosophy. I like to use the term *moral theory* to describe most of this aspect of moral philosophy. By now, even religious ethicists find it impossible to discuss our distinctive versions of ethics without reference to this core moral theory vocabulary.

Moral theory mainly functions at four levels: ***descriptive, critical, normative,*** and ***metaethical***. These terms surface again and again in the field.

Some aspects of moral theory simply attempt to name and *describe* with accuracy aspects of human moral thinking and behavior.

Normative (sometimes called *constructive*) moral theories go further. They make proposals as to how human beings *should* structure their moral thinking and behavior. Some of the most famous terms in all of ethics, such as ***deontology, teleology, utilitarianism,*** and the ***categorical imperative***, represent broad normative proposals about morality. Normative ethics happens whenever anyone makes a "should" statement about how people should think and act, either in relation to specific real-world issues (sometimes called **applied ethics**) or as an overall rule of life, as in moral theories like utilitarianism.

Critical-level ethics happens when moral norms, theories, or behaviors are assessed according to a standard, such as intellectual coherence, rationality, fit with human nature, feasibility, helpfulness, justice, or faithfulness to a religious value or revelation.

Metaethics happens when scholars comment about how moral vocabulary is used and moral arguments made, or when they reflect on metaphysical or theoretical questions such as whether there is moral reality, or objective moral truth, and if so, what its source might be.

Here is an example in which you can see all four levels.

In many countries of the world, the belief that sex belongs only in marriage has been abandoned both in theory and in practice. That is a *descriptive* claim, testable by public opinion polling and behavioral measurement. Some ethicists and religious leaders have critiqued the sex-in-marriage-only standard as unrealistic or unhelpful, while others have decried the abandonment of the older norm. When either group does this, they are working at the *critical* level. Different norms for sexual conduct have been proposed, including mutual consent, reciprocity, and a covenantal standard. Now we are at the *normative* or constructive level. Ethicists argue over the proper definition of terms such as marriage, consent, and covenant, and what to make of stark cultural differences on these issues. That finally moves us to the *metaethical* level.

We will return to sexual ethics later in this book. Hopefully, this little foray has whetted your appetite a bit.

2.2 Driving Down the Ethics Highway

I have found some success in making sense of moral theory by using a highway metaphor. Say you have made vacation plans and soon will embark on a long road trip by car. As you undertake your trip, you are mainly thinking about your destination and what awaits you there.

Whatever your destination, though, you cannot let your mind wander too much because every moment of your trip is governed by rules of the road. If you violate these rules you could face significant penalties.

Further, you must attend to the actions of other drivers because you are not on the road alone. You must also be deeply aware of the condition of your vehicle and of yourself as the driver. Is the automobile up to the journey? Are you currently sane, sober, and alert?

Put this road trip metaphor together, and you can see that we have noted goals, rules, others, and self. We are already not too far away from some of the not-so-small questions noted in the last chapter. What are the goals? What are the rules? What serves the needs of people and relationships? What kind of people should we be? This sets us up nicely to understand some of the most important technical vocabulary in ethics as well as a few key moral theories.

2.3 The Goal Dimension of Ethics

Much of human behavior is goal driven. We are always seeking to attain goals that we consider important. A term in technical ethics for morally significant goals is ends (*teloi*, in Greek). Some moral theories ask about the ends that human beings seek, and what ends we should seek. Overall, this aspect of moral life is called teleology. Those who focus ethics on goals or ends are doing ***teleological ethics***.

For example, if our fundamental end in life is seeking our self-interest, we can be described as egoists. Such description is rarely offered as praise, though surely everyone pursues their self-interest in various ways each day. However, if we believe it is good and proper that all people should be motivated fundamentally or exclusively by self-interest, we have graduated to a moral theory called ***ethical egoism***.

If, on the other hand, we wake up each day seeking to serve other people, we can be described as embracing ***ethical altruism***. Christians can easily justify such a life from scripture: "It is more blessed to give than to receive" (Acts 20). An interesting wrinkle to discuss here is what to make of how some people find their greatest pleasure in doing good for others. If my highest end is to make you happy, and doing that makes *me* happy, does that mean for me ethical altruism is a form of ethical egoism?

One major moral theory suggests that, at least for social ethics and government policy, the proper goal is to achieve the greatest good (or happiness) for the greatest number of people. This theory is called utilitarianism, and it was refined by British philosopher John Stuart Mill (1806–1873) in his 1861 book by that name, after a cruder version proposed by Jeremy Bentham (1748–1832). Utilitarianism has had a long and productive life and remains significant today.

It is hard to argue with the idea that we should act in such a way as to seek the greatest good for the greatest number of people. (Happiness as the goal is a little more complicated, though defining "good" is no small feat either.) Some approach like utilitarianism does govern policymaking in many arenas, from health care to national defense to traffic law.

A somewhat different vocabulary for a similar goal is ***seeking the common good***, which is essentially the best outcome for the whole community, by contrast with the good of one or a few. Some moral theories focus on advancing every individual's well-being and say that the right goal is collective and individual ***human flourishing***. The common good and human flourishing are important teleological approaches in contemporary Christian ethics.

The strength of teleological theories is the way they build on the fact that all meaningful human actions pursue goals. Assessing the moral quality of the goals that people seek makes sense. Directing actions based on their success in achieving morally significant goals also makes sense. It is morally more worthy to seek the common good than private good, to serve all rather than just the privileged or the solitary self. The actions of almost every leader and every institution are best evaluated based on whether they set and meet worthy goals that benefit everyone in the community.

Teleological moral thinking goes wrong when people forget or dismiss the significance of other dimensions of ethics, such as the humble but indispensable moral rule, and when they forget the significance of the needs and rights of each person. Goal-directed behavior is fine, but like all kinds of behavior it must be governed by rules, and every individual matters.

2.4 The Rule Dimension of Ethics

Some of the most elaborate vocabulary in moral theory has to do with ***moral rules***, the concrete commands that govern human life in many sectors.

There is no question that rules dominate many areas of our lives. Most of them are established by human beings and imposed on communities ranging from families to schools to nations. They are more likely to be accepted if they are developed by those who are governed by them, or at least in consultation with them, but this is certainly not always the case. From childhood, we discover, sometimes painfully, authorities who impose and enforce rules upon us.

Rules come in different gradations of strength and enforcement. Consider a spectrum from rules that come as orders, dictates, commands, or laws, and contrast these with action-guides that are more like suggestions or guidelines. Notice that in the most important contexts that people traditionally encounter, like law and religion, rules tend to be framed at high strength, with punishments attached for violation, in this world or the next.

Religious and philosophical ethics has had a long and rich debate about where rules ultimately originate. If we believe moral rules come from God—and especially if we believe that God's will is what makes things right and wrong—we are into some form of *divine command* ethics. Overall, ethical systems that treat rules as coming from outside ourselves are called *heteronomous*, by contrast with the belief that we can or should come up with our moral rules *autonomously*. Moral rules believed to be of divine origin are usually given strong vocabulary such as *moral commands* or *moral laws*. This is certainly a major strand of religious ethics, especially in the Abrahamic traditions of Judaism, Christianity, and Islam.

But it is also possible to speak of moral commands or moral laws and not ground them in divine will. Immanuel Kant (1724–1804), the great German philosopher, proposed the categorical imperative as a kind of secular moral law. In his famous 1788 book called *The Critique of Practical Reason*, he put it this way: "Act only according to that maxim by which you can at the same time will that it should become a universal law." That basically amounts to the idea that only if we could reasonably desire that every person in the world act upon the same basis that we are acting upon are we acting properly. This is sometimes called the *principle of universalizability*. Notice that the categorical imperative pretty much replaces large numbers of specific rules with one overarching rule.

Kant strongly emphasized that moral maturity involves imposing such *moral duties* on oneself based on the dictates of reason rather than the command of God. He rejected heteronomous ethics because he believed such externally imposed commands to be unworthy of human rationality and *dignity*. That's what children do—obey rules imposed by more powerful others. Grownups impose morally rigorous demands on themselves. This move was a major part of the turn from religious ethics to rationalist ethics during the Enlightenment. In retrospect, it is clear both that the human desire for externally imposed moral order never went away, despite Kant, and that autonomous rationalist ethics was no less susceptible to error than any other ethics.

Moral rules become **moral principles** when they move out one level of abstraction. The way Stassen and I put it in *Kingdom Ethics* is that rules tell us concretely what to do and what not to do, while principles offer more abstract or general underlying reasons for rules. If you impose a rule on someone and can't tell them the principle that grounds the rule, they will not find it very convincing. Principles like honesty, respect for persons, and autonomy ground many rules. In medical ethics, for example, the rule-governed practices that patients be told the truth about their condition, be given all reasonable treatment options, and be allowed to choose for themselves what option to take, are grounded in these principles.

Underneath core principles are even more **basic convictions**. In traffic law, for example, the law might be that the speed limit is 70 mph. The key principle underneath the law is protecting public safety. The basic conviction underneath the principle is that human life matters. If someone, in turn, asks why human life matters, the answers become theological or visceral. That's when you know you have reached bedrock, the basic convictions level.

I still like the quadruple-decker model we offer in *Kingdom Ethics* that makes basic convictions foundational, then one level up is principles, another level up is rules, and at the top come **particular judgments** in specific situations. People are not always explicit that this is how they are reasoning morally, but often they could identify this thought structure if pressed.

This model has analytical power as well. For example, notice that people who don't have much use for rules tend to jump from basic convictions to particular judgments, skipping over rules and often over principles as well. One group like this were the **situationists**, whose ideas were popularized by Joseph Fletcher (1905–1991) in his 1966 book called *Situation Ethics*. For Fletcher, the only relevant basic conviction is love, and therefore the only relevant action-guide is to act to advance love. My view is that while situations matter deeply in ethics, and love is always a relevant moral principle, situationism as a theory doesn't work that well in practice because even love needs moral structure around it.

On the other end of the spectrum, we find **legalists**, who focus tightly on rules and miss everything "beneath" or even "above" in moral decision-making contexts. Moral **intuitionists** just feel their way in specific situations without any underlying thought structure at all. Medical ethics tends to live at the principles level and to generate rules from there, so their ethical approach is sometimes called *principlism*. And so on.

A technical term for ethical theories based on rules, duties, or obligations is *deontological ethics*. While there are many forms of deontological ethics, their shared idea is that the rightness or wrongness of an action is not based on its consequences but on the nature of the action itself or in terms of the relevant rules that apply.

Here's an example. Abusing an elderly person is awful. It has bad consequences. We wouldn't want to live in a society filled with elder abuse. There are many rules and laws against it. But the fundamental reason not to mistreat an elderly person is because it is intrinsically wrong. How do we know this? We just know it, deep in our viscera, as evidenced by our outrage when we see it happen. The widespread agreement about the wrongness of abusing the elderly may offer some evidence of a natural or God-given moral consciousness that resides in human beings. *Moral conscience* is sometimes described as the voice of this moral consciousness that arises when we are considering its violation. But even moral conscience can go wrong because it can be damaged, suppressed, or malformed (see Chapter 7).

Another dimension of rule-ethics is the question of absoluteness. Much effort has gone into considering whether rules are absolute, to be obeyed one hundred percent of the time, or whether *moral exceptions* can be considered. While there is a long tradition of *rule-absolutism* in moral theory—the belief that moral rules are exceptionless—most ethicists today agree that many moral rules admit of exceptions, largely because of the consequences of not admitting them.

But that doesn't cover *all* moral rules, and exceptions are not handed out like free candy. We can lie to save a life, it is widely agreed, but it is also widely agreed that we must not ever torture children for any reason. On every moral issue that we deal with, we face the question of the relevant moral rules and any possible exceptions.

The Latins get a gold star for inventing the term *prima facie* to add as a qualifier in front of moral rules that might admit exceptions. That term means "at first appearance." An example is the idea that lying is wrong at first appearance, but there might be exceptions. The one proposing the exception is responsible for showing why an exception was justified in this case. That's how the idea of *prima facie* moral rules works. The concept is also significant in legal settings, where it means that "at first appearance" there seems to be sufficient evidence to proceed with a legal case.

2.5 A Detour into Metaethics

We saw earlier that people who absolutize rules or tend to operate entirely at the rules level are sometimes called legalists, and there are plenty of them in religious life. On the other hand, many would argue that moral norms have weakened in recent decades, especially in Western culture. Certainly, it is true that any social consensus about moral norms has weakened, if it ever existed.

But questioning about moral norms goes further than that. Many very smart philosophers have doubted moral reality itself or, if there is a God, what God has to do with it. Their critiques are so significant that it looks like we need to take a detour into metaethics before continuing down the ethics highway.

Let's start off with one of the oldest issues in divine command ethics, which surfaced as far back as Plato. It has been called the *Euthyphro Dilemma*, from one of Plato's famous Dialogues of Socrates. The dilemma is this: Does God forbid X because X is intrinsically wrong, or is X wrong just because God forbids it? The problem with taking the first option is that this admits a moral standard that exists independent of God's command. The problem with taking the second path is that God could arbitrarily command any atrocity and that would make it right. When we think of the many murderous religious zealots of history, this becomes more than a theoretical problem.

That's one kind of metaethical problem. But an entirely different level is reached when people doubt whether morality is anything other than subjective human opinion.

One way to understand the *ethical skepticism* that became visible in the early 20th century and remains with us today is as a response to growing awareness of cultural moral differences. It is true that discovering the vast differences between moral beliefs and practices across cultures and among individuals can be highly disorienting.

Paying close attention to the differences in moral rules and norms across cultures and eras is sometimes called *descriptive moral relativism*. Its recognition of cultural differences in moral norms is simply accurate—the Nazis believed in killing "subhumans." Hopefully, no one reading this book believes "subhuman" is a proper way to describe anyone, let alone that it might be permissible to kill those so designated. This reminds us that it is quite a leap to move from descriptive to **normative moral relativism**, which is the belief that there does not exist an objective or transcendent standard of right or wrong and so we must learn to tolerate moral difference without passing judgment. This once-trendy view should not have survived the discovery of Auschwitz.

When we see both how much people disagree about morality, and how emotional they get, it can be tempting to conclude that moral statements merely express feelings or attitudes rather than describing anything in the world. This **noncognitivism** essentially reduces to the idea that there is no true moral knowledge, and certainly no objective right and wrong. Instead, there are only attitudes or dispositions; or, in a theory called **emotivism**, moral norm statements are viewed as just expressions of human emotion.

Moral skeptic J. L. Mackie (1917–1981), in his *Ethics: Inventing Right and Wrong* (1977), argued that human morality is indeed simply invented. Mackie was an atheist who argued that there is no objective or transcendent morality, and that moral rules and norms are entirely a human creation.

My own view about these metaethical matters can be sketched briefly as follows. I believe that there is indeed a moral structure to the world and that God is the Creator of this moral structure like everything else. God has always sought to communicate this moral structure to human beings, for our good, and has done so through both **general revelation** available to all people and **special revelation** available through divine self-disclosure at specific moments of salvation history. More on this in the next chapter.

The human ability to discover, hear, and obey God's commands and goals is damaged by sin, which surfaces powerfully in cultural systems of all kinds and in every human heart. Our effort to articulate moral rules and goals, even those which we believe come from God, is often deeply compromised, and we frequently find that we were wrong.

In that sense, I believe both in objective God-given morality that transcends cultures and in our grave human difficulty in discovering, hearing, and obeying it. I certainly accept that many human moral norm statements are flawed, sometimes disastrously so.

Still, I do believe that the core of the moral dimension of human existence is a discovery rather than an invention. It's like how all of us humans have the good fortune to be born into a world with plants, animals, and colors, all abundant and diverse. We did not invent plants, animals, and colors, but we surely need language to describe what we so blessedly discover. Ethics is a language for describing what we have discovered in the moral dimension of life.

2.6 Consequences, Others, and Character

Having taken our detour into metaethics, let us return to the ethics highway. We have thus far discussed both that the reason we get in our vehicles is to speed our way toward a goal, and that our pathway toward that goal must be governed by binding rules. People who lose sight of the goal as they get buried in rule minutiae might never get to their destination. These are the legalists. But people who absolutize the goal and dismiss all rules make for dangerous drivers. These are the *antinomians*. Both on the highway and in life they are resolutely to be avoided.

We have yet to speak about the other drivers, and that driver who is yourself. We also need to tie down a loose end related to an ethical theory called *consequentialism*. Let's add these considerations as we conclude our trip down the ethics highway.

A highway full of cars is a community—a community of strangers, but yes, a community. It is a community of people whose individual identity and behavior do not matter all that much—until they matter acutely, when we find ourselves, or others, dead or injured. Then strangers can become intimately acquainted indeed.

Ethics is always partly about the consequences of our actions. When I am making my twice-weekly trip back and forth between Atlanta and Macon, Georgia, and I see someone driving 100 mph and weaving between cars, his actions matter a great deal to me—because if that person slightly miscalculates, my car and my body might end up paying dearly for it. Morally responsible people consider the potential consequences of their choices. This is an aspect of character that matters deeply to everybody whose life intersects with other lives—which is everybody.

Consequences matter in ethics. This theme gets elevated to a moral theory by the—wait for it—*consequentialists*, who believe that the rightness or wrongness of an action is not intrinsic to the action but depends on the effects or consequences of the action. What makes an action right or wrong is what effect it has on others or self. When you are trying to decide what to do, you know what is right by anticipating the likely consequences and making the best available decision.

Of course, I believe that reducing normative ethics to consequences goes too far—but attending to consequences is indeed important in ethics. I drive carefully in part because I understand the potential consequences for many people if I choose not to do so. Anticipating the potential consequences of various courses of action is what morally responsible people do. While we do not always know what the exact or even likely outcome of our choices will be, we must do the calculation anyway as part of any serious moral discernment process.

People who act, heedless to the consequences, earn our negative judgment of their character. They are not safe drivers on the ethics highway. They are not demonstrating proper respect or care for others. They are harming (or risking) the well-being of the community. When they "crash" it costs a great deal to all concerned.

Virtue ethics comes in here, though we need not say that much more about it, as we will give it thorough attention in a later chapter. I want to reinforce the original point, that the condition of the car and the driver must be a consideration before any road trip, and the metaphor extends broadly to life. One reason we must have at least a reasonable level of introspection is because the state of our character affects others. We are not alone. We are interconnected with many. If we care about what happens to them, we must care about the state of our moral selves. We must always be open to self-correction. In *Kingdom Ethics* we call this **continuous repentance**.

One reason I get up early every morning to study scripture, pray, and journal is so that I can be my best self in facing the moral challenges of each day. Call it soul maintenance for the ethics highway. Many accidents are caused by incapacitated drivers.

2.7 Jesus and Moral Theory

Jesus never declared himself a teleologist, deontologist, or virtue ethicist. He didn't report his vote on the categorical imperative or utilitarianism. His ethics was theological rather than philosophical, and his vocabulary was rooted in the soil of Israel.

I do, however, think we can turn to Jesus and see a path to avoiding the absolutizing of any of the specific moral theories we have considered here—while also connecting to the value of their best insights.

With the teleologists, I see Jesus as a deeply goal-driven person. I will argue that his central stated social-ethical goal was the kingdom of God. He also offered a laser focus on doing God's will as his stated goal. He was deeply committed to a goal of lifting the burdens of legalism on religiously marginalized people. He lived and died for the salvation of the world.

With the deontologists, Jesus offered stern ethical imperatives in the form of negative prohibitions and positive injunctions. His followers were not to divorce, not to return evil for evil, not to hate their enemies, not to swear oaths, not to gaze lustfully at others, and much more. They were to tell the truth, practice peacemaking, show mercy like the Good Samaritan, and give alms, though not for show. We will examine these moral teachings throughout this book.

One of the tragedies of much of the Christianity I have encountered is an inability to get this issue of concrete moral demands right. Rule-focused souls, often conservative, are right to emphasize biblical commands, but all too often fixate on minutiae and slide into legalism. Goal-oriented souls, often liberal, are right to focus on the grand ends such as social justice, as Jesus did. But sometimes they develop an allergy to moral commands, as if articulating any rules at all is somehow oppressive.

Jesus never seemed to have this problem. He lived by moral commands which he believed came from God and yet he never lost sight of the big picture—the reign of God, the deliverance of the oppressed, the priorities of justice, mercy, and love. The way of Jesus makes actual demands on people. But those demands are never just pointless rules or religion for religion's sake. They are always clearly grounded in a bigger picture of God's purposes in this world.

So, even in relation to moral theory, the correct answer is always to look to Jesus first. We will still face considerable ethical ambiguity and complexity, and we do see through a glass darkly. But Jesus offers a path forward, in which goals, rules, consequences, responsibilities, community, and character all find a place.

Discussion Questions

1. What would you say is the moral tendency (or default setting) of yourself or your religious community when it comes to the choice between a focus on rules or goals in ethics?

2. Discuss the quadruple-layer paradigm of basic convictions, principles, rules, and particular judgments. See if you understand it and if it makes sense to you. What is your preferred operating level?

3. What explains the tendency toward legalism in much of Christianity? Have you encountered it? What are its effects? Is the greater danger in your specific context legalism or antinomianism?

4. Are certain acts wrong because God says so, or does God say so because they are wrong? This is called the Euthyphro Dilemma. Have fun with it.

5. Do you find yourself troubled by the skeptics, relativists, and noncognitivists who doubt the reality of any transcendent right and wrong?

To watch Dr. Gushee deliver

**Lecture 3: How Do We Find Out How
We Should Live?**

Follow this link:

https://youtu.be/e-HAK98Oiy4

Or scan the QR code.

To listen to the audio, follow this link:

https://qrco.de/bcLtbu

Or scan the QR code.

To scan a QR code, download a QR reader from the app store on your device, open the application, follow the directions, and point your device's camera at the code.

CHAPTER 3

How Do We Find Out
How We Should Live?

Much of the argument in ethics is not about content but about process. I guess that is true of most other academic disciplines when you get to know them. There is the matter of what the field has concluded, but there is also the matter of how the field has concluded it. The arguments are usually at least as intense about process as they are about content.

This chapter is about process. It is about the process of determining moral norms in Christian ethics. It could be said that this is a discussion of ***ethical method***, and that would not be wrong. But here we are especially focused on issues of sourcing and ***moral authority***. In the effort to determine how Christians should live, what sources do we consult? What people, institutions, written works, and other moral guidance sources will count as authoritative when Christians go about the task of moral discernment?

3.1 General Human Moral Sources

This issue of sources of authority is an area in which the differences between general human ethics, the ethics of different religious traditions, and Christian ethics show up in a big way. It would be interesting to start a discussion at this point about how ordinary nonreligious people make moral decisions. What sources do they consult? What authorities do they trust?

I remember that my mother, who was a committed Catholic, used to read the advice columnist Ann Landers (1918–2002) in every morning's newspaper. Ann Landers answered questions from readers, often at the borderline between ethics and *etiquette*. These are etymologically related words, by the way. Can you see the family resemblance? Ethics is about right and wrong. Etiquette is also about right and wrong, though mainly at the level of culture, social tradition, and custom rather than big-time moral issues. Mom took Ann Landers seriously as a kind of authority source for life. (Here is how you set a table for a fancy dinner party. Here is what you do with your second wife at your daughter's wedding. Etc.) Millions of other confused mid-20th-century folks did the same.

My father never bothered with Ann Landers. He was a chemical engineer, working as an energy and environmental policy analyst for the federal government. He lived in the world of data-driven research and the (disputed) moral values that go into government policymaking. His job was to analyze the best available science, study existing government policies and industry standards, and lay out policy options toward achieving all the relevant values, such as clean air, a vibrant economy, and fair, enforceable laws.

Notice the sources already at play in our discussion so far: cultural custom, advice columnists, newspapers, science, empirical research, reason, and a sense of the common good within the modern nation-state.

Downshift a bit and consider other sources that everyday people listen to. What would you add to this list? Parents, friends, partners, impulses, an inner voice, instincts, feelings, celebrities, entertainers, politicians, astrology, fortune cookies, conspiracy theories, TV news/opinion figures, well-known authors ...

We should probably also add that a lot of what people decide to do seems to be sourced in places unknown even to themselves. Whenever we say, "I don't know why I think that—or why I did that," we are in that realm of moral intuition or impulse. Meanwhile, there are many occasions in life when a snap decision is required of us. No sources can be consulted because there is no time. These are some of the most important moral decisions of all. Sometimes they are the truest revelations of our character.

3.2 Religious Moral Sources

Each of the world's religious traditions adds to all these general human moral sources its own repertoire of religious sources. In most of these traditions, these religious sources function in an authoritative manner that we do not usually see with nonreligious moral sources. They are elevated to a place of sacredness. This sacred authority can be grounded in claims about the divine origin and inspiration of these authorities, their great antiquity, or simply the unique role that these sources play in the traditional belief and practice of religious communities.

While every religious tradition is unique, it is possible to identify certain common types of religious sources. These include sacred scriptural texts, recognized religious authority structures and offices, post-scriptural depositories of influential teaching, and an authoritative religious-community *ethos* or way of life. Religious traditions of some vintage carry authority in part due to their antiquity itself—"for thousands of years we have believed and done it this way." Compelling religious traditions teach not just what to think, but how to think. Or, especially in more authoritarian traditions, they resolve the authority question by doing the thinking for believers in advance. If we want to know how we should live, we just open the book(s) to the proper place(s), or consult the tradition(s), or have a meeting with the leader(s), and we are set. That is a powerful resource for believers, and for many it is one of the reasons why they believe.

It is a helpful exercise for those attempting to think critically about religious life to examine and then try to describe the way in which moral authority functions in quite specific religious communities. This task is complicated because there may well be a gap between the official moral authority posture of a religious community and what really happens in that community or in the life of its individual adherents. Especially in open, free, modern (or postmodern) cultures, longstanding religious moral authority structures find considerable competition even in the hearts of their own believers.

3.3 A Chastened Post-Evangelical: Moral Conflict, Failure, Confusion, Quest

In various places in my writing, including *Kingdom Ethics* and especially my 2020 book *After Evangelicalism*, I consider the repertoire of Christian moral authorities at length. One last time, in this book I will take a run at this significant question.

My mature approach to this matter has been deeply chastened by a career filled with intense experiences of moral conflict within the Christian community, both in the U.S. and around the world. On issues ranging from the role of women in the churches, to abortion, to divorce and remarriage, to race, torture, human rights, climate change, sexuality, and Christian engagement with secular politics, I have taken a career-long bath in internecine Christian moral conflict.

My thinking has also been marked by studying numerous cases in which Christians have failed to behave in a manner remotely close to our stated moral values: in Christian Europe during the Holocaust (see my first book, *Righteous Gentiles of the Holocaust*), in the heavily Christian Yugoslavia while it was dissolving, in Christian Rwanda during the 1994 genocide, in Christian slaveholding America, and so on.

I have seen my own views change on several issues, while also witnessing agonizing moral confusion on the part of both individuals and faith communities, from congregations up to the church writ large. The communications I have received from Christians asking me to help them sort out their moral confusion are too many to count.

How long ago seem the days in which I could join others who said that if Christians would just "study the scriptures" or be "truly biblical" all would be well. It must be more difficult than that because it never quite works out as easily as such slogans might suggest. One reason I am a self-described post-evangelical Christian is because I can no longer accept the central evangelical claim that just reading the Bible resolves all questions related to the Christian moral life. Nor have I moved over to a tradition-oriented Roman Catholic or Eastern Orthodox approach and substituted popes, bishops, church councils, or metropolitans as the authorities who resolve all moral questions. I take both scripture and tradition very seriously but cannot read them as their most uncritical adherents do.

I have had to embrace the idea that Christians join with other uncertain souls of all human sorts in our effort to "see through a glass darkly" (1 Cor 13:12, KJV) toward moral discernment and action. We Christians should draw carefully on our unique sources while also attending to the broader human moral quest to know and do what is right. All human beings must regularly make decisions and act on them, but wise people recognize the provisional and error-prone nature of all our judgments. Christians should join others in a posture of seeking truth urgently while always being willing to reconsider and take a new path.

Despite endless efforts on all sides to avoid the problem, there is no way to forestall the fallibility of human judgment by somehow getting our moral sourcing right. It is never just a matter of more Bible, more tradition, or more whatever. *We* are always the ones accessing whatever sources we consult, and we are always fallible. And indeed, our sources, because of the human imprint on them, reveal the traces both of divine inspiration and of human fallibility.

3.4 Considering the Christian Moral Sources

Consider what follows a modest proposal for best moral sourcing practices to be undertaken by fallible Christians. This, at least, is what I will attempt.

A place to begin is with a claim to a theology of revelation. God created us, God loves us, God has spoken and still speaks to us, God in grace wants us to know how we should live. The "us" here is all of humanity, and our Christian tradition (more in some branches than others) expresses confidence that God has inscribed his will on the human heart and makes it known through the perceptible moral structure of the world. As noted in the last chapter, this is often called general revelation. Of course, even the existence and purported content of general revelation is itself debated.

Christians stand in a line of religious tradition that adds to general revelation claims about God's special revelation to Israel and then the church, God's covenant peoples who share a large portion of sacred scripture attesting to God's acts and commands. We Christians also claim that Jesus of Nazareth, the Messiah of Israel and God Incarnate, is the ultimate form of God's communication to humanity. Christians are, by definition, those who believe this about Jesus and who consider Jesus our ultimate moral source.

In that sense, the right answer to every Christian moral sourcing question is to refer it back to Jesus. That does not simply resolve every moral question. But it gives us our starting place—our preeminent moral source is not a text, tradition, or practice, but a Person, not just someone we read about but the Savior who redeems us and the Lord to whom we pledge our very lives.

If we center on Jesus for ethics, we need to look not just to his words and deeds but also the way he used the sources available in his own tradition. In *Kingdom Ethics*, Glen Stassen and I conclude that Jesus related to his sources much like the prophets of Israel in whose lineage he stood. He took Jewish scripture as authoritative, but he read the texts through a prophetic rather than cultic/legalist lens, he emphasized God's justice as siding with those trampled by the powers of this world, and he lived within an apocalyptic-eschatological kingdom-of-God frame that we will discuss in a later chapter.

It is also important to note that Jesus built upon but dramatically exceeded all prior prophetic manifestations of supernatural power through the Spirit of God at work in him. Jesus read scripture, engaged people, and wrangled with current tradition and religious leaders in ways all marked by his identity as Spirit-anointed Son of God (Mt 3:16–17). This left him notably free from and sometimes deeply critical of a religious traditionalism that harmed people in the name of God. If we take the historical Jesus seriously as a source for our ethics, we will need to be open to the supernatural in a way that is uncomfortable for many who live on this side of the Enlightenment. We will also need to hold tradition somewhat more loosely than many religious traditionalists are inclined to do.

As we look back from a distance of two thousand years, we see many layers of tradition and practice standing between us and the Jesus we meet in the Gospels. We must face the fact that world Christianity is a massive but divided faith community, with some aspects of a shared moral tradition and method, but many distinctive and conflicting beliefs.

In terms of scripture, we have not just the Hebrew Bible that was Jesus' Bible, and not only the Gospels that tell the story of Jesus, but also the New Testament with its various refractions on the story of Jesus and of the church, and its various accounts of the moral life. The discontinuities in method and moral vision between the Jesus of the Synoptic Gospels (Mt/Mk/Lk) and the Jesus of Paul, Acts, the Johannine tradition, and the pastoral epistles are real. The Christian ethics of the non-Synoptic New Testament (with the lone exception of the Epistle of James) elevates the suffering, death, and resurrection of Jesus but not his teachings or his version of kingdom theology. This has created fractures within accounts of Christian ethics from the very beginning.

I continue to believe that Christian ethics needs to be morally sourced in a serious and central way by sacred scripture, and all my work reflects this commitment. But we need an honest reckoning with the vast diversity of scripture in relation to morality. Every deployment of scripture for moral discernment involves substantial choices as to which authors, sections, genres, periods, and motifs of scripture will be taken as central. I continue to favor a Jesus-centered through-line that leans Hebraic, prophetic, justice-oriented, and kingdom-of-God-as-social-salvation. This places me in line with some strands of Christian ethics—notably Social Gospel, modern Catholic Social Teaching, and some types of liberationism—and significantly out of step with other versions of Christian ethics that tend toward a focus on Old Testament law, Paul, or the pastoral epistles.

An interesting question for all students to consider is whether you have faced the diversity, and not just the unity, of scripture's ethical witness, and where you find yourself landing in your own scriptural focus. Even asking that question, and considering the range of alternatives, ought to put to rest any pretensions to infallibility in one's own interpretation of scripture. We cannot even agree on which parts of scripture to center for ethics, let alone how to interpret the specific passages that we might select.

Moral tradition is defined in *Kingdom Ethics* as "a group of moral norms and convictions … that a community forms and passes on across generations. These traditions themselves then come to carry a kind of moral authority" (*KE* Glossary, p. 456). A fascinating split within Christian traditions themselves (consider Roman Catholicism, Eastern Orthodoxy, and Protestantism here) is the extent to which they acknowledge that they are, in fact, traditions, rather than just "Biblical Christianity" or even Truth Itself.

The older Catholic and Eastern churches view themselves as traditions, or even Tradition, and consciously build consultation with (or submission to) the tradition's great ideas, documents, and figures into their moral sourcing repertoire today. The idea is that God's Spirit spoke to the church Fathers (and sometimes Mothers). Their literary remains reflect that and must be respected. The older Protestant traditions like Lutheranism, Calvinism, and Anglicanism reflect this same spirit. But newer, more populist, sometimes quite idiosyncratic Protestant churches more often attempt to reconnect with primitive Christianity with each new iteration, leaping over two millennia in the process. But give them a generation or two and you can count on internal moral traditions arising in these other churches too. It is just what communities do. They create traditions.

Our attitude toward the written evidence of two thousand years of Christian tradition is up to us. The options range from complete submission to total disrespect. Somewhere in the middle makes the most sense. The way Jesus both embraced some traditions and wholeheartedly rejected others carries great authority for me. A middle position also fits with what we see when we actually engage specific bits of Christian moral tradition. Sometimes it offers a distilled and enduring wisdom visible from age to age. Other times, it looks more like the product of a particular culture or era, perhaps treated with too much reverence due to its old age.

Compare the church's historic understanding of forgiveness, on the one hand, with its centuries of antisemitism, on the other. Both are ancient, both are distinctly Christian traditions, and both have major theologians and documents associated with them. One gives life, and the other has, quite literally, taken it. Rosemary Radford Ruether's 1974 book *Faith and Fratricide* made it impossible for me to doubt the antiquity or depth of ancient Christian antisemitism, and Martin Luther's shocking 1543 screed *On the Jews and Their Lies* showed that Christian hatred of Jews carried forward into Protestantism with deadly force.

In the phenomenal farewell address section of the Gospel of John (Jn 14–17), Jesus offers the confident and reassuring promise to his disciples that after his departure the Holy Spirit "will teach you everything" (Jn 14:26). This passage is just one of several upon which Christians have sometimes based a moral sourcing theory emphasizing the ongoing inspiration of the Holy Spirit for Christians today. Soft versions of this idea are everywhere in Christianity. More intense versions tend to be found in Quaker, pietistic, charismatic, and Pentecostal Christianity.

It does make perfect sense from a certain perspective. The New Testament teaches that Jesus was raised from the dead and ascended to the right hand of the Father. He has bequeathed the Holy Spirit to the church for all its needs today, including moral discernment. If we want to know God's moral will for us, we do not have to just read the Bible or consult tradition on our own. We should instead do these things asking for the Spirit's help. We also should do other things, like praying earnestly, worshipping, listening for God's voice, gathering in small groups for communal discernment with the Spirit's help, and so on. Most Christians can report some experience in which they were quite sure that the Holy Spirit illuminated, inspired, convicted, directed, or transformed them and their perspective on things. I certainly have had such experiences, though I could not say they are an everyday matter.

When the Holy Spirit moves in this way, it is wonderful. But the Spirit "blows where it chooses" (Jn 3:8). Christians can't make a program out of evoking the Spirit's guidance. Efforts to do so tend toward manipulation and abuse. And far too often, Christians who report the Spirit's direction seem to hear different voices saying different things. Who is to adjudicate disputes among Christians over the Spirit's invisible and inaudible direction?

One solution is to say that all claims about the Spirit's guidance should be tested by Jesus' words and by scripture more broadly (Jn 14:26b). Sure. But what if we disagree about how we think the Spirit is telling us to read scripture? What could be more certain than the Holy Spirit of God telling us something? It seems surefire. Except for when it's not.

Maybe religious leaders are the answer. Just get some saved, sanctified, anointed, well-trained pastors, bishops, cardinals, and reverend doctors, and let them make the decisions about morality. They become the ultimate source of moral authority.

As a practical matter, in almost every Christian community some group of leaders plays a powerful role in sourcing morality. In the more authoritarian traditions, they may play the exclusive role. And, of course, scholars who specialize in ethics carry disproportionate authority for the area of Christian morality—at least, some of us think they should! There are several church bodies, mainly of some size, hierarchy, and antiquity, that have developed offices for moral reflection and for the development of official moral doctrine. These are usually staffed, and sometimes led, by trained ethicists, sometimes also called *moral theologians.*

Recognized Christian leaders usually do take the primary role in deciding how moral sourcing should work, in interpreting recognized moral sources, and in leading communities of faith in moral discernment processes. Even if clergy are not especially interested in this part of ministry, ministry will, in fact, require it of them. Just look what happens when there is a major moral issue that emerges in the congregation, denomination, or local community. We will say more about this special role for the minister in the later chapter on the work of Sondra Wheeler.

One other challenging thought comes to us by way of liberationist and womanist ethics. These traditions, emerging from historically marginalized communities, are deeply affected by histories of abusive readings of the Bible directed against their well-being. These are resistance ethics emerging from descendants of the formerly colonized, subjugated, and enslaved. These traditions remind us strongly that the power of "leaders" to interpret authority sources such as Bible and tradition is a power that can be and often has been used to harm subjugated people. These authors demand and reclaim the power to interpret the sources for themselves.

This is a reminder that the question of how we should live as Christians must ultimately be understood as a communal matter, belonging neither solely to individual Christians nor to pastoral or scholarly authorities. It is the Christian Church as a whole, the churches in every configuration, and believers from every social location, that must do the work of moral discernment. "We" are the inheritors of the sacred sources of our faith tradition and we cannot avoid taking responsibility for what we do with them in our time. Specialists play a certain role, as do recognized church leaders, but in the end the faithful will determine what we will believe, teach, and practice. At least, that is my very Baptist belief. Sometimes the people are the ones who tell the leaders that it is time for further doctrinal development. I believe we can see that happen in most every generation.

3.5 Conclusion: Entering the Argument

Morality matters greatly to people. We do not like moral uncertainty, and most of us deeply dislike moral conflict. There is a kind of religious mentality that demands absolute certainty in doctrine and morality. Almost always that demand filters backward to claims about the absolute certainty and trustworthiness of one or another of the authority sources we have discussed here.

Over a long career, my discovery has been *both* that moral certainty and consensus matter greatly to people *and* that at least the latter is rare. Even though I believe God knows what God's moral will is, we are not God. We are just us, seeking, questing human beings trying to feel our way in the semi-dark. I want Christian ethics students to arrive at confident moral convictions upon which they are willing to stake their livelihoods and even their lives. But I never want them to believe they have arrived, in principle, at unquestionable and absolute truth. Christianity, including ethics, is a series of long arguments involving shared sources, all ultimately about figuring out what it looks like to be Christ's people. We enter an argument when we become serious Christian thinkers and leaders of religious communities. Others will come after us and will do the same. Welcome aboard.

Discussion Questions

1. How do the nonreligious people that you know source their moral decisions? Where do they turn for guidance?

2. Do you find it compelling when people cite tradition as a major source for Christian moral beliefs?

3. To what extent should Christians attend to general human knowledge sources?

4. Discuss instances in which you have found yourself in intense argument with other Christians over "what the Bible clearly teaches."

5. What do you make of claims to the Holy Spirit's direction when these are made in moral argument? Have you ever seen such claims conflict?

6. Do you wish that we could have absolute certainty in moral discernment? Why or why not?

To watch Dr. Gushee deliver

Lecture 4: Jesus from Below:
      Engaging Howard Thurman's
      Jesus and the Disinherited

Follow this link:

https://youtu.be/49jgl6BqTC0

Or scan the QR code.

To listen to the audio, follow this link:

https://qrco.de/bcLtkH

Or scan the QR code.

To scan a QR code, download a QR reader from the app store on your device, open the application, follow the directions, and point your device's camera at the code.

CHAPTER 4

Jesus from Below:
Engaging Howard Thurman's
Jesus and the Disinherited

4.1 Introducing Howard Thurman

At this point in my Introduction to Christian Ethics course, I always engage *Jesus and the Disinherited*, an extraordinarily significant 1949 book by a distinguished African American scholar-pastor named Howard Thurman (1899–1981). I first started having students engage Thurman because I thought his account of Jesus' ministry in its precise historical context very helpfully supplemented what Glen Stassen and I say about this issue in *Kingdom Ethics*.

Decades later, I now understand much more fully Howard Thurman's pivotal role as a forerunner and encourager of both the U.S. civil rights movement and antiracist Christian theology. I now read *Jesus and the Disinherited* as a major statement of resistance to what went wrong with predominant forms of white European and American Christianity, damaged by misused political power, by violence, and by racism.

To the best of my ability, I want my version of Christian ethics, in practice and not just in theory, to be a part of the resistance tradition that Thurman helped to pioneer rather than the oppressive tradition that Thurman so powerfully critiqued.

Regardless of my success or failure on that front, there are certain specific elements of Thurman's understanding of Jesus and his ethics that have

become a permanent part of my faith and my ethics, as will be shown in
what follows.

My primary guide to the life story of Howard Thurman is a wonderful 2020 book called *Howard Thurman and the Disinherited: A Religious
Biography*, by historian Paul Harvey. Here is a synopsis.

Howard Thurman was born in Daytona Beach, Florida in the last year of
the 19th century. His grandmother had been a slave, and Thurman's childhood and youth were spent in the vicious post-Civil War "Jim Crow" South,
at the height of the era of lynching. That evil practice—extrajudicial torture and murder—shadows this book as it shadowed African American life
during that nightmarish era. Thurman often spoke of the profound scarring
that racism and segregation inflicted upon him from his earliest days, and
his efforts to find a path to psychic peace.

Against all odds, Thurman managed to get a high school education, to
excel there, and then to attend the famous, historically Black Morehouse
College in Atlanta, graduating as valedictorian. He went north in 1923 to
attend Rochester Theological Seminary in upstate New York. This was a
school of Baptist lineage mainly famous at the time for having been the academic home of the recently deceased Walter Rauschenbusch (1861–1918),
the key leader of the Social Gospel movement, and author of *Christianity
and the Social Crisis* (1907) and other deeply influential works that emphasized the social change mission of Jesus and not just spirituality, worship,
and personal salvation.

By the time Thurman finished his education, his theological and spiritual
vision had solidified. He appreciated but had left behind the conservative
Black Baptist church of his upbringing. At a time when fundamentalists and
modernists were splitting the Protestant world, he landed on the modernist
side in his biblical interpretation and theology.

Thurman's most remarked characteristics were his deep mysticism and
his commitment to action for social justice as flowing out of that mysticism.
He was a pacifist, deeply attracted to Mohandas Gandhi's (1869–1948) spiritually grounded social justice efforts in India (he later led a delegation to
India that included several hours with Gandhi). Thurman loved Jesus but
saw him more as model and paradigm than as the lone Savior of the world.
He appreciated all spiritually serious paths that led both to God and human
brotherhood.

Thurman began his ministry in 1926 as pastor of Mount Zion Baptist Church in Oberlin, Ohio. Thurman's ministry at Mount Zion was brief but impressive, and he began developing a national profile during this time.

Because his young wife Katie's health was failing, the Thurmans moved back to Atlanta where Howard took up a professorship in philosophy and religion at Morehouse and its sister school, Spelman. Not long afterwards, based on his rising reputation, Thurman was offered the post of dean of the chapel at Howard University, another leading historically Black college, located in the nation's capital. He occupied this position from 1932 to 1944. Meanwhile, he crisscrossed the country giving sermons and lectures.

In 1944, Thurman felt called to help start one of the first intentionally interracial and multicultural Christian churches in America. Called the Church for the Fellowship of All Peoples, this exciting new venture was initiated far away in San Francisco, a city that Howard and his second wife, Sue, came to love and to which they retired. This church began as a co-pastored effort between Thurman and white Presbyterian minister Alfred Fisk. After two years, the overshadowed Fisk left, and Fellowship Church became the nationally recognized pulpit of Howard Thurman.

It was during Thurman's years in San Francisco that his prolific pen began to pour forth important books. The most famous of these is the book we are about to consider, *Jesus and the Disinherited*.

Now a superstar, in 1953 Thurman moved to Boston, where he assumed a dean of chapel post again, this time at historically white Boston University. He taught and ministered there until 1965.

Among Thurman's acquaintances at Boston was a young man named Martin Luther King Jr. (1929–1968). Other future leaders of the civil rights movement learned under him, including James Farmer (1920–1999), a fearless Freedom Rider and one of the founders of the Congress of Racial Equality (CORE). Thurman's ideas and pastoral counsel mentored the generation that hit the streets with campaigns of Gandhian-style nonviolent civil disobedience in the name of Jesus.

Howard Thurman was a forerunner, almost a John-the-Baptist figure. He was a forerunner to the civil rights movement. He was a forerunner of intentionally interracial churches and the breaching of the color line in white Christian academia. He was a forerunner of postcolonial theologies. He was also a forerunner to **liberation theology**, which "emphasizes God's intent to liberate, or set free, those who are enslaved, imprisoned, and oppressed by unjust social structures" (*KE* Glossary, p. 462). Liberation theology includes the critique that much of Christianity, as it has evolved, stands directly against the liberative teachings and spirit of Jesus himself. This means that if one wants to follow Jesus one must oppose much of organized Christianity. Thurman said this explicitly.

Thurman believed that Jesus came from, and for, the "disinherited" of the Earth, those—in his famous formulation—who spend their lives with their "backs against the wall" (*Jesus and the Disinherited*, p. 1). This insight was a breakthrough in modern biblical study. It is a conviction that I fully embrace.

So now, let us turn to this unforgettable book.

4.2 Thurman's Jesus as One of the Disinherited

Thurman claims in the first chapter of *Jesus and the Disinherited* that the global perception of Jesus has been disastrously misshaped as a legacy of the West. Most of the darker-skinned peoples of the world have encountered Jesus through white missionaries from Europe (and the U.S.). But these missionaries offered a version of Christianity completely detached from the Jesus who walked the dusty roads of Palestine. Western missionary Christianity, says Thurman, was a religion of and for the majority, the powerful, the rulers of the world. But Jesus was a Jew, a member of a minority group under the humiliations of Roman occupation, one who was poor, subjugated, and lacking political rights or power.

The issue with colonial (and Southern U.S. white) Christianity is not just the horrific and religiously discrediting evils done in the name of Christ. It is also the legacy of a completely inverted understanding of Jesus himself. Conquering Christianity brought the sword in the name of Jesus—and carried an understanding of Christ Triumphant to match.

But Jesus himself—as a "religious subject" (p. 5), in Thurman's words—was among the subjugated of the world. If we would even understand Jesus, let alone claim to follow him, we must enter (at least imaginatively) what today we would call Jesus' ***social location***, the political, class, and economic position he occupied in his own time and place.

Thurman's gently communicated but foundational claim is that conquerors and those who still benefit from those conquests are not in the best position to understand the teachings of one of the conquered of the Earth. They (we?) stand too far removed from Jesus' social situation. If we would understand what he is saying, we will need to listen to those who share a life experience that more resembles his. Howard Thurman, a Black pastor/ scholar from the Jim Crow South, has a word to offer. And he does not just speak from and for himself. He speaks from and for his people.

With this move the axis of the theological world shifted just a bit, presaging a revolution in theology that began the de-centering of the interpretations offered by the most privileged of the world.

4.3 Jesus for the Disinherited

Thurman claims that no truly human Jesus could have lived in his context of oppression and not be affected by it. Nor could Jesus have hoped to speak a relevant word to a Jewish community under Roman oppression if he did not attempt to address the powder keg situation that all his compatriots were facing. Tensions were such that barely 30 years after Jesus, a massive failed Jewish revolt beginning in 66 CE led to the destruction of Jerusalem, including the Temple, and the deaths of countless Jews.

To interpret Jesus' teachings in that context, Thurman explicitly draws on his own experience of oppression and lessons learned from traveling in India and other parts of the dominated world.

For the politically oppressed, says Thurman, the fundamental daily question is this: "under what terms is survival possible?" (p. 10). In the case of first-century Jews, the Roman boot was on their necks, the Roman soldiers were in the Holy Land itself, and at any moment they could be nailed to a Roman cross without legal rights to protect them.

In such situations there are really two main options, says Thurman— nonresistance or resistance.

Nonresistance can look like assimilation, surrender, or collaboration, all options that involve abandoning dignity in the hope of survival—or perhaps some advantages. Thurman places the Sadducees and the Herodians in this camp. Oppressors almost always buy off a privileged but corrupted minority of the oppressed.

Nonresistance can also look like a retreat to cultural isolation, having as little to do with the oppressor as is humanly possible and attempting to retain culture and dignity by withdrawing to be left alone. Thurman pegs this as the path that the Pharisees took.

Resistance, on the other hand, obviously can take the form of arming, training, and preparing for war—usually both against local turncoats and the major enemy, in this case, Rome. This was the Zealot option. The upside of this path is that dignity is retained; the downside is that in situations of power imbalances resistance is usually bloody and futile.

Thurman says that Jesus was a resister, but he resisted using spiritual weapons, not physical ones. It is that unique Jesus-resistance that Thurman tries to unpack.

As Thurman ends the first chapter, he offers a provocative interpretation of the difference between Jesus and Paul. Jesus was powerless under Roman rule, but because he was a Roman citizen, Paul was not. Offering a close contextual reading of both Paul and Jesus, Thurman suggests (quite innovatively at the time) that the power differential between them helps explain the differences in their teachings.

Making a point that was not uncommon in Black church life, but was most unexpected for white readers at the time, Thurman essentially identifies Jesus (but not Paul) with Black people: "The striking similarity between the social position of Jesus in Palestine and that of the vast majority of American Negroes is obvious to anyone who tarries long over the facts. We are dealing here with conditions that produce essentially the same psychology" (p. 23).

About twenty years later, James Cone (1938–2018), in his groundbreaking 1970 book *A Black Theology of Liberation*, took the next step in describing God as Black, in the sense that "God has made the oppressed condition [of Blacks] God's own condition" (p. 63). Later, in his 1975 *God of the Oppressed*, Cone also claimed Jesus as Black, "because and only because Christ *really* enters into our world where the poor, the despised, and the [B]lack are, disclosing that he is with them, enduring their humiliation and pain and transforming oppressed slaves into liberated servants" (p. 133, italics original). And, as liberation theology unfolded, it became clear that Jesus could be identified as Brown, Indigenous, and poor; that is, Jesus comes from and for the crushed of the Earth, and whatever we mean by "salvation" must make sense to them.

4.4 Fear, Deception, Hate, and Love

In the next three chapters, Thurman takes on three fundamental conditions of the grossly disinherited: fear, deception, and hate. In each case, Thurman begins with a description of the condition and why it is inevitable under oppression. He gives examples drawn from the experiences of many groups, but the experience of Black people in Jim Crow America is always in view. He carefully places Jesus as coming from the same kind of life situation and therefore the same natural starting point—fear, deception, and hate. But then Thurman seeks to show how Jesus, in his deep spiritual genius, both models and teaches a way past what comes naturally—a way toward love.

Thurman argues that the weak and dominated, the isolated and helpless, learn to live in constant fear as a defense against harm. Always on the alert to danger, simply seeking to get through each day without deadly violence coming upon them and their children, the oppressed "commit to memory ways of behaving that will tend to reduce their exposure to violence" (Thurman, p. 30). They also teach their children whatever lessons in survival that they have learned along the way.

With the horrors of lynching clearly in view, but also the plight of Jews under Roman oppression, Thurman describes situations in which certain groups of people have few if any rights, civil authorities are no help but are instead co-conspirators in oppression, and there is "no available and recognized protection from violence" (p. 27).

This description makes me think about what it was like to be a Communist, Socialist, Sinti/Roma, handicapped, homosexual, or Jew in Nazi Germany, even before the Holocaust—as well as what it is like to be "other" in many parts of the world even today. Anywhere that people can just do anything to you because you are the underclass, the less-than, is the kind of situation of oppression that Thurman has in mind.

Learning to live in fear of random, imminent, degrading violence and death has grave consequences for the oppressed. These consequences include humiliation, the loss of self-respect and dignity, and the profound sense that one's life simply does not matter. The constant state of fear has negative physical effects as well as emotional ones. When reinforced by religion, the sense of worthlessness deepens because (supposedly) it has been sanctioned by God. Thurman says this fear finally can become a kind of "death for the self" (p. 35) even if physical survival continues.

This is the situation in which Jesus and his people found themselves. And, says Thurman, Jesus addressed it directly. His message was simply that "man is a child of God" (p. 38), that "God is mindful of the individual" (p. 39), and that no power on Earth can take away God's decision to love and value every person—including, perhaps especially, the disinherited whom others devalue so grotesquely.

Thurman says that Jesus teaches this: You matter. You are a child of God.
Do not believe what others say about you. You have dignity. You are sacred.
You have talents and can make a mark on the world. Believe in God, believe
in yourself, believe in life.

These core convictions give the oppressed the inner spiritual and moral
power to overcome some of the most crippling effects of mistreatment. It is
partly a choice: *I choose to believe that I matter to God, and I will not fear you
or anybody.*

Even a moment's consideration of Jesus' way of interacting with people
reveals that he practiced what he preached. No one made Jesus cower. He
feared no one other than God, whom he knew as his beloved and loving
Father.

Still, Thurman understands from hard experience that in situations of
oppression it is generally not safe to tell the truth from below to above. In
the Jim Crow Southern U.S., Black people needed to pretend that they were
perfectly happy with their lives, perfectly well-treated by their white bosses,
perfectly satisfied with their second-class social status.

You're happy working for me, aren't you, Sam?
Oh, yes sir, perfectly happy, couldn't be happier, Mr. Jones.

Deception, says Thurman, is the way of the weak in relation to the strong,
the prey in relation to predators. It is the way of children in relation to
the wrathful power of their parents, wives with husbands under patriarchal
systems, and even animals as they hide from their hunters.

The problem with settling into a pattern of deception is that it requires
daily violation of what Thurman calls our "inner imperative" to tell the truth
and is intrinsically degrading. Still, when the need to survive bumps up
against the imperative to tell the truth, it is usually the latter that gives way.
Indeed, oppressed communities sometimes develop entire cultures of deception, dissembling, coded talk, and so on.

Thurman argues that Jesus' teaching in the Sermon on the Mount about
letting our "yes" be "yes" and "no" be "no" (Mt 5:37–42, Thurman, p. 60)
must be understood from within this context of oppression and the deception that frequently follows. Reading Jesus that way lights up the passage
with fantastic clarity.

Thurman's Jesus is declaring to the oppressed that they should live with
a "complete and devastating sincerity" (p. 59) in all relationships, even with
those who can kill them (you). Thurman is entirely aware that this does not

come naturally under these conditions. Indeed, he has already reviewed two other options for beaten-down people in relation to deception—they can lie freely in relation to the oppressor, assuming the oppressor does not deserve the truth, or they can lie selectively in certain areas while trying to protect other areas where they will not lie. The problem with either of these options is that they are degrading, humiliating, and morally damaging. The truth matters so much that having to violate it regularly is soul-killing.

This is the reason why Jesus counsels a fearless commitment to telling the truth regardless of power imbalances. This is for self-respect, for integrity, for a reintegration of the oppressed person of their relation to God with their relation to others.

But also, says Thurman, fearless truthfulness might also have a surprisingly transformative effect on the oppressor. Powerful people who are not accustomed to being told the truth by those who are "beneath" them can be thrown off balance by no longer being able to validate themselves based on their power. If I say, "No, today, I will tell the truth and I will not be pushed around," the oppressor may lash out with further abuse of power, sure— but he/she may also be shaken loose from their own bondage, potentially changed for the better by this surprising move on our part. We, meanwhile, the abused, will have made a great breakthrough toward viewing ourselves, and maybe even toward being treated, with the dignity that every person deserves.

In Thurman's view, the fearless, oppressed Jesus counsels choosing the possibility of a shorter life over the inevitability of soul self-destruction through constant lying to save one's own skin. When one reviews Jesus' own life with this in view, we see that this is exactly what Jesus did. He told the truth fearlessly, to all and sundry. He was dead by 33. Yet surely it was his utter fearlessness and truth-speaking that so attracted people to Jesus.

Thurman is never better in this book than in his gritty and realistic treatment of the development of hate in the lives of the oppressed.

Jesus teaches his followers to love rather than hate their enemies (Mt 5:43–48). But Thurman understands that hatred, when it comes from the disinherited, is a fully understandable response to oppression. When a group of people is spitting on you and yours, discriminating against you, and even periodically murdering you, not to feel anything in response is to surrender. Hatred, from below, says Thurman, becomes a primary path to self-validation, self-respect, and resistance. To hate someone who treats you like you are worthless is to refuse to accept your supposed worthlessness.

In situations of group-on-group oppression, like Roman occupation, hate is therefore normal, natural, and to be expected. It is what the oppressed feel, in order not to be broken by their oppression.

Thurman, of course, acknowledges that Jesus teaches love—not just of neighbors but of enemies. How in the world could he do that? Does he not know what it is like to be oppressed? Well, yes, of course he does.

Jesus, though, also knows that "hatred destroys finally the life of the hater" (p. 76). It brings disintegration from the inside as all creative energies are dried up. Hatred may bring temporary self-validation but at the ultimate cost of inner spiritual death.

So Jesus teaches love. This is not a sentimental love. Love here is a decision. It is a decision not to let that inner spiritual death get the last word. But you must work your way through the hate to get to the love.

Thurman offers certain practical strategies for disciplining the impulse to hate. We can recall that no evil deed inflicted upon us represents the full intent of the doer. We can remember that those who inflict harm on us ultimately have that harm double back on themselves. And we can humbly acknowledge that God forgives us of our own misdeeds. We choose love.

When we do this, we open the door to the possibility of transforming hateful situations—and oppressors. We may be able to create the opportunity for a breakthrough on their part. We certainly will find it an inner breakthrough on *our* part—and in the end, that is reason enough to choose love.

4.5 Conclusion: Thurman and the Dream of a Kingdom

Howard Thurman accomplished so many important things with *Jesus and the Disinherited*, a book that is now seven decades old and as compelling as ever. His book permanently affected my approach to Christian ethics in the following ways:

- Rooting Jesus in his Jewish, Palestinian, Roman-occupied, concrete historical situation;

- Studying the Sermon on the Mount closely and taking Jesus' teachings seriously as a path to transcendence and empowerment amid real-life hardship and struggle;

- Bringing the hard-fought spiritual lessons learned over three centuries of the Southern U.S. Black Christian tradition to a central place in global theology and ethics;
- Articulating Christian ethics as leaning into the dream of a better world, as "kingdom ethics."

Notice how Thurman describes it:

> Living in a climate of deep insecurity, Jesus, faced with so narrow a margin of civil guarantees, had to find some other basis upon which to establish a sense of well-being. He knew that the goals of religion could never be worked out within the then-established order. Deep from within that order he projected a dream, the logic of which would give to all the needful security. There would be room for all, and no man need would be a threat to his brother. 'The kingdom of God is within you' (Thurman, p. 24).

Thurman's version of the kingdom of God here is more mystical and inward than what Glen Stassen and I offer in *Kingdom Ethics*.

We argue that Jesus taught about a new kind of world dawning with his coming, a kingdom of God filled with justice, peace, and healing.

Thurman's emphasis in this book is more on the dawning of a new *inner world*, powerful enough to transcend a still deeply broken outer world— with, perhaps, occasional victories in that outer world.

Howard Thurman's kingdom of God looks less like a world transformed beyond its injustice and more like oppressed people themselves transformed despite the injustice that continues.

As I look back on thirty years of personal experience and world history, Thurman's approach looks better than ever.

I once hoped for a world transformed. Chastened, today I mainly hope for the formation of communities of Christ-followers who will live in the way of Jesus regardless of the direction of world history.

The next chapter will offer a full (re)consideration of the role of the kingdom of God in Christian ethics.

Discussion Questions:

1. If Jesus' teachings are best understood by those who also suffer oppression, what are privileged people supposed to do with them—or even to understand them?

2. Many of us have been taught to read all figures and voices in the Bible as having the same authority or even as saying the same thing. But consider what Thurman says about Jesus by comparison with Paul. Discuss.

3. What do you think about the idea that even though fear, deception, and even hate are perfectly natural responses to oppression, Jesus says we must ultimately reject all three? Is Thurman reading Jesus correctly? If so, do we still care to follow Jesus?

4. Which do you think is a more relevant vision: the kingdom of God as global moral transformation, or as a kind of inner vision regardless of what happens in the outer world?

To watch Dr. Gushee deliver

**Lecture 5: The Kingdom of God as the
              Narrative Frame for Christian Ethics**

Follow this link:

https://youtu.be/vc7QU-_gwr4

Or scan the QR code.

To listen to the audio, follow this link:

https://qrco.de/bcLtnx

Or scan the QR code.

To scan a QR code, download a QR reader from the app store on your device, open the application, follow the directions, and point your device's camera at the code.

CHAPTER 5

The Kingdom of God as the Narrative Frame for Christian Ethics

5.1 Storytelling Creatures, Narrative Theology

Human beings are storytelling creatures. This is one of the things that most definitely sets us apart from other creatures. We make up stories, mundane and fantastical, from childhood forward. "Once upon a time ..."

It is amazing to watch my 6-year-old grandson Jonah switch instantaneously from regular time to story time. One moment he is just back from school and getting some pretzels and juice. The next minute he is cutting up a cardboard box to make himself imaginary rotors for the helicopter he will strap to his back when he flies away. No one has to ask him to do this. We would have to ask him *not* to do this. He's a natural storyteller. It is delightful.

Humans tell stories to make meaning of our lives. Maybe not all of us, and certainly not all the time, but most of us, some of the time, think of our lives in terms of a story. "My parents were ... I was born in ... I found my sense of direction when ... we were married on a scorching hot August day ... the cold January night that Holly was born we were living in New York and ... I am hoping to end my story this way ..."

Narrative theology is a term adopted in the 1980s by so-called postliberal theologians to describe the articulation of religious beliefs by living religious communities using their own central stories, in their own linguistic categories. Narrative theology was a breakthrough past the fundamentalist-liberal split in Protestantism, because it saw both as modern projects—in that both had left the Christian narrative behind as they reduced Christianity either to divinely revealed dogma on the fundamentalist side or rationally defensible husks of Christian belief on the modernist side. Narrative theology was developed primarily by Yale Divinity School theologians Hans Frei (1920–1988; *The Eclipse of Biblical Narrative*, 1974), and George Lindbeck (1923–2018; *The Nature of Doctrine*, 1984). It was brought into ethics under the influence of Yale-trained Stanley Hauerwas. I recommend his co-edited 1989 work, with L. Gregory Jones, called *Why Narrative?*

Narrative theologians are determined to speak about Christianity in terms of the scriptural story, and stories. They see Christian existence as fundamentally being about learning to narrate our lives within the frame of the biblical story, or the story of Jesus, and to live in a manner befitting for those who are part of that story.

I like narrative theology because I think it fits with scripture. Surely the Bible contains much more than narratives, or one big narrative—but the canon in its final shape does have a narrative through-line. It looks something like this: God made a good world, human beings sinned and tragically disrupted the goodness of God's world, God grieved, punished, but then began a long history of acting to redeem our broken selves and broken world. God elected Israel as covenant partner and light to the nations, shepherding the Jewish people through a long, winding history that included slavery, rescue, lawgiving, wilderness wandering, conquest of the promised land, kingship, division, defeat, exile, return, and restoration. God took human flesh in the Jew Jesus to culminate the story of Israel's salvation and extend it to all the world. Jesus was born, preached the good news of God's kingdom, healed, exorcised, loved, suffered, was crucified and buried, and raised from the dead. Jesus founded the church to continue his ministry until he returns at the end of the age.

All theological claims made within Christian faith are secondary to this Story and should be organically derived from it.

5.2 Rationalist/Experiential vs. Narrative Ethics

Narrative ethics is a term that we can use to describe ways of "doing ethics" that are explicitly rooted in a story, or stories, such as what we find in the Bible.

It is certainly not necessary to situate the work of ethics within a narrative frame. Indeed, it can seem that the moral dimension of human experience is more-or-less timeless. While moral problems arise for each individual within the context of his or her uniquely personal story, the moral dimension of life as a whole seems perennial, ubiquitous, and constant. People always and everywhere encounter moral challenges such as how to relate to their parents, siblings, and children, what goals to seek as they craft the direction of their lives, how to deal with crisis situations like unwanted pregnancies or ruptured marriages, how to relate to social inequalities and prejudices, how to organize public life, whether to kill when the tribe or the nation demand it, and whether to tell the truth even when it brings personal embarrassment.

Many traditions of ethical reflection have emerged in contexts without an especially strong or compelling shared narrative, religious or otherwise. The ancient Greek philosophers—Socrates, Plato, and Aristotle—who founded a critically important part of the Western ethical tradition, did not seriously contextualize their ethical analysis or moral counsel within a religious narrative frame. While they were situated within a particular cultural context with its own particular religious stories, they did not articulate their ethics in religious-narrative terms. Instead, they spoke to what they believed to be enduring aspects of human nature and the human predicament on this Earth.

Modern Enlightenment moral philosophers such as John Stuart Mill and Immanuel Kant, though they were inheritors of the Western Christian tradition and reflected its impact, attempted to offer ethics of principles/theories that any rational person could accept upon reflection. There was no narrative frame to their theories. These were rationally deduced maxims that, supposedly, could be applied always and everywhere.

I am arguing that several of the major strands of the Western moral tradition are rationalistic, perhaps also experiential, but explicitly non-narrative. Human beings learn what to do through reason and maybe also through experience, and the lessons learned apply always and everywhere, until the big asteroid strikes, the sun explodes, or Jesus returns.

Jewish narrative ethics, however, situates Jewish moral obligation within the frame of the Jewish narrative, especially as found in the Hebrew Bible, the giving of Torah, and the covenant of God with the Jewish people. Christian narrative ethics embraces the Hebrew Bible and its narrative but also includes, and of course centers on, the narrative of Jesus Christ. In both cases, moral obligations are not derived merely from reason or broad human experience but instead are situated within the framework of the biblical story, and specific stories.

For Christians also, moral norms, principles, virtues, goals, responsibilities, obligations, and so on, do not just hang in the air independently, and are not just derived from reason or experience, but are situated within the story of Jesus and all that this signifies. We conduct ourselves in such-and-such a manner because this is how characters who are a part of the story of Jesus must live. That is the grand insight of narrative ethics, which is just a fancy recent way of recalling that Christianity is a story, not just a belief system or a set of rules and principles.

5.3 Kingdom Ethics as an Apocalyptic Christian Narrative Ethics

Anyone who reads our book *Kingdom Ethics* is immediately plunged into a distinctive form of Christian narrative ethics. Glen Stassen and I claim, based on the authority and example of Jesus as recorded in three of the four Gospels, that the kingdom of God constituted the narrative frame for our Lord's moral teachings and that it should function in the same way for Christians today. Let me now rehearse that argument, which was sourced in biblical scholarship by major figures such as W.D. Davies (1911–2001, *The Setting of the Sermon on the Mount*, 1964), N.T. Wright (*Jesus and the Victory of God*, 1996), and Bruce Chilton (*Pure Kingdom*, 1996).

"The good news of the kingdom of God" (Mt 4:17) was the substance of Jesus' message—his "gospel." This message had Old Testament roots, especially passages from the prophet Isaiah that were especially influential in shaping Jesus' own vision (Is 9:2–7, 35:5–10, 60:17–19, etc.). Jesus clearly situated his own ministry within the prophetic hope, and promise, of a future redemption of Israel, and the world, in which sinful human (and demonic) rebellion against God is defeated and God will reign in all creation as the Creator-King rightly deserves.

Jesus reflected the this-worldly orientation of the Jewish tradition in viewing God's redemptive triumph as consisting in deliverance from captivity, justice prevailing over injustice, peace ending war, inclusion overcoming exclusion, healing beating sickness and death, and joy finally winning out over sorrow as God comes in power to rule. "God shall wipe away every tear from their eyes ..." (Is 25/Rev 21). We call these characteristics of God's reign the "seven marks of the kingdom."

This kingdom-of-God narrative is **apocalyptic** in that it "purports to unveil the meaning of past, present, or future historical events as part of God's redemptive plan" (*KE* Glossary, p. 450). Jesus chose to focus on, adopt, and reframe not just the prophetic part of the Jewish tradition but the apocalyptic component of some of the prophets. It is also **eschatological**, in that it has to do with the decisive events scheduled by God for the end of time.

We suggest that the teachings of Jesus about the kingdom of God not only offer a narrative frame for the moral lives of his disciples, but also specify a large number of moral norms, practices, and virtues that are suitable—fitting—for those living within this narrative. Moreover, we suggest an **inaugurated eschatology** approach to Jesus and the kingdom, in which Jesus' coming initiates the "End of Days," which will be fully consummated at Jesus' return. This gives Christians both a strong motivation and a clear time horizon for our moral living. The motivation is this: every time we do an act of justice, peacemaking, deliverance, inclusion, healing, or whatever, we are participating in the advance of the kingdom of God. Our story joins Jesus' story and helps to advance it. The time horizon is this: we, the church, will participate in kingdom advancement until the end.

Another way to conceptualize this is that the eschaton is reaching back toward us from the future, and we glimpse it, taste it, even help bring it into reality in our world as we live kingdom-of-God lives. This is sometimes called **proleptic theology/ethics** and is associated with the work of Ted Peters, especially his 1992 book, *God: The World's Future*. Peters says that we participate in the coming future by living according to its terms right now. In this way the future breaks into the present, through us.

This kingdom-focused narrative framing puts Christian morality into a cosmic, Jesus-centered narrative frame. It provides a deep grounding for a social justice and world peace orientation that addresses vast social sins with a Social Gospel. In this approach there is no arena of life that is exempt from searching kingdom-of-God reflection and action, leading to a clearer moral purpose for the average local church, and a deeper emphasis on Christian mission as being about moral action in this world as well as preparing souls to meet God and enter eternal life.

5.4 Problems with a Kingdom Ethics Narrative Frame

It seems fitting to address some of the problems, or at least challenges, that can arise in relation to the kingdom-of-God frame for Christian ethics.

1. It can be disputed whether Jesus himself really believed that his own story was an inaugurated eschatology. Perhaps he believed that his coming was going to trigger the end of the age immediately, or at least imminently. The evidence for this includes statements in the Gospel accounts in which he suggests that the end is at hand or that people who are listening will not die before they see it (cf. Mk 13:30 and parallels).

2. As Jewish scholars routinely point out, while the Jewish hope of redemption was and is this-worldly and does indeed involve the comprehensive healing of this broken world (in Hebrew, *tikkun olam*) neither the earthly Jesus nor the church achieved anything like this redemption. Children are still murdered, economic injustice is still rampant, bigotry still poisons relationships. It is hard to accept that Jesus has "inaugurated" a new age when the evidence of the promised change is so sparse.

3. Apocalyptic literature is among the most fantastical, some might say desperate, in all the Bible. It emerges from people in crisis, and— it can be argued—deals with deep suffering and broken dreams by projecting vengeance-and-rescue scenarios. In other words, many believers in many religions have gone wrong reading apocalyptic sacred texts as if they provide sure guidance for action in the real world. For this reason, some argue, these texts really do not provide a secure basis for everyday Christian ethics.

4. The idea that Christians get to participate in advancing God's kingdom might inappropriately shift the balance between God's redemptive actions and our own. *We* become the ones who bring in the kingdom, through what *we* do. Now, the counter to this argument is that God has always invited cooperation from obedient believers in bringing redemption—look at Noah, or Abraham and Sarah, or Moses, or David, or Paul. Stassen and I say in *Kingdom Ethics* that ***participative grace*** is God's recurring pattern toward us, not overpowering divine action to which we simply surrender. Still, some worry that this approach is too human-centered.

5. It has been easy for Christians to over-identify their understanding of moral progress with God's own kingdom. Peace is temporarily negotiated between Iceland and Greenland and we see a victory for the kingdom. Social insurance is enacted that provides a better safety net for the poor and we claim a kingdom win. Or worse: A revolution topples the czar in Russia and some call it a victory for God's reign, despite the abundant bloodshed that follows. Don't we need a way to think about morality, even social justice efforts, that is smaller, more incremental, and this-worldly, that sees good reasons to do good moral work in the world, but without sweeping everything up into the massive story of the coming of God's kingdom? Who are we to say that this or that thing that happens is a victory, or defeat, for God's own kingdom?

6. Kingdom-of-God thinking has been pegged as a temptation to a wild-eyed *millenarianism*. This is the term for the belief by a religious, social, or political group or movement in a coming fundamental transformation of society, after which all things will be better. Visions of global transformation can tempt fanatics and revolutionaries to topple thrones and powers in the name of their dream. And what happens when millenarian dreams go sour, and their adherents plunge into despair?

7. It is very difficult to maintain a time-urgent eschatological vision when Jesus keeps *not* returning and history keeps *not* ending. Historical theologians can easily document how quickly mainstream Christianity quieted its apocalyptic fervor after Jesus' ministry. The seemingly unreachable kingdom dream of global moral transformation changed into a more imaginable dream of a seedling of new humanity coming to exist in the Church of Jesus Christ. Indeed, over time, language about the "kingdom of God" either dwindled to insignificance or shifted to mean, variously, a) the church, b) heaven, or c) earthly Christian kingdoms, from Constantine forward. This can be critiqued as a great loss of the church's primal moral vision, and it was thus critiqued by Walter Rauschenbusch and other early 20th century leaders of the Social Gospel movement. But the problem remains, that human nature bucks hard against eschatological visions when they never yield the eschaton.

8. Finally, some theologians and moral thinkers have concluded that it is sounder to focus on what God *has already done* in Christ than on what will purportedly one day happen, at the end of time. Dietrich Bonhoeffer (1906–1945) is a major example of a Christian thinker who never ceased to focus on Jesus Christ, but whose grand narrative was of God's having become human, *which has already happened*, instead of the coming of the kingdom in the future. For Bonhoeffer, because God became human in Christ, humanity is reclaimed, the image of God is restored, and humans are invited to accept re-formation into the image of Christ that was always God's plan for human flourishing.

In terms of narrative, Bonhoeffer offers a kind of **realized eschatology**, centering on the implications of what God has already done in Christ. Bonhoeffer explicitly rejected rooting Christian ethics in the narrative frame of the kingdom of God, which he identified with the end of the world. He writes: "no one has the responsibility to turn the world into the kingdom of God, but only of taking the next necessary step that corresponds to God's becoming human in Christ" (Bonhoeffer, *Ethics*, 224–225). Jens Zimmermann, in his magisterial 2019 book *Dietrich Bonhoeffer's Christian Humanism*, offers the best recent account of how Bonhoeffer's theological ethics are structured in this way.

But what are we to make of the stubborn fact that Jesus came preaching the kingdom of God? This is the reason why many find themselves embracing a "kingdom ethics." Because Jesus himself did so.

5.5 Narrative Frames in Christian Ethics Today

In the final section of this chapter, I want to take you on a brief tour of some other important voices in Christian ethics to see what narrative frame they seem to adopt.

Martin Luther King projected the appealing vision of the "Beloved Community," a concept that goes back a hundred years in Western liberal theology but that he transformed into something like a kingdom-of-God-comes-to-racist-America eschatological vision. King's education involved serious study of the Social Gospel movement, and his vision was steeped in the long, rich legacy of Black Christianity in America. We have already noted the influence of his Boston University chaplain, Howard Thurman, as well. King's narrative frame certainly had a deeply eschatological dimension, though the story he invited Americans to live into was mainly its transformation into a country that resembles its own proclaimed values.

Liberation theology, as developed by figures such as James Cone and Gustavo Gutierrez (beginning with his *Theology of Liberation*, 1971), centers especially on the Exodus narrative to claim that God's essential character is as liberator of the oppressed of this world. While liberation theology takes various forms, it can be viewed within the narrative frame of an apocalyptic, eschatological, or kingdom ethic, because it sets forth a vision of a world transformed through political and social liberation efforts in which God and people cooperate. You could say that liberationists take liberation-from-oppression to be the fundamental mark of the activity and reign of God in this world.

Womanist theology is a powerful, progressive Black feminist approach born in the 1980s in dialogue with James Cone, with its earliest major voices including Katie Cannon (1950–2018; *Black Womanist Ethics*, 1988), Renita Weems (*Just a Sister Away*, 1988), Jacquelyn Grant (*White Women's Christ and Black Women's Jesus*, 1989), and Emilie Townes (*Womanist Justice, Womanist Hope*, 1993). Reflecting deeply on the experience of Black women in the United States especially, womanist theologians and ethicists generally do not name liberation as their fundamental moral norm or goal, but instead something more like *survival with unbroken dignity in community* amid circumstances of often crushing sexual, racial, and economic oppression. Womanists routinely press for a much more just world, but the narrative frame of their ethics is more the Black female experience in the United States than a kingdom-of-God world transformation story. A 2011 edited work, *Womanist Theological Ethics*, is a significant recent compilation.

Miguel De La Torre, a Cuban American Baptist ethicist, for several decades described his ethics as liberationist. (See his 2013 *Ethics: A Liberative Approach*.) However, in a relatively recent turn in his thought, he has provocatively rejected either a kingdom-of-God or liberationist narrative frame and instead embraced what he would describe as the honest hopelessness of the irremediably oppressed (De La Torre, *Embracing Hopelessness*, 2017). De La Torre does not believe that any global transformation or divine kingdom is coming, but he calls the oppressed to continue to fight for their rights and for justice. De La Torre's move here is a reminder that many motivations can lead to work for justice, rights, and dignity, and that an eschatological narrative frame is not required.

The teaching of the Roman Catholic Church is that the kingdom of God should be viewed as simultaneously a past, present, and future reality. In the official *Catechism of the Catholic Church* (#2816–2821), the kingdom is described as having "come in Christ's death and resurrection," as "in our midst" in the Eucharist, and as "coming in glory when Christ hands it over to his Father" after his return. The Catholic Church claims that when Jesus taught us to pray "Thy kingdom come" he was primarily referring to this final coming of God's reign. But meanwhile "far from distracting the church from her mission in this present world, this desire commits her to it all the more strongly." The Holy Spirit, given at Pentecost, is the One who does the work of the Reign of God, though the battle continues in us and around us for the Spirit's triumph over sin and the flesh. The Spirit assists the church in "distinguish[ing] between the growth of the Reign of God and the progress of the culture and society in which [we] are involved." But "this distinction is not a separation. Man's vocation to eternal life does not suppress, but actually reinforces, his duty to put into action in this world the energies and means received from the Creator to serve justice and peace."

Overall, this careful both/and Catholic synthesis situates the kingdom-of-God narrative frame as more supplemental than central to the Christian moral life. The church situates its moral teachings in the Catechism not under the heading of the kingdom of God but instead under "life in Christ," "the dignity of the human person" and the proper shape of the "human community." Eschatology is not central to the presentation offered.

5.6 Conclusion: Timeless Challenges and the Kingdom of God

My own reading of scripture—which centers on the Story of, and stories about, Jesus—makes it impossible for me to jettison the narrative frame of the kingdom of God. However, I am much more wary than I used to be about entirely situating Christian ethics within a kingdom narrative. The errors into which many believers have drifted when turning to apocalyptic scenarios are all too clear. Human nature and human moral challenges do have a certain timeless quality to them and perhaps are best addressed within the broader, less apocalyptic frame of creation, fall, covenant, and redemption.

And yet, that dream, that vision, of a perfected and renewed world never goes away—especially for those who need it most badly. A central place that we see Jesus projecting that dream, and teaching people to live into it, is in his Sermon on the Mount. That is our next stop on the journey.

Discussion Questions:

1. What is the difference between a narrative ethic and a rationalist or experiential one?

2. Inaugurated eschatology and participative grace are two important technical terms that help explain the narrative frame of "kingdom ethics." What do these terms mean and how do they fit together?

3. Does the "kingdom ethics" narrative frame inspire you, work for you, make sense to you? Would it make sense to the people of your church?

4. What are the most important concerns about or objections to making the kingdom narrative central to Christian ethics?

5. Of the options named in the last section of the chapter, which one or ones do you find most interesting or worth further exploration?

To watch Dr. Gushee deliver

**Lecture 6: The Sermon on the Mount
and Christian Ethics**

Follow this link:

https://youtu.be/bSSZYb2BvIg

Or scan the QR code.

To listen to the audio, follow this link:

https://qrco.de/bcOl17

Or scan the QR code.

To scan a QR code, download a QR reader from the app store on your device, open the application, follow the directions, and point your device's camera at the code.

CHAPTER 6

The Sermon on the Mount and Christian Ethics

6.1 The Mountain of the Sermon on the Mount

The Sermon on the Mount is the single most important biblical text in the history of Christian ethics. It is the longest single block of Jesus' teaching that we have in the Synoptic Gospels. It focuses on how people are supposed to live. It was central in the moral instruction of large sections of the early church, once the canon was completed.

The Sermon has been central in shaping the moral vision of many specific Christian groups and movements, ranging from the Anabaptists of the 16th and 17th centuries to today's Christian pacifists, radicals, and peace-and-justice advocates. It has a kind of constitutional role in such communities. On the other hand, it has proved to be a stumbling block to many Christians who do not find its teachings congenial or realistic. But even those who do not like the Sermon on the Mount have to deal with it, by finding some way to reinterpret, evade, or dismiss it.

The Sermon on the Mount is, indeed, something like a mountain. Those of us who say we are Christians can't miss it. We must deal with it.

6.2 Reviewing the Content of the Sermon on the Mount

The Sermon on the Mount is found only in Matthew, though Luke 6:20–48 offers considerable parallel material, and certain sayings found in the Sermon float elsewhere in other Gospels.

Matthew constructs his account of Jesus' ministry in a way that basically launches with the Sermon on the Mount. After the birth narrative (Mt 1–2), we meet John the Baptist and Jesus is baptized by him (Mt 3). Then Jesus is led by the Spirit into the wilderness and enters his 40-day fast and temptation experience (Mt 4:1–11). John the Baptist is arrested and Jesus moves from Nazareth to Capernaum to begin his ministry, starting with proclamation of the dawning kingdom (Mt 4:12–17). He calls his first four disciples (Mt 4:18–22). Jesus' ministry expands throughout Galilee, and a summary includes preaching, healing, and exorcism (Mt 4:23–25).

Crowds gather from everywhere. Then immediately comes the Sermon, which is offered on "the mountain" (Mt 5:1). The narrative slows down suddenly, and we experience Jesus offering extended authoritative teaching. The mountain setting, as well as all the references within the Sermon to Jewish law and tradition, certainly suggests to a knowledgeable Jewish reader that Jesus is a Moses figure, delivering God's Law from the mountain.

Matthew 5:3–12 the "Beatitudes," which open the Sermon, can be interpreted in various ways. At one level, they can be read as statements of desirable virtues and practices—humility, mourning, meekness, hunger for justice, mercy, purity of heart, peacemaking, endurance of persecution for justice and the kingdom. In *Kingdom Ethics* Glen Stassen and I argue that these sayings should be interpreted in a more dynamic, prophetic, kingdom-tinged way. Jesus is saying that God is acting now to deliver the world. The kinds of people who are ready to participate in God's deliverance— indeed, who are perhaps already participating—live like this.

Matthew 5:13–16, the "salt and light" passage, has normally been interpreted by Christians to speak to the distinctive, world-preserving, world-changing, way of life of followers of Jesus. In *Kingdom Ethics*, we suggest that those who do what Jesus teaches are the ones functioning as the world-preserving, world-changing, Christ-witnessing community.

Matthew 5:17–20 situates Jesus' teaching in relation to "the law and the prophets," that is, the Old Testament canon, Jewish law, and perhaps even Jewish tradition. The teaching is paradoxical. Matthew's Jesus comes to fulfill, not abolish, Jewish law. Jesus comes not to annul or displace that law but to "exceed" or even perfect it. Awareness of the tensions in early Christian communities over Jewish law as it pertains to Gentile converts makes one wonder whether this is an argument from the "conservative," retain-Jewish-law side. Or it could be what Jesus really taught. Or both. We can complicate the matter further by reminding ourselves that one person's "fulfillment" of a tradition is another's annulment.

Matthew 5:21–48, sometimes called the "antitheses," contains six sayings framed with the repeated "You have heard that it was said (to those of ancient times), but I say to you ..." Most Christians have been taught to read this central part of the Sermon as setting aside, annulling, or at least radically intensifying Old Testament passages or even Law. But in 5:17–20 Jesus had just said that he was not abolishing or annulling the Law. If we take this claim at face value, the Sermon on the Mount is going to offer an intensification, but not annulment, of Jewish Law.

Christians have generally been taught to read the intensification this way: Not just murder is banned, but anger, insults, and name-calling (5:21–26). Not just adultery is wrong, but also looking with lust (5:27–30). The Old Testament teaching permitting divorce if a proper certificate is offered the wife is intensified by banning divorce except for *porneia* (5:31–32; usually translated as unchastity). The teaching banning false oaths becomes a command not to swear oaths at all (5:33–37). The authorization of strictly proportional retaliatory violence is replaced by the command to turn the other cheek (5:38–42), and the traditional practice of loving neighbors and hating enemies becomes a command to love your enemies (5:43–48).

Matthew 6:1–18 is an exhortation to continue with core Jewish practices of **almsgiving**, fasting, and prayer, with strong emphasis on doing so only for God and not to be seen by others. During the instruction on prayer, famously known as the Lord's Prayer, Jesus also offers an unequivocal command to forgive and links it to God forgiving us. We will return to this teaching later.

Matthew 6:19-34 focuses on material possessions. Jesus teaches treasuring heavenly rather than earthly treasures, avoiding greed (or even wealth), not worrying about daily material needs, trusting God, and striving for God's kingdom.

Finally, Matthew 7 bans judging others and instead urges humble self-correction (1–5). Jesus teaches trusting prayer as if God is a good father—because that is what God is—rather than, in our insecurity, placing our trust in those who are not worthy of it (6–11). Jesus gives us the Golden Rule in v. 12: "In everything do to others as you would have them do to you." This is one of the most significant moral teachings ever.

In his peroration (13–27) Jesus says the way to "life" is narrow rather than wide, that we need to beware of many false prophets, that actions flow from character and a life is tested by its fruits, that practicing his teachings rather than merely calling him 'Lord' is what matters to Jesus. He promises that a life built on his words will stand every stress, while, as the hymn says, "all other ground is sinking sand."

6.3 Obedience or Evasion in Response to the Sermon

Glen Stassen convinced me from his historical research that there are really two fundamental kinds of responses to the Sermon on the Mount among Christians—efforts to obey and efforts to evade. The efforts to obey came first. The efforts to evade came later, but eventually triumphed.

When we dive into the Sermon on the Mount and see what the fuss is about, it becomes clear that the focus of conflict is really Matthew 5:21–48, the so-called antitheses, and to a lesser extent Matthew 6:19–34, related to wealth and trust. Christians do not argue with the same intensity about the other parts.

The crux of the concern is that the teachings of Jesus in these sections are—it is claimed—not natural, possible, realistic, or perhaps even desirable for human beings. It is not natural or possible to avoid all anger, especially when we have been harmed. It is not natural or realistic to demand that we never look with sexual desire on someone who is not our spouse. It is not realistic or desirable to restrict divorce to grounds of sexual misconduct—think of the violence in some marriages! It is not natural, possible, or desirable to ask human beings to refrain from self-defense and to demand that we replace hatred for enemies with love. It is not realistic never to worry about having enough to eat, clothes to wear, or money in the bank, and not desirable to have that attitude if we are responsible for other people.

If this is how you read the Sermon on the Mount, but you want to appear to take both Jesus and the Bible seriously, you have some work to do. Stassen is right that this "work" has generally taken the form of finding some way to evade the Sermon's clear teachings, usually by supposing some kind of *moral dualism*—splitting off the teachings of the Sermon from the real world of real people today.

We can, for example, argue that Jesus was addressing *private* life, and not *public* life, and thus exempt public officials from the teachings.

We can say that Jesus was addressing the *inner* realm of our attitudes rather than the *outer* realm of our actions, and thus we can exempt our actions from the teachings. (For example, in the setting of war: "I don't hate you, but I will kill you if I must.")

We can follow old-school **dispensational theology** and say that Jesus was *not addressing the world of now*, the current "dispensation," but instead the world after he comes back, and thus we can exempt the present from the reach of his teachings.

We can say that Jesus desired *not obedience but repentance*, as in "I know I can't obey these teachings, and this is sinful; I admit my need for forgiveness of sins through Christ." We keep on sinning, but we are grateful for grace.

We can say that Jesus' teachings apply to Christians in the realm of the *church*, but in the realm of the *world* even Christians must play by other rules. Consider a perfectly devout Christian family person who teaches Sunday school—and who also happens to be president, and at this moment is signing off on a decision to bomb another country.

We can imagine the Sermon as **counsels of perfection**, as the Catholic Church historically did, suggesting that only a monastic or clerical class, set apart from real world living, can attempt to apply them in their cloistered realm.

Stassen was convinced that all these evasions and dualisms constituted a systematic effort to avoid obeying what Jesus taught. Because Christians are, by my definition and by his, people who are defined by their decision to follow Jesus and serve him as Lord, such evasion and dualism represent a fundamental negation of Christian identity.

Stassen was also convinced that much of what has gone wrong in the history of Christianity is tied to this evasion of Jesus' central body of moral teachings. Jesus taught a countercultural way of deliverance from all that is so wrong in the human heart and in the world. But we choose to ignore him while claiming to be his followers. This helps account for why thoughtful people like Mahatma Gandhi, who deeply honored Jesus and the Sermon on the Mount, have said that they would be happy to become Christians, if they could ever meet one. (A wonderful resource offering Gandhi's take on these matters is a 1991 edited collection called *Gandhi on Christianity*.)

Okay, fair enough. But what about all these objections? Are they simply to be dismissed as a historic wrong turn? Is it indeed possible, realistic, or desirable to attempt to bind ourselves to obey commands like never being angry, turning the other cheek, loving our enemies, and abandoning any concern for material possessions?

6.4 Glen Stassen on the Sermon on the Mount

Glen Stassen attempted to address the crux of these objections with his trailblazing *transforming initiatives* interpretation of the Sermon. It was one of his greatest contributions to biblical studies and Christian ethics. This interpretation dominates the discussion of the Sermon in *Kingdom Ethics*, both the first and second edition. It is well worth taking some time to review his argument.

The trajectory of his interpretation was set in part by his reading of the Sermon on the Mount as a manifesto for participation in the dawning kingdom of God. If, as we know, Jesus began his ministry by proclaiming "Repent, for the kingdom of heaven has come near" (Mt 4:17), it makes sense to believe that his teaching is both part of that message and preparation for the kingdom. If the Sermon on the Mount is a message that helps people repent, prepare for, and participate in God's kingdom of deliverance, justice, peace, healing, and renewed community, then we will not be quite as surprised by what Jesus offers there.

Further, if we accept the internal claim of the Sermon that Jesus' teachings are not meant as annulments of Jewish law but as true fulfillments, we pick up another important piece to the puzzle. We should look for teachings that both return to the wellspring of God's dealings with Israel in the past and also lead toward the redemption of Israel and of all the nations, long promised but not yet fulfilled.

The linguistic discovery that helped unlock a new interpretation of the Sermon for Stassen was his find that it is possible—he would say not just possible but clearly preferable—for the Sermon to be read not as antitheses, but as triads. In other words, at least Matthew 5:21–48 but ultimately Matthew 5:21-7:11 should be read not as old/new antithetical dyads but as 14 triads containing a) traditional righteousness, b) sinful pattern, and c) transforming initiative (see *KE* Glossary, pp. 471, 473–474). Stassen's linguistic evidence included the pivotal fact that, especially in Matthew 5:21–48, the passages contain more than just "they said/but now I say," and the "more" includes an imperative verb that climaxes each saying and should be what draws our attention.

Thus, in Matthew 5:21–48 Jesus begins with a restatement of traditional teaching in v. 21: Do not murder. It's in the Ten Commandments. Jesus believes in it and wants us to obey it. He then lays out the escalating anger and hateful words that take people perilously toward violence (v. 22). Stassen called this the "sinful pattern" of how anger moves up the ladder to violence, a routine, awful feature of human life which Jesus diagnoses realistically. He then concludes the teaching with the climactic imperative to drop everything, even your once-a-year sacrificial gift at the altar of the temple, to go make an effort at reconciliation with your offended brother or sister (v. 23–24).

If we both want to obey God's Law and participate in the dawning of God's reign, this is what we must do—develop the practice of proactive peacemaking. There is nothing unrealistic, impossible, or undesirable about that. Indeed, Stassen loved to give historical and personal examples of conflicted situations resolved through this practice. Yes, it seems hard, maybe even unnatural, to drop our proverbial or literal swords and go try to make peace. And yes, it does not always work, because others do not always respond accordingly.

But sometimes when we surprise someone from whom we are estranged by taking an initiative to heal the breach, our brokenness can be transformed into renewed friendship. Who can deny that this is both possible and desirable? *Surprising—transforming—initiatives.* That was Stassen's great discovery, and his proposal for how to read the Sermon on the Mount. Look not for impossible ideals but transforming initiatives.

As Glen Stassen also loved to point out, isn't that exactly what God offered the world in Jesus Christ? God didn't offer us ideals or impossible teachings. God offered us reconciliation through Jesus Christ. "Rarely will anyone die for a righteous person—though perhaps for a good person someone might actually dare to die. But God proves his love for us in that while we still were sinners Christ died for us" (Rom 5:7-8).

Stassen's claim was that the entire Sermon on the Mount (that is, 5:21–7:12) is structured in this triadic way, featuring transforming initiatives as the climactic teaching.

I think this claim is quite persuasive in relation to the teaching on oaths (5:33–37), where Jesus turns a sinful pattern of playing games with promises to God and others into a straightforward demand for honesty in all relationships. It also seems compelling in relation to the sinful pattern of religion becoming a showpiece rather than a true expression of devotion to God (6:1–18). The transforming initiative here is to do pious practices privately rather than publicly. In relation to the human tendency to get materialistic or wrapped up in material worries (6:19–34), Stassen saw the transforming initiative as a kingdom-focused and generous life—by shifting our focus to God's project on Earth, material possessions lose their grip on our hearts.

Not everyone is persuaded that the teaching on adultery (5:27–30) contains a persuasive transforming initiative. Stassen's proposal was that Jesus' hyperbolic language of cutting off hands and plucking out eyes represents a transforming initiative teaching his male listeners to remove themselves from temptation—rather than blaming and cloistering women, as was and is so common. Likewise, Jesus' teaching on divorce (5:31–32) does not contain a transforming initiative, so Stassen reached over to 1 Corinthians 7:11 for Paul's (implicit) command to seek reconciliation in marriage. It is also possible to see Jesus' tightening of the legitimate grounds for divorce and rules for remarriage as something of a transforming initiative in a context in which loose legal interpretation was becoming a license for men to abandon their wives.

The teachings on turning the other cheek and enemy-love (5:38–48) only work as transforming initiatives if we interpret them in a strategic rather than passive way—as a strategy of transforming initiative rather than surrender.

Most English Bible translations certainly seem to translate Jesus' teachings as a counsel of sunny nonresistance. If someone hits you, if someone has become an enemy to you, "do not resist" (5:39, NRSV)—instead, give them the other cheek to slug, and love them anyway (5:43). This interpretation is probably the main source of various efforts to evade the Sermon on the Mount, because it seems degrading and impossible.

Stassen claimed that the Greek here better supports a translation of "do not retaliate revengefully by evil means" (*KE*, p. 98), that is, by using violence. Instead, surprise your enemies by returning good for evil. This is a strategy that raises the dignity of the oppressed and opens the possibility for a transformation of the situation toward nonviolence and equality. This passage was embraced by the civil rights movement. Note the connection with Howard Thurman's interpretation, described in Chapter 4.

Indeed, Thurman's reminder of Jesus' context of grinding foreign occupation helps complete the picture here. The Romans want to humiliate you and tempt you to respond with fruitless violence. Surprise them by returning good for evil. Work on your heart by praying for them (5:44), doing good for them, and loving them as God loves God's enemies (5:45–48), rather than nurturing violent fantasies. This is the way of deliverance that can break us out of that dismal, global, deeply sinful human pattern of returning evil for evil as the body counts rise. It also has the deep spiritual benefit of enabling us to set our own course in life, even in relation to our enemies, rather than constantly being in a posture of angry response to what other people do. There is freedom along this route, but it requires considerable internal strength and resilience.

6.5 Where I Now Stand on the Sermon on the Mount

Here is where I now stand on the majestic Sermon on the Mount.

Jesus wants God's will to "be done on earth as it is in heaven" (Mt 6:10). When God's will is done on earth, as it is in heaven, then and only then will the kingdom of God be fully present.

The Beatitudes (5:3–12) honor and encourage the formation of a community within the human family—originally drawn from within the Jewish people, but now open to all peoples—who want God's kingdom with a fierce hunger and who are open to changing everything and dropping everything to bring it to fruition. These are the people who preserve and enliven human existence as salt, and who by their deeds bring light—the light of God's presence—into a dark and violent world (5:13–16).

Jesus honors the Hebrew Bible and Torah as faithfully reflecting God's will. And yet he is convinced that prevailing interpretations and practices at his time did not chart a path to the kingdom of God (5:17–20). That version of righteousness needs to be fulfilled and exceeded.

Jesus' moral vision is holistic. He is very much concerned about broken relationships, oppression, and violence (5:21–26, 38–48). He offers a path of proactive reconciliation and peacemaking that simultaneously changes the dynamics of oppression and raises the dignity of the oppressed. The path he offers does not guarantee an end to the subjugation of some groups by others, but does offer the most promising route to nonviolent, dignified, potentially transformative resistance. His teachings are not impossible, but they are demanding. They require spiritual grounding and moral self-discipline. And, when you think of it, they do create a life that is more God-resembling, because God does in fact demonstrate even-handed love in this world both to friends and enemies.

Jesus taught a male-dominated society sexual self-control and covenant-keeping, which neither exploits nor abandons women (5:27–32). Especially in light of the continued power and practices of patriarchal societies, his teachings remain just and potentially transformative. But they feel alien to a society mainly focused on personal freedom.

Jesus, like so many other prophets, had a nose for religious pretense, hypocrisy, and misdirection. His teachings on religious oaths (5:33–37), almsgiving, fasting, and prayer (6:1–18), and judging others (7:1–5) are incisive and purifying. He bans oaths, bans showy religious practices of all types, and bans a moral judgmentalism so often motivated by religion. Jesus wants piety to purify motives rather than confuse or worsen them.

Jesus is very much aware of the power both of economic need and economic greed (6:19–34, 7:6–11). He never says that humans don't need the basics—but he does say God can be trusted to provide them. He commends a path toward stripping material greed out of our hearts. Perhaps he is also implying (as his brother James affirmed later) that one of the primary motives of violent oppression in this world is material greed (Jas 4:1–3). Those who have abandoned greed and learned to live simply have no need to hurt others to obtain more belongings.

Finally, Jesus teaches a way of life that he knows is not the common human or even religious way (7:13–29). He understands that typical patterns of believing and behaving merely reinforce all the disastrous sinful patterns already present in human life. He knows that religious teachers can always be found who will reinforce precisely the patterns that violate God's revealed will. He knows that declarations of religious loyalty are cheap and easy, when what he really wants is for people to live the way he commands.

This is what I believe about the Sermon on the Mount. These are not impossible teachings to be cleverly evaded, though some are certainly quite challenging, especially in roles of public responsibility. Jesus teaches the world a way of life to be assiduously cultivated and performed. He teaches it as the way of deliverance from our sinful patterns—as the way to, and of, the kingdom of God.

Discussion Questions

1. What has been the significance of the Sermon on the Mount in your religious community? Is it featured as central in the moral formation efforts of your church?

2. Think of examples of times when you have heard Christians, perhaps even preachers and teachers, teach you to evade or make a dualistic reading of the Sermon. To answer this question, go through the various dualism and evasion strategies discussed here.

3. Do you find the transforming-initiatives reading of the Sermon persuasive? Why or why not?

4. Do you believe Jesus' teaching in the Sermon represents an annulment and/or a fulfillment of the Hebrew Bible's teachings?

5. Can people exercising public responsibility really practice the teachings of the Sermon?

To watch Dr. Gushee deliver

Lecture 7: Christian Virtue Ethics

Follow this link:

https://youtu.be/lc2Clebja4A

Or scan the QR code.

To listen to the audio, follow this link:

https://qrco.de/bcOl5G

Or scan the QR code.

To scan a QR code, download a QR reader from the app store on your device, open the application, follow the directions, and point your device's camera at the code.

CHAPTER 7

Christian Virtue Ethics

7.1 Scenes With My Father

Virtue ethics is one of the oldest dimensions of moral philosophy and one of the most significant. Its questions are asked in every culture and in every thoughtful community: What is a good person? What qualities of character make an individual or a community flourish?

This chapter was drafted on the cold December 2020 day after I rescued my ailing 90-year-old father from another miserable hospital stay and returned him home under hospice care here in Atlanta. We were beginning the last leg of life's journey with him.

At my father's final stage of life, my sisters and I were told that we had three choices, all made worse by COVID lockdowns.

We could have sent him to a nursing home, where his daily needs would have been met but we would not have been able to see him except through glass. He would have died physically separated from his family.

We could have packed up his things and moved him to an assisted living facility with onsite nursing care, where we might again have been separated from him for the rest of his life.

Or we could return him to his own apartment at an independent senior-living community, call in hospice to help manage his last-stage medical care, and offer 24/7 accompaniment until he died.

The choices we faced with Dad call to mind that ultimate question of ethics, "How should we live?"

Most of the six not-so-small questions from Chapter 1 could have proven helpful in analyzing what to do for Dad. But at that moment, the question that struck me as most relevant was the character question: "What kind of people should we be?" More specifically: "What kind of son do I strive to be in relation to my father at this last stage of his precious life?"

Given all relevant factors at that precise moment, for both of my sisters and for me, the idea of doing anything other than bringing Dad back to his own apartment, under our loving care, seemed inconceivable *in terms of the kind of persons we wanted to be*. And so that is what we did.

7.2 The Sculpting of Souls

The most basic insight of character ethics is that moral being precedes and even determines moral doing. We do what we are.

Behind this claim is a certain view of human nature. That view—which goes back to the Greek philosophers and is grounded both in centuries of experience and moral theory—is that humans are sculpted into a certain moral form over the course of a lifetime.

In children we can easily see both inherent personality traits and also their great sensitivity to their environment. For a long period of time, the clay is still quite malleable.

As children mature, they gain greater power to make choices that will affect the ultimate outcome of their character. Rather than being mainly sculpted by others, they begin to sculpt themselves. Their character gradually takes a more definite shape, and as that happens, the predictability of their behavior grows. There is a kind of essence to them, and people who know them well can give a good account of it.

As Larry Rasmussen and Bruce Birch pointed out in their *Bible and Ethics in the Christian Life*, the English word **character** comes directly from the Greek word *charakter*, a term describing the imprint left by the mark stamped on official documents (p. 74). Character is the distinctive imprint left by a unique human life. While people can surprise us even in middle age with tremendous moral growth (or decline), most often continuity of character is visible.

7.3 Character in Community

This basic account of character formation should be immediately recognizable to anyone who has ever loved a romantic partner, raised a child, or taught a room full of teenagers. Its truth has been recognized by every community that cares about its own survival.

Indeed, character and community are deeply intertwined. Character is formed in communities, most of which have very definite ideas regarding the traits they believe essential for community well-being. The technical term, deriving from Greek philosophical ethics, for the character qualities deemed desirable by communities, is *virtue*: "qualities of a person that make that person a good person in community and that contribute to the good of the community" (*KE* Glossary, pp. 474–475).

Communities constantly deploy strategies for shaping character in the directions they consider most important. People are considered virtuous if their character develops in the direction that their community considers beneficial. Parents, educators, and religious leaders are among the frontline workers in shaping the character of the young.

This is a bit scary when you think about it. It would be nice to believe that there is a more-or-less universal set of virtues that people everywhere recognize and affirm. People should be kind, merciful, and forgiving, or honest, diligent, and hardworking, or humble, other-centered, and sacrificial, or ...

Even cursory attention to these three virtue triads reveals that in substance they differ quite meaningfully. And these are all solid virtue lists. When we then zoom out and consider some of the worst societies in human history, looking at the "virtues" they embraced, we see some truly awful results.

One of the best examples of such toxicity was in Nazi Germany, from 1933 to 1945. As authors like Peter Haas (*Morality After Auschwitz*, 1988), David Jones (*Moral Responsibility in the Holocaust*, 1999), and Richard Weikart (*Hitler's Ethic*, 2009) have shown, Nazism had a definite ethic, even a character ethic. This totalitarian state intentionally sought to crush Christian virtues like mercy and compassion and replace them with new "virtues" like ruthlessness, race-struggle, eugenics, ultranationalism, "hardness" in the face of Jewish suffering, and loyalty to Adolf Hitler. While the Nazis themselves admitted with frustration that they were never entirely successful in uprooting the character-formation traditions of the older German Christian culture, they made enough progress to create thousands of young race-warriors ready to slash and burn their way across Europe during World War II.

7.4 Virtue as Embodiment of the Good for Which God Designed Us

One of the very oldest accounts of virtue was that generated by the Greek philosopher Aristotle. His version of *virtue ethics* was refined in ancient Christianity and today is embraced by Christian ethicists of various traditions, though still being especially featured in Catholic ethics.

The Aristotelian-Thomistic virtue ethics tradition (Thomism is named for the towering Catholic theologian Thomas Aquinas, 1225–1274) refuses to concede that a virtue simply equals a desirable character trait as defined by this or that community. Instead, it believes that virtues are character traits that fit with human nature, especially "the good for which humans are designed" (*KE* Glossary, p. 474). The idea is that humans do have a *design*—let's adopt the Christian version of this view and describe it as a *divine* design. On this view, virtues are character traits that conform with the good for which God designed us, while *vices* are traits that hinder or fail to conform with that divine design.

Consider the claim that God designed humans for loving relationships of various types. We flourish when we love and are loved. Virtuous character, in this dimension, would look like attitudes, dispositions, emotions, urgings of conscience, habits, and practices that tend toward the building and sustaining of loving relationships. Relevant virtues might include commitment, resilience, patience, forgiveness, and self-control.

This account does not accept that such positive traits are virtues merely because they have been declared such by specific communities. Quite the opposite—these character traits have been valued by decent, functional, and wise communities because they have discovered how humans were designed and have developed moral traditions that respond accordingly. Communities, like Nazi Germany, that attempt to invert what generations of humans have discovered about the God-given human good and the path to human flourishing end up destroying themselves and others.

7.5 Virtue and Happiness

An interesting paradox in virtue ethics is the role of the concept of happiness. The basic claim is that the good life is the virtuous life, which is the happiest possible life. In technical ethics language, this is called **eudaimonistic ethics**, from the Greek word *eudaimonia*, for happiness or flourishing.

We can look around and see that many of the happiest people we know are those who exhibit the most mature virtues. These people seem to have the most profound intimate relationships and the virtues required to sustain them. The good, the right, the natural, and the happy all seem to align for such people. Truly, such people are blessed, and a blessing to others.

One can easily conclude that being virtuous is what makes for (true) happiness. If we add the theological conviction that God is good to us and wants humans to flourish by experiencing true happiness, then virtue ethics ends up having the joyful implication that morality is not about God imposing odious demands but instead nudging us toward our own highest happiness.

This seems perfectly lovely, and yet we do see many cases in which a virtuous life is not in fact a happy life—or even a long one. Sometimes virtue can be costly and sacrificial. We also see that many seemingly happy people do not give much evidence of being virtuous. This problem is already raised in scripture, perhaps never more acutely than in the book of Job—and, of course, in the unjust death of Jesus.

7.6 Virtue and the Natural

The use of the term "natural" is often deployed in relation to virtue theory—and in ethics generally. The term is so central to the tradition I am describing that it is sometimes called **natural law** ethics, which has been a central term in Catholic ethics and largely rejected on the Protestant side. The idea is that the world has a rationally discernible, God-given, law-like, created/natural order, and that human flourishing is achieved through conforming our actions to that order. We have already seen that much of Christian virtue ethics seems to be built on this assumption.

But this all gets quite complicated when you push a bit deeper.

For example, it certainly does seem as if God created us, and thus that it is "natural," to seek a flourishing life through meaningful intimate relationships. But what do we make of how our drive for relationships can become obsessive? Or how we can become too dependent on one person, or ask a person to be what only God should be? These tendencies recur so frequently in human life that they too can be called "natural." Right? But how would the "natural" in that sense relate to how God created us?

The issue comes up everywhere in life. We were created to need and to enjoy food, but why does gluttony also come so naturally? We were created to want sexual satisfaction, but why does our natural sexual desire sometimes take such unnatural forms?

Gay people naturally desire sexual bonding with a member of the same sex. Yet the natural law tradition historically has claimed that homosexual desire and activity is intrinsically unnatural, and millions of gay people have been told this over many centuries. How does God's creation relate to the concepts of the natural and unnatural here? Who decides whether same-sex desire conforms with God's created order, and/or is natural or unnatural? We are sent back to authority questions at this point.

We can perhaps see why the status of the term "natural" is one of the most disputed concepts in Christian ethics. Even if it appears that human life exhibits many traces of divine design, it also appears to be damaged and disordered. And we see plenty of confusion and disagreement about that design, as well as about which patterns of behavior should be described as natural or unnatural.

Dietrich Bonhoeffer's essay on "Natural Life" in his *Ethics* has proven decisive in my understanding of these issues. He splits the categories of creation and nature/the natural, arguing that God's creation became "nature" through the primal fall of humankind into sin. Since then, everything human is open to both use and misuse through human choices. When in our relative freedom humans choose rightly in areas such as sexuality and family relations, that can be described as conformity with the (post-fall) natural; when we choose wrongly, that can be described as unnatural. Choosing the natural preserves and rightly orders life until the coming of Christ, while choosing the unnatural damages, disorders, or destroys natural life.

Bonhoeffer agrees that human reason is the part of natural life that has the capacity to "[perceive] the natural in its givenness" (p. 174). However, human reason should be understood as "entangled in the fall" rather than having retained its "essential integrity" (p. 175, fn1). For Bonhoeffer, then, not only do we not live in God's pre-fall creation order, we do not have access even to reliable thinking about it. What we have is post-fall natural life and a rational capacity to think about it that has also been damaged by sin.

This means that what we see when we think we see the natural is cloudy and subject to error. *How* we see is also cloudy and subject to error. Overall,

Bonhoeffer's approach means that virtue cannot just be conformity of character with God's creational design, but something more elusive—conformity of character with what is natural, with what preserves and orders life, in a world made by God, damaged by sin, and being redeemed in Jesus Christ until he comes again. This can be described as a chastened Protestant, or at least Bonhoefferian, version of the "natural" and therefore of virtue ethics.

7.7 The Components of Character

Did you notice earlier when I ran quickly through these words—attitudes, dispositions, emotions, conscience, habits, and practices? Let's use this list as a working summary of the components of character and camp out here for just a moment.

One of the most interesting things about virtue ethics as a subfield of ethics is the way it overlaps so deeply with psychology. (Indeed, this area is sometimes called *moral psychology*.) Virtue ethics attempts to specify some of the most important elements of whatever we call that which lies at the very center of the self—mind, soul, spirit, heart, or simply, character. These days we most often turn to psychology and related fields to describe all that stuff going on inside the infinitely mysterious human person. But it's part of the tradition of ethical reflection too.

We can try to break down these components of the moral self by using words like:

a) attitudes: enduring internal mental/emotional postures toward life in general or particular arenas of life; e.g., positive, hopeful, pessimistic, conspiratorial.

b) dispositions: characteristics that tend to shape people's behavior across multiple situations; e.g., selfishness, greed, service-orientation, insecurity, suspicion, violence.

c) emotions: mental reactions experienced as strong feelings, which include physiological reactions; e.g., anger, fear, sadness, gladness.

d) conscience: an inner feeling, voice, or guide related to the rightness or wrongness of a feeling or course of action.

e) habits: deeply ingrained learned behaviors that become essentially automatic, often tied to specific contexts; e.g., brushing teeth, putting a napkin on one's lap, bedtime routines.

f) practices: intentionally repeated acts, behaviors or activities; e.g., giving money to charity every month, going to church, exercising every other day.

There are deep complexities here. If I were writing as a psychologist, I would have to be much more detailed and consider various accounts of each of these components.

Conscience is especially interesting because, though its function is intrinsically moral, the fact that one "has a conscience" guarantees little or nothing as to its reliability. And it is possible to view it as a sign of human brokenness that we even need a conscience.

The concept of practices has also gained considerable attention in recent ethics, graduating to become an organizing category for the moral life, especially of communities. We can know the state of an individual or community's character based on its most characteristic practices.

There is also a feedback loop between practices and the inner moral self. When behaviors graduate to become practices, they can become so formative that they loop back around and shape our character at its core. Consider how a weekly practice of serving the poor or visiting those in prison can reshape attitudes, emotions, and dispositions.

Notice the searching interiority of these kinds of considerations. This is ethics as deep internal self-reflectiveness. It exempts almost no aspect of the inner life from the moral realm and seeks growth toward wholeness—or holiness—in each area. Some of us were taught that "all feelings are acceptable" and so on, but virtue ethics does not rest content with problematic or unvirtuous attitudes or practices even when it comes to emotions. Virtue ethics understands that in the moral arena sometimes the highest mountains to climb are those inside the self.

Character ethics has attracted the criticism that it involves far too much navel-gazing and can easily lead to a kind of morbid perfectionism. There is even a term in old-school Catholic moral theology called **scrupulosity** to describe excessive moral self-reflection and guilt associated with a hyperactive conscience.

Birch and Rasmussen remind us that Martin Luther (1483–1546) famously said that the true movement of the Christian life is "not from vice to virtue but from vice *and* virtue to grace" (*Bible and Ethics in the Christian Life*, p. 46). He believed this partly because he found his earlier monastic lifestyle to produce scrupulosity, and because he found in the good news of God's forgiving grace through Jesus his path to inner peace. To this day one is far more likely to find suspicion of character ethics on the Protestant side than on the Catholic side.

7.8 Three Notable New Testament Virtue Clusters

I want to briefly consider three important strands of tradition in the New Testament, each specifying a vision of normative character. They are related to each other, but each strikes its own distinctive notes.

7.8.1 Paul and the Fruit of the Spirit

One of the most memorable accounts of the virtues is offered by the Apostle Paul—even though he does not use the word "virtue" or "character" to describe what he is talking about.

In Galatians 5:13–26, Paul draws a contrast between life in the flesh (*sarx*) versus life in the Spirit (*pneuma*). Paul's theory of virtue is that "those who belong to Christ Jesus have crucified the flesh ... [and instead] live by the Spirit" (Gal 5:24–25a). The "fruit" of the Spirit consists of an attractive array of virtues: "love, joy, peace, patience, kindness, generosity, faithfulness, gentleness, and self-control" (Gal 5:22–23a; cf. Col 3:12–17). While Paul does counsel moral effort toward such virtues (cf. Gal 5:25), he more strongly emphasizes that desirable moral qualities emerge supernaturally for those who dwell in Christ (Gal 5:6), and Christ in them (Gal 2:20). For the Apostle Paul, what we might call virtues are more like spiritual-behavioral evidence of what Christ has already done than a product of our efforts toward moral growth.

7.8.2 The Ministerial Virtues in Acts 20 and the Pastoral Epistles

As a seminary professor, I have always thought it important to call out for attention the "ministerial virtues" strand of New Testament teaching. Two of the most relevant passages for developing a list of virtues for ministers are Acts 20, where Paul is saying farewell to the Ephesian church elders, and 1 Timothy 3:1–8, the latter with parallels elsewhere in the Pastoral Epistles of 2 Timothy and Titus.

I think Acts 20:17–35 is a hidden gem in scripture. I urge every seminarian to spend some time with this passage. In a strikingly passionate meeting with leaders of a church that he founded and loved, Paul reviews his approach to ministry with that community. For Paul, the ministerial virtues include passion, humility, Gospel commitment, an urgent sense of responsibility for the church, comprehensive and truthful preaching, alertness, hard work, indifference to material possessions, non-covetousness, helpfulness to the weak, a giving spirit, and a willingness to leave when God calls. This is now my favorite text to preach at an ordination service.

The Pastoral Epistles are noticeably more conservative than the undisputed Pauline letters and have a more hierarchical feel. They are often deployed to bounce women out of ministry. That is not how I use a text like 1 Timothy 3:1–7. The ministerial virtue list here directs living above moral reproach, faithfulness in marriage, sobriety of thinking, sobriety in relation to alcohol, self-control, respectability, hospitality, teaching ability, gentleness, peaceableness, non-covetousness, good family management, and maturity.

Whatever virtues one might add or subtract from this list, part of its value is in making ministerial students consider the moral gravity of the role. We will discuss such issues in more detail when we consider the work of Sondra Wheeler's book, *The Minister as Moral Theologian*, a bit later.

7.8.3 The Beatitudes as a Kingdom of God Readiness List

In *Kingdom Ethics*, Glen Stassen and I treat the Beatitudes (Mt 5:3–12) in a very distinctive way. Rather than simply accepting the standard claim that Jesus was teaching timeless virtues such as humility, meekness, mercy, purity of heart, and peacemaking, we situate this opening salvo of the Sermon on the Mount within the kingdom-of-God narrative frame that we discussed earlier.

The Beatitudes are a prophetic-eschatological declaration, in which Jesus is announcing that the kingdom of God is dawning. The Beatitudes track very closely with Isaiah 61:1–11 (as does Jesus' inaugural address in Lk 4:16–30, by the way). Isaiah 61 was a prophetic statement of God's coming deliverance of the oppressed, poor, brokenhearted, imprisoned, mournful, and abused Jewish exiles. Jesus was offering parallel good news to the similarly oppressed Jewish people of his day. He was also calling his hearers to celebrate and get ready for the deliverance that God was promising imminently.

Luke's version of the Beatitudes (Lk 6:20–26) reads like a straightforward announcement that God is acting to reverse the existing social order, with those on the bottom about to be moved right to the top. ("Blessed are you who are poor, for yours is the kingdom of God ... Woe to you who are rich, for you have received your consolation" Lk 6:20, 24). Matthew's nuance is that Jesus is not just announcing the coming deliverance but also inviting participation on the part of his listeners. ("Blessed are the peacemakers, for they will be called children of God" Mt 5:9.) The Beatitudes are not a statement of timeless virtues, but instead a dynamic, prophetic, eschatological teaching: if you want to participate in the spread of God's reign, be a peace-maker, and so on.

7.9 Jesus as the Center of New Testament Virtue Ethics

One of the best reasons to develop a fulsome ethics of Christian character is that the New Testament clearly does so. The Hebrew Bible had often described the character of God and in various ways called the Jewish people toward imitation—"Be holy, for I am holy" (Lev 11:44, cf. 1 Pt 1:16). But this *imitatio Dei* (imitation of God) theme explodes in significance in the New Testament, where it becomes *imitatio Christi*—the imitation of Christ. That is one of the most powerful implications of a religion in which God becomes human and lives a human existence—indeed, the perfect human life. "The Word became flesh and lived among us ... full of grace and truth" (Jn 1:14). New Testament authors constantly point their readers back to the example of Jesus Christ himself. My favorite example is the so-called Christ-hymn from Philippians 2:

Let the same mind be in you that was in Christ Jesus,

Who, though he was in the form of God,
    did not regard equality with God
    as something to be exploited,
    but emptied himself,
    taking the form of a slave,
    being born in human likeness.
And being found in human form,
    he humbled himself
    and became obedient to the point of death—
    even death on a cross.

Therefore God also highly exalted him
    and gave him the name
    that is above every name,
    so that at the name of Jesus
    every knee should bend,
    in heaven and on earth and under the earth,
    and every tongue should confess
    that Jesus Christ is LORD,
    to the glory of God the Father.

The goal of Christian virtue ethics is ultimately ***christomorphism***—that, by God's grace and in the Spirit's power, those who claim to follow Jesus Christ will gradually come to resemble him.

Discussion Questions

1. Do you agree that the basic moral character of most people is pretty much set by the time they are young adults?

2. What virtues were emphasized by the most important people of your childhood and youth?

3. Do you believe that the virtuous life leads to happiness? Why or why not?

4. What do you think of the idea that there is a created moral order to the world and that it can be accessed by anyone through reason? What do you think of Bonhoeffer's critique?

5. What are some of the aspects of Jesus' character that you find most compelling?

To watch Dr. Gushee deliver
Lecture 8: Truthfulness
Follow this link:
https://youtu.be/87HCl1qUsso
Or scan the QR code.

To listen to the audio, follow this link:
https://qrco.de/bcOl7j
Or scan the QR code.

To scan a QR code, download a QR reader from the app store on your device, open the application, follow the directions, and point your device's camera at the code.

CHAPTER 8

Truthfulness

8.1 The Moral Core: Truthfulness, Sacredness, Justice, Love, and Forgiveness

In the next five chapters, we will consider five moral norms that are so important that they provide a kind of moral core to Christian ethics. These norms are truthfulness, sacredness of life, justice, love, and forgiveness. At one level these are virtues that any morally serious Christian parent will seek to teach their children. At another level they can be seen as the moral core of Christian living and as applicable to all specific moral issues.

Recall that I am taking a lifecycle approach to arranging the chapters in this book. So far, I have thought of my reader as the serious Christian young adult attempting to access and understand the vocabulary, methods, sources, and traditions of Christian ethics. Now I picture that adult having gotten married and been blessed with children. She wants to nurture her children in the way of Christ and so she has just happily read about virtue ethics. Now she needs some specific content as to the moral norms that she should teach her children, and the moral virtues that she should seek to model for them. Thus, she is overjoyed now to discover these chapters on truthfulness, sacredness, justice, love, and forgiveness, five absolutely core elements of the Christian moral life.

8.2 Why Truth, Truthfulness, and Truthtelling Need a Comeback

When Glen Stassen and I published the first edition of *Kingdom Ethics* in 2003, we began with a study of over 50 existing Christian ethics textbooks. Only six contained any discussion of the nature of truth, the virtue of truthfulness, or the extent of the moral obligation to tell the truth. Notice that threefold breakdown of what we are talking about in this chapter: truth, truthfulness, and truthtelling. They are related but not identical.

We found that most ethics textbooks that did address the ethics of truth focused on technical arguments over whether it is ever morally permissible to lie. That familiar question in ethics *can* prove illuminating in terms of how one thinks about the nature of moral obligations. Moral absolutists won't lie even to save life; others will lie in such extreme cases, but if so, they must then account for why lying is both wrong and yet permissible. This discussion opens the door for helpful clarification of the nature of *prima facie* moral obligations.

But don't miss this: The heart of this classic back-and-forth over possible emergency permissions to lie assumes social agreement about a strict moral rule against lying, only asking whether exceptions can be made. This old discussion of the ethics of truthtelling did not imagine a social reality in which lying has become routine. That would change the context entirely.

When *Kingdom Ethics* briefly touched on situations of systemic lying from the very top of society, these were treated as happening in tyrannies like Nazi Germany or the USSR. We did not think that this line, from our last paragraph, would ever seem so relevant to contemporary Europe or the United States:

> The Scriptures remind us of occasions in which "truth has perished" (Jer 7:28) or truth has "stumbled in the public square" (Is 59:14). In such times justice, righteousness, and human life itself can become supremely threatened. Those who hold power are called especially to live in truth and to be aware of the many temptations they face to resort to duplicity, dishonesty and truth's suppression (p. 388).

Systemic lying from elected government leaders, torrents of disinformation and misinformation on social media, ideologically fractured accounts of reality, the loss of a social norm of truthtelling, the abandonment of the virtue of truthfulness … this is where we find ourselves in many nations today. We are long past just debating about emergency situations where lying might be okay. Truth itself needs a comeback.

8.3 What is Truth?

In a famous draft essay called "What Is Meant By 'Telling the Truth'" which is included in the 1995 English edition of his *Ethics*, Dietrich Bonhoeffer claims that "the real is to be expressed in words. This is what constitutes truthful speech" (p. 360). He goes on to complicate the matter by suggesting that the nature of the relationship that exists between people helps determine what "the right word" is on each occasion. But he did not fiddle around with the definition of truth. To speak the truth is to express reality in words.

Bonhoeffer's shorthand definition reflects the commonsense understanding that truth is *correspondence with reality*. More formally, truth is the property of being in accord with reality or fact. This is called the **correspondence theory of truth**. If I say x, x is only true if x corresponds with the fact or reality to which x refers. If I say, "I was late because of unusually heavy traffic," that statement is only true if the reason I was late was because of unusually heavy traffic.

If we accept that telling the truth is at least a *prima facie* moral obligation, this must mean that it is morally significant that people offer statements that correspond with reality. The reason we do not talk about this simple fact very often is that it is taken for granted—unless a problem arises.

Philosophers have offered several competing approaches to this correspondence theory of truth. That's partly because not every statement really intends (or purports) to be a description of reality. It's also because not everybody agrees that there is such a thing as a shared reality available to be described. And it's because philosophers never accept the obvious without challenging it.

Pragmatic theories of truth suggest that truth is that which is verified when tested and/or put into practice. Truth is not once and for all established, but instead provisionally verified or disconfirmed by constant examination, trial and error, and self-correction. Truth is the hard-won achievement of a community of rigorous inquiry. This approach to truth seems especially relevant in the sciences.

Coherence theories of truth claim that statements are true insofar as they fit with and are interdependent with others within a broader whole. This allows statements to be evaluated for their truthfulness within the context of the system within which they are made. This approach seems most appropriate within self-enclosed systems such as theologies, or even games. "It is normally wrong to punt on third down" makes sense only within the game of American football. "The Spirit proceeds from the Father *and* the Son, and not the Father only," has coherence within the realm of a certain version of classic Christian theology. And so on.

Constructivist theories of truth suggest that truth is a social construct, linked to power. What is "true" is that which has been declared true by those who hold power. The cynical yet familiar expression "history is written by the winners" gets at this concept.

Skeptical theories of truth all have in common that they (attempt to) poke holes in the correspondence theory. Examples include:

The *performative theory*, which claims that when we say that something is true, we are merely performing a speech-act that signals our endorsement of another statement.

The *consensus theory of truth* simply says that truth is whatever a particular group agrees is true. This approach seems to abandon the idea of any reality beyond a shared group perception.

Deflationary and redundancy theories assert that truth claims do not denote a real property in the world, or they are merely redundant reinforcements of assertions.

Finally, *pluralist theories* suggest that different types of propositions might relate to different kinds of truth. Correspondence, pragmatic, constructivist, coherence, or other approaches might make sense in some areas but not in others.

For most everyday purposes, the correspondence theory of truth offers what we need. A truthful statement corresponds with reality. When people's statements routinely do not correspond with the facts to which their words refer, they have become liars, embracing a vice that violates the truthfulness upon which community depends.

8.4 Scriptural Wisdom: From Truth to the Virtue of Truthfulness

When one digs around a bit in the Bible, it becomes clear that scriptural writers think of truthfulness as a virtue at least as much as truth as correspondence with reality and truthtelling as a moral obligation. Indeed, in keeping with that key insight of virtue ethics, the Bible often treats truthful character as the presupposition for even the possibility of truthtelling.

The Hebrew word that is normally translated as "truth" in English is *emeth*. The Hebrew word *emunah* also can be translated as "truth" or as "truthfulness." These key Hebrew words are translated in an astonishing range of ways. What I find interesting is how often the best translation seems to be about truthful character rather than truth or speaking the truth.

> The Rock, his work is perfect, and all his ways are just. A faithful (emunah) God, without deceit, just and upright is he.
>
> **—Dt 32:4, NRSV**

Persons, beginning with the Divine, are true (or not). The actions of persons who are true will be truthful. Such people, and their actions, can also be described as faithful, right, just, firm, sound, steady, and so on. Those who are true at their core develop truthfulness as a virtue. Others come to rely on this.

The Old Testament treatment of truth is richly insightful. If truth at its core is about character properties, and not about statement properties, then our thinking about the subject is turned on its head. The main question moves from "what is true?" to "who is true?"

Further development continues in the New Testament. The principal New Testament Greek word for truth is *aletheia*. The term is certainly used to describe statements that correspond with reality, the truthful character of God and the expectation of truthful character in Christ's people, and the obligation to tell the truth.

Most interestingly, though, some New Testament treatments of truth add a *mystical, participatory,* and *eschatological* dimension. Truth is an aspect of God's character revealed at this eschatological moment that wills to enter and transform receptive human beings. This theme is especially apparent in the literature associated with the Apostle John.

John's treatment of truth is eschatological, in that truth marks the ful-fillment of God's redemptive plan, now breaking into human life. It is participatory, in that truth enters willing humans and we in turn dwell in truth and truth in us (Jn 14:17, 1 Jn 1:8). It is mystical, in that truth is a spiritual reality, a supernatural force that makes us holy and new (Jn 17:17, Rev. 21:5).

For the Johannine tradition, followers of Jesus know the truth (1 Jn 2:21) and tell the truth (Jn 19:35). But more profoundly, disciples are "from the truth" (1 Jn 3:19) and "in the truth" (2 Jn 1:1); the "truth abides in [them]" (2 Jn 1:2). They are made holy, or sanctified, "in the truth" (Jn 17:17). Out of this spiritual-characterological state flow truthful lives. Disciples "walk in the truth" (2 Jn 1:4; 3 Jn 3–4). Those who claim knowledge of Christ but do not obey his commands reveal that there is an absence of truth in them (1 Jn 2:4; cf. Jn 14:15).

A spiritually empowered and deeply felt commitment to Christ is the foundation of a character that dwells in truth, and a way of life walking in the truth, here at the eschatological moment when the Truth Himself has entered human history.

8.5 Truthfulness, Covenant, and Christian Community

> So then, putting away falsehood, let all of us speak the truth to our neighbors, for we are members of one another. Be angry but do not sin; do not let the sun go down on your anger, and do not make room for the devil ... Let no evil talk come out of your mouths, but only what is useful for building up, as there is need, so that your words may give grace to those who hear. And do not grieve the Holy Spirit of God, with which you were marked with a seal for the day of redemption. Put away from you all bitterness and wrath and anger and wrangling and slander, together with all malice, and be kind to one another, tenderhearted, forgiving one another, as God in Christ has forgiven you.

> —*Eph 4:25-32*

Truth is a theme for other New Testament writers as well. This passage from Ephesians, believed to be written by the Apostle Paul, suggests that truth is *interpersonal* and *covenantal*. Truth exists between people, in their relationships. Indeed, truth binds people together. Likewise, lies corrode relationships, not least in the church.

Ephesians 4 bans lies and commands truthfulness because, "we are all members of one another." In the church, we are spiritually, mystically, interpersonally connected. A different way to say it is that part of the covenant that binds members of the church with Christ and one another is a shared commitment to nurture truthful character and to tell the truth to one another.

Notice that lying is named alongside other kinds of self-harming activities in the Body of Christ—unmitigated anger, evil talk, slander, malice. What makes these verbal sins so bad is that they harm the community. They tear down rather than build up.

Lying is a speech-sin that harms people and relationships, and in the Body of Christ that is an attack on Christ himself. This idea that lying is harmful to people and relationships is obviously true of lies that themselves constitute attacks on others, such as slander, mentioned in this passage, and perjury ("bearing false witness") mentioned in the Ten Commandments itself (Ex 20:16). Slander is character assassination using words. Bearing false witness, such as in a capital trial, can constitute judicial assassination.

Zoom in a bit and think about the truth that binds together our most intimate relationships. I am thinking about my marriage to Jeanie, now of 37 years. There is an interpersonal truth that exists between us and helps bind us together. It consists of truthful memory of our long journey together, consistent patterns of promise-keeping, and truthful communication in a thousand little daily interactions. But it also looks like not the slightest deviation into misdirection, deceit, or dissembling.

This is true not just of intimate relationships.

When we tell someone something, we are implying, just by the very act of speech, that we respect them and will tell them the truth. If we speak to them as if we were telling them the truth, we owe them the actual truth. Every conversation between free people who live in dignity involves an implicit covenant to tell the truth. *A covenantal web invisibly binds me together with the persons to whom I am speaking.* There can be no human community without the trust that follows from consistent truthtelling.

If we had to double-check every word that even one person spoke to us each day, we would not have time to do anything else. Indeed, we would lose our minds. Reality is so important to human functioning that those who consistently lie to us threaten not just their relationship with us but our relationship with reality, and thus perhaps our very sanity. This is the meaning and gravity suggested by the term *gaslighting*. And the chief way to gaslight someone is to lie to them a lot, making them doubt their own grip on reality.

Community runs on truthtelling covenants, even when we forget about them. We mainly notice the problem when people start breaking those covenants.

8.6 The Covenant of Truth in Public Life

The idea that truth is interpersonal and covenantal applies in public life and not just in private life. When "truth stumbles in the public square," it is almost always correlated with grave losses for justice and advances for evil.

I remember thinking about this on January 20, 2017 when the new U.S. president, Donald Trump, raised his right hand, put his left hand on a Bible, and swore his presidential oath of office. I did not have high confidence that a man with his track record could be trusted to keep his oath to "preserve, protect, and defend the Constitution of the United States." Little did I know how bad it would finally get.

Trump was making a covenant with the American people, as all presidents before him had done. Covenant declarations are speech-acts that verbally perform covenant commitments into existence. Think about what happens when people marry. They say vows that perform covenant commitments.

In the Bible, and today, covenants can be between people only, or between people and God. But even covenants between people often call upon God as witness, guarantor, or avenger if the covenant is broken. Covenant promises bind the behavior of those making them. Having made sacred vows, the covenant partners are obligated to act accordingly.

Undergirding any public covenant making is the largely implicit covenant to speak truthfully. Vows mean nothing if words mean nothing and truth does not matter. *People who do not speak truthfully cannot make reliable covenant promises.*

Every nation needs government leaders who contemplate deeply the nature of their covenant obligations. When nations pick leaders, they should carefully consider whether candidates have a covenantal vision of the office—and whether they have a track record of truthful character and truthtelling in earlier roles and relationships. Christians used to know this.

Under mendacious regimes, truth is concealed, redefined, and controlled by the Leader, Party, or State. Under tyranny, the manipulation of truth, the creation of an enforced empire of lies, is brutally enforced. *You will agree that 2 + 2 = 5, because we say so, and we will enforce our redefinition of truth until we break you.* In these most tyrannical of states, you can get killed simply for refusing to say that 2 + 2 = 5.

But truth can be threatened not just under tyranny and torture, but instead simply by a steady bath of lies from the top of the state.

In U.S. public life over the period 2017–2021, we witnessed a reign of lies. *The Washington Post* concluded that Donald Trump made over 30,000 false or misleading statements in his four years in office. Roughly one-third of the public believed the lies. Many others did not believe the lies—but they accommodated the liar out of fear and expedience.

The most interesting people to watch during this awful time were not Democrats, whose party affiliation and ideology made it easy for them to perceive Donald Trump clearly. Instead, it was the population of Republicans who had to decide whether they would submit to a regime of lies when they knew what it was. The most impressive in this group are those who suffered real costs for choosing bedrock truth over Trumpian power. But there were not enough of them. The U.S. body politic remains fractured because of Donald Trump's lies, the most dangerous of which proved to be the claim that the election had been stolen from him.

8.7 The Intertwining of Lies with Social Evil

Such lies can be deadly.

Every fall semester at Mercer I teach a course on ***genocide***—the intentional effort to destroy a national, ethnic, racial, or religious group.

In every genocide we study, we see that a torrent of lies preceded, accompanied, and followed the evil events. Start with Nazi Germany and go from there.

It appears to be an iron law that there is no genocide apart from massive, systematic lying. First there are the lies told by regimes about the supposed dangers and evils of the targeted groups. Then there are the lies about the nature and consequences of the destructive policies that these regimes begin to implement against the groups. Next come the lies about what is happening to the groups after their members begin to disappear. Afterwards, there are the lying denials, the evasions and dissembling—and finally (perhaps) the snarling moral justifications of the atrocities once they are undeniable.

During the genocide in the former Yugoslavia, journalist Peter Maass was able to get an interview with Slobodan Milošević (1941–2006), who (mis)ruled that land from 1989 until 2000 and was indicted by the International Criminal Tribunal for Yugoslavia for war crimes. Maass was struck by the comprehensive nature of Milošević's lying. This is from his riveting 1997 book called *Love Thy Neighbor: A Story of War*:

> Milošević existed in a different dimension, a twilight zone of lies, and I was mucking about in the dimension of facts. He had spent his entire life in the world of communism, and he had become a master, an absolute master, at fabrication. Of course my verbal punches went right through him. It was as though I pointed to a black wall and asked Milošević what color it was. White, he says. No, I reply, look at it, that wall there, it is black, it is five feet away from us. He looks at it, then at me, and says, The wall is white, my friend, maybe you should have your eyes checked. He does not shout in anger. He sounds concerned for my eyesight (p. 213).

Maass goes on to say that because he had spent so much time covering the war and genocide in the former Yugoslavia, he knew exactly what color the wall was. Milošević's lies did not deceive this grizzled reporter. Maass went right on reporting the truth. But the lies confused some, delayed others from getting at the truth, and provided a convenient false narrative for Milošević's people to believe in.

Genocide is the worst form of organized, usually state-sponsored, evil. But the point applies down the line to less extreme forms of public or governmental wrongdoing. Systemic falsehood and systemic wrongdoing are inextricably related. Lies and injustice go together; truth and justice do so as well.

8.8 Christians as Seekers of Truth

Glen Stassen talked about "information integrity" as crucial for Christian ethics, and it surfaces in the first edition of *Kingdom Ethics* (p. 67). This term seems to have come out of the computer security world. Information integrity is the dependability and trustworthiness of information and the processes by which it is obtained.

Glen selected the term to describe how Christian moral discernment should work. We cannot think well in the realm of Christian ethics if we do not have information integrity. If we process our moral choices based on undependable or untrustworthy information, our bad inputs will produce bad outputs. If where we go to get our information, and the way in which we process information, lacks integrity, we will consistently get bad results.

Instead, if we are urgently committed to seeking truth and doing justice, then we will clean up our information processes, systems, and content. We will improve the dependability and trustworthiness of our information. We will not listen to inveterate liars, even if they tell us things that we wish were true. We will value truth, seek truth, and love truth as a core aspect of being followers of Jesus Christ who is the Truth.

Truth is an important issue in Christian ethics, even part of our moral core. It is not just a philosophical conundrum, theological claim, or interesting moral puzzle. Truth is also a fundamentally significant social ethical issue—indeed, a matter of life and death.

We need a fresh commitment to truth and need to stop toying with cynicism about truth's meaning.

We need a recovery of the centrality of truthfulness as an aspect both of God's character and of the expected character of God's people.

We need a reclaiming of an old-fashioned moral obligation to tell the truth in everyday life.

We need to be able to expect people, including ourselves, to keep the covenants they make.

And yes, we need an expectation that anyone who exercises leadership in major social institutions can be counted on to tell the truth except when they are forbidden to do so based on other fiduciary duties. Political and moral renewal in those nations that need it requires a recommitment to truth itself.

Discussion Questions

1. Do you perceive a "crisis of truth" in your national/social context?

2. Discuss the difference between truth as a propositional or cognitive reality and truth as a property of character, whether of God or of people.

3. Discuss the connection between systemic lying and social evils like genocide.

4. How are Christians in your social context doing with their information integrity practices?

To watch Dr. Gushee deliver

Lecture 9: Sacredness

Follow this link:

https://youtu.be/Ubw7Of1DIw4

Or scan the QR code.

To listen to the audio, follow this link:

https://qrco.de/bcOlAe

Or scan the QR code.

To scan a QR code, download a QR reader from the app store on your device, open the application, follow the directions, and point your device's camera at the code.

CHAPTER 9

Sacredness

Human life is sacred: this means that God has consecrated each and every human being—without exception and in all circumstances—as a unique, incalculably precious being of elevated status and dignity. Through God's revelation in Scripture and incarnation in Jesus Christ, God has declared and demonstrated the sacred worth of human beings and will hold us accountable for responding appropriately. Such a response begins by adopting a posture of reverence and by accepting responsibility for the sacred gift that is a human life. It includes offering due respect and care to each human being that we encounter. It extends to an obligation to protect human life from wanton destruction, desecration, or the violation of human rights. A full embrace of the sacredness of human life leads to a full-hearted commitment to foster human flourishing.

—David P. Gushee, *The Sacredness of Human Life*, 2013

9.1 Why I Elevate the Norm of "Sacredness" in Christian Ethics

In early 2013, I published a lengthy book on the concept that human life is sacred to God and that this sacredness is the ground of our most important moral obligations to one another. Since undertaking the research for that book, I have been sure that the sacredness of life should be treated as part of the moral core of Christian ethics—one of the first things we teach our children, one of the values we hold most dear.

There are three reasons why I felt the need to offer a substantial treatment of the idea that human life is sacred. These continue to hold true for me today, and underlie the sketch offered in this chapter.

At the political level, in the United States sacredness-of-life language has been discredited by conservative hypocrisy. The term tends to be deployed most often by American Christian conservatives to express opposition to abortion but in relation to no other issue in which human life is also at stake, like war or the death penalty. It is avoided by American Christian liberals as tainted by association. The concept of life's sacredness deserves better.

At the theological level, liberal Protestants generally avoid sacredness language and prefer justice language, while conservative Protestants generally deploy sacredness language that they have borrowed from Catholicism and upon which they have done little independent reflection. Inspired by Pope John Paul II's (1920–2005) beautiful 1995 encyclical *The Gospel of Life*, I aim to offer a treatment of the sacredness of life that makes sense in various Christian communities but is rooted in a recognizably Protestant divine-command theology.

At the academic level, I believe that scholars need to attend with precision to this critically important ethical norm. My work intends to get to the roots of the idea that human life is sacred, to understand what it really means and where it comes from, and to determine if a contemporary articulation of it is helpful for ethics today.

9.2 Sacredness as a Moral Status Ascribed and Commanded by God

To ascribe sacredness to something is to venerate it, often because of its connection with God and always because of its differentiation from the ordinary. Human beings show a consistent tendency to ascribe sacredness in this way to various things—to places (like Jerusalem, or Mecca, or where we became Christian), objects (like crucifixes, or sacred relics), documents (like the original Declaration of Independence, or a trove of love letters), ideas (equality, freedom), people (royalty, or ancestors), and God, or gods. It is a deep human impulse. But is it more than an impulse? Is there something of God in it?

In Christian moral tradition, when believers ascribe sacredness to human life, we do so because we believe that we have received divine revelation that God has ascribed such sacred worth to life. We place immense value on human life because God does—and because God has commanded that we do so. We treat all persons with reverence, respect, and responsibility because God has revealed that this is what we must do. We refuse to look with indifference on any human life, because the eyes of God look with love on all human lives. Perceiving and treating life as sacred is divine revelation and divine command.

In Christian terms, human life is sacred not merely on its own, because of something intrinsic to it, but because of its connection with the God who created it and who values it as such. We love human beings, we reverence and respect and seek to care for each person, not because of who they are but because of who God is and what God has commanded. This is by far the surest basis for a sacredness-of-life ethic.

Many secular theories try to teach humans to value other humans because of some *capacity* or *characteristic* that most humans share and that (purportedly) sets us apart from non-humans, such as our rationality, spirituality, or agency. This makes sense at one level, because we do rightly stand in awe at the most sublime capacities of the human being, and our tradition has often identified one or more of these capacities as central to what it means to have been made in the **imago Dei**, the image of God (Gen 1:27–28).

However, the problems with ascribing sacred worth based on capacities such as rationality and agency are abundant. These capacities are not present in utero, they develop slowly during childhood, they never fully develop for some, and they often erode to near nonexistence at the end of life. The variability of the realization of these sublime capacities in the lives of actual human beings places at risk the moral status—even the *human* status—of a substantial minority of the human population. If someone judges us as lacking one of these capacities, they can lower us right out of the human species or at least out of the range of moral concern.

This is an issue that will surface when we consider moral issues that emerge at the edges of life, such as abortion and euthanasia. It also shows up when we consider the inhumane way that people are often treated in prisons, partly based on the assumption that prisoners have demonstrated that they do not have the highest human capacities and should be treated as such.

The long and sordid history of racism also demonstrates that entire populations have been defined as "less than," as sub- or non-human, based on spurious negative judgments of their supposed rationality, spirituality, or agency. Some of us can choose to believe that others of us are not quite human—this is a perennial human temptation. Many people have been maimed and murdered based on such judgments.

Besides the witness of scripture, these are some of the reasons why I hold that the sacredness of human lives must not be based on any observable quality or capacity of a human life. *The foundation for viewing and treating every human being as sacred is not our observation but God's command.* Efforts to retain some idea of **_human dignity_** (a term often substituted for sacredness of life) while abandoning this theological underpinning have proved vulnerable to incoherence, rejection, or collapse—though these efforts continue apace today.

Still, I believe we are best served by returning to the biblical roots of the idea that human life is sacred and staking our flag there.

9.3 The Hebrew Bible on the Sacredness of Life

The Hebrew Bible teaches the sacredness of human life across its genres—not without complications, including areas where some biblical texts fall short of the Bible's own deepest truths, for example, in the acceptance of slavery, and in war's brutalities. Still, in its account of God's creation, Exodus and deliverance events, legal materials, and prophetic exhortations, the sacred worth of human life is implied, taught, reinforced, legislated, and demanded.

9.3.1 Creation Themes

The most primal claim of the biblical tradition is that human life is created by God and has a consequent sacred worth. Genesis 1–2 tells us that humans do not come from nowhere but are the creative handiwork of God. (What is true about humans is also true of all other creatures on the planet, each in their own way.)

Further, God is *equally* the Creator of *all* humans. The dignity, blessings, and tasks given to human beings are given to all. There is one God who makes one humanity. This is a pivotal element of biblical creation theology, and it contributes at least an implicit primal egalitarianism and human unity at the very foundations of biblical theology and ethics.

Genesis 2 offers an account in which God begins to create humanity by creating one man first. The first woman is then formed out of the first man. From these first parents come everyone else. In this story we are all kin, all part of one vast human family. We all have the same divine Creator and the same earthly forebears. This theme, reinforced in the New Testament (Acts 17:26), should have made the development of any Christian racism or hierarchical thinking quite impossible. We are sisters, we are brothers, to all human beings.

The creation narrative also teaches that human beings are made in the image of God (Gen 1:28). Few concepts have been more important in elevating and equalizing the status of human beings, birthing a human rights tradition, and dignifying human life. This is so even though theologians have often disagreed about the precise meaning of the *imago Dei*, and have sometimes strayed into the "capacities" interpretation, with the problems described earlier.

9.3.2 Exodus and Deliverance

The Bible records that God's universal care for creation and humanity took a focused form in God's compassionate response to the suffering of Israel when they were enslaved and threatened with genocide (Ex 1–15). God's deliverance of the Hebrew people from the Egyptians profoundly shaped Jewish identity, theology, and ethics. They were and are a rescued people, saved by a God who hears the cries of the oppressed. Their God is a liberator, motivated by compassion, justice, and covenant faithfulness.

The concept of a God who demonstrates impartial love for all people is a clear biblical theme, and yet it stands in some tension with the idea of a God whose ear inclines especially to the oppressed, as in the Exodus. But in an unjust world, justice requires special help for those whose "backs are against the wall." Some must be lifted up—even at the price of confrontation—to join the others who are already blessed with the privilege of standing up straight.

9.3.3 Covenant and Law

The Old Testament narrative moves from Exodus to Sinai, from God's miraculous deliverance of the covenant people to God's giving of the laws that shall govern Israel. Several justifications for a strong sacredness-of-human-life ethic can be noted in biblical law.

The entire framework of Torah as recorded in the Hebrew Bible demands recognition of God as Lawgiver. The law descends from God to people rather than being developed by people alone. Whatever one may make of this idea historically, its implication is that God is the ultimate source of law in Israel, God's own dignity transfers to the law, and God holds people accountable for their obedience.

This elevation of a divinely transcendent legal/moral standard over human life creates great momentum toward human equality. Law levels the playing field, weakening the strong and strengthening the weak. All stand equal before the law and before those human courts charged with enforcing it. Of course, this only works if enforcers of the law protect this vision from corruption. This also is commanded in biblical law.

9.3.4 The Demands and Dreams of the Prophets

One of the Old Testament's key resources for a sacredness-of-life ethic is found in the demand, and the yearning, for a transformed world of justice and peace. *Shalom*, or true peace, happens when people live in security, flourish in the exercise of their capacities, and the sacredness of every human life is recognized. The prophets both demand shalom now and yearn for it in the future.

Taking shalom seriously points us toward what it really means for human beings to flourish. Shalom means everyone has a place in a community that values them. Everyone has enough to eat and drink. Everyone has the means to work successfully and meet their own needs and that of their loved ones.

Shalom means the healing of broken bodies and spirits, an end of tears and an eruption of joy. The prophets remind Israel that this was always God's intent, not just for the chosen people, but for all people. Creation, deliverance, law, and prophetic demands and dreams thus all unite around a common theme—God's good world is a sacred place full of creatures whom God values, with human beings at the pinnacle, but all creatures having their own proper part. Our charge is to build, repair, and protect communities in which God's exalted vision can be fulfilled.

9.4 The New Testament on the Sacredness of Life

The New Testament proclaims that the *shalom* promised by the Old Testament prophets has dawned in Jesus Christ, who called it the kingdom of God. The Old Testament strands that had contributed to the sacredness ethic are *personalized* in the ministry of Jesus Christ. Jesus incarnates the message of human life's sacred worth, and he intensifies it through his teaching that how we treat the most vulnerable human being is how we treat God (Matt. 25:31–46).

Jesus carries forward all four themes noted above. He offers a creation theology affirming God as Creator and God's loving care for human beings, while employing his power over creation to heal, rescue, and raise people from the dead. He teaches and exhibits the compassionate deliverance for suffering people that God had exhibited to Israel. He offers a rendering of Jewish legal and moral norms that affirms and heightens the protections offered in Torah. He both articulates and embodies the prophetic vision of an eschatological shalom in God's coming future.

A central commitment in the sacredness of human life ethic is to the protection of human life from wanton destruction. Jesus rejects human violence, despite the abundant provocation to violence that existed for all Jews under Roman occupation.

Jesus says that God pays attention even to the life of a sparrow, and all the more attends to providing for our material needs—therefore freeing us to trust him and serve others (Mt 6:26). He describes God as a loving Father who can be counted on to care for his children.

As Howard Thurman so beautifully articulated, Jesus teaches and demonstrates that every individual matters to him and therefore to God. No groups are less than, none are greater than. His example pushes Christians toward an ethic of indiscriminate love toward all, with special care for outcasts and those viewed as "below."

Further, New Testament reflection on the Story of Jesus Christ himself—his birth, ministry, death, resurrection, and ascension—ties all of human existence to the sacred journey of the God-man, Jesus. As Dietrich Bonhoeffer emphasized, and Jens Zimmermann has noted, the incarnation of God in the human Jesus becomes the basis for a new dignifying of human life and a renewal of human character (Zimmermann, *Dietrich Bonhoeffer's Christian Humanism*, pp. 94–99). The concept of the image of God takes on profound new possibilities when it is reframed as the ***imago Christi***, the image of Christ. Christ embodied what it means to be fully human. We are invited to participate in his life and come into conformity with it (Rom 12:1–2). Here sacredness becomes ***moral sanctity***, or ***holiness***, as a human life begins to show forth the moral goodness that God intended for all of us.

The early church taught and often practiced a strikingly countercultural ethic of honoring life. Because of its marginality, the first churches could not hope to affect the major directions of imperial state policy, but they could carve out a distinctive way of life that overcame the hierarchy, prejudice, violence, and cruelty of their cultures. In the church, slaves, ex-slaves, and free Roman citizens gathered in one community. Jews and Gentiles learned how to live as part of one body. Cruelty, status hierarchies, and violence were rejected. The sick and abandoned were cared for. The hungry were fed. No one was viewed as worth more than anyone else. There were the seedlings of a new creation and a new humanity. Though the church sometimes fell short of its best self, by all accounts it was this tender communal ethos that led to the surprising spread of Christianity in the Greco-Roman world.

9.5 Christian Failures and the Sacredness-of-Life Ethic

Christians did not always live out their convictions about life's sacredness. When the Roman Empire became officially Christian after the Emperor Constantine converted in the fourth century, the church began to make compromises to its ethic—most notably, accepting state violence; most egregiously, using violence to root out heresy and stamp out schism. Those moral compromises deepened when the Roman Empire became officially Christian, setting the trajectory toward official, established Christianity—first in Europe and later wherever Europeans colonized. Christendom became the new face of Christianity in the world.

Many have rightly wondered whether it was the church or the state that was truly converted in the fourth century CE. Despite some gains achieved through alliance with the state—such as the end of accepted *infanticide* and gladiatorial combats—the church's prior nonviolence was largely surrendered. Christianity, Christian regimes, and Christian people ended up with much blood on their hands. Many people around the world do not think of the sacredness of life when they think of Christianity. They instead think of heresy trials, inquisitions, crusades, wars of religion, colonialism, conquest, and slavery.

It helps a bit to remember that there were always Christians who fiercely resisted these corruptions. The life-revering resources of scripture and tradition could be submerged by supposedly Christian regimes but never destroyed within Christian people. The sacred worth of each person as created in God's image, human dignity, and God-given human rights continued to be defended by Christians during the age of Christendom.

Often the most powerful dissents were offered by subaltern Christians themselves, who understood the deepest meaning of the religion that was being used to harm them. Consider again the versions of Christianity that developed among the enslaved and colonized peoples of the New World, today leaving a legacy in Black theology, womanist theology, Indigenous theology, liberation theology, and more.

Eventually, repeated Christian failures contributed to the discrediting of Christianity, the gradual collapse of official Christianity, and a growing cultural secularism. The early modern period saw demands for religious and intellectual freedom, recognition of human rights, incipient democracy, and the dethroning of state religion.

In its earliest stage these themes were not rejections of the Christian moral tradition but instead efforts to protect its best insights while preventing the church from politically enforcing its orthodoxy. Eventually, though, Christianity paid a high price for its sins—a loss of credibility in cultures that had seen too many Christians who did not understand the true meaning of their own moral tradition. This is still where we find ourselves in many lands.

Christians are surrounded by people who do not trust the church because of our many historic failures, but who, ironically, continue to benefit from cultural commitments that originated within Jewish and Christian scripture and tradition.

Post-Christian cultures generally still elevate human dignity as a broad cultural standard. They institutionalize concern for the most vulnerable through every kind of social welfare program. They offer expansive civil rights. They are filled with people working to advance social justice.

Every time someone draws a contrast between how the world should be and the world as it is—every time someone speaks of a dream, of a world in which all tears are wiped away, in which all flourish—we are still being nourished by the biblical vision of the way God intended the world to be. That is, as a sacred world, created and sustained by both divine and human love, every life valued beyond measure.

To take the God-given sacredness of human life seriously is to learn to see each human being as a kind of royalty, a person of high dignity and ineffable worth. It demands a spirit of reverence toward all persons, respecting each in the uniqueness of their own personality and life story. An ethic of the sacredness of human life works itself out in various sectors of life, from parenting to policing, from education to health care, and far beyond. Where people are the most vulnerable, a commitment to life's sacredness is most critical. Treating life as sacred reaches toward the highest potential in human relations.

Human life can become whatever we make it. When we choose to live in cesspools of coarseness, prejudice, and violence, we turn our world into a hellscape. When we instead go high, treating others as the sacred beings they are, we dignify ourselves and beautify our world.

Discussion Questions

1. Do you recognize the idea that we tend to select certain objects, places, or persons as sacred? Discuss any such sacred things in your life.

2. Have you been taught the belief that human life is sacred? What about all creaturely life? If so, what applications of this idea were suggested?

3. According to this chapter, what exactly is it that makes human life sacred?

4. Discuss the strengths but also potential problems of the idea that elevated human worth is tied to certain human capacities such as rationality and agency.

To watch Dr. Gushee deliver

Lecture 10: Justice

Follow this link:

https://youtu.be/pJD5m2EVlbg

Or scan the QR code.

To listen to the audio, follow this link:

https://qrco.de/bcOlEh

Or scan the QR code.

To scan a QR code, download a QR reader from the app store on your device, open the application, follow the directions, and point your device's camera at the code.

CHAPTER 10

Justice

You shall appoint judges and officials throughout your tribes, in all your towns
that the LORD your God is giving you, and they shall render just decisions for
the people. You must not distort justice; you must not show partiality; and you
must not accept bribes, for a bribe blinds the eyes of the wise and subverts the
cause of those who are in the right. Justice, and only justice, you shall pursue, so
that you may live and occupy the land that the LORD your God is giving you.

—Dt 16:18–20

10.1 Justice as Memory

Prominently displayed in my home office is a wall hanging that is drawn
from the passage cited above. It says, in English and Hebrew, "Justice, justice,
shalt thou pursue." This cherished gift was given to me by Holocaust survivor Fred Gross, whom I assisted in finding a publisher for his 2009 memoir,
One Step Ahead of Hitler (Mercer University Press). This riveting book tells
the story of how Fred and his family barely escaped the Holocaust when the
Nazis overran Belgium, and then France, during World War II.

Fred gave me this wall hanging because he believes that my teaching
about the Nazi assault on the Jewish people is an expression of justice. My
dissertation focused on the small minority of non-Jews who risked their
lives to save Jews from the Nazis. That book was *The Righteous Gentiles of the*
Holocaust.

The Jewish community never experienced anything like "justice" in relation to the destruction of their European Jewish civilization and the murder
of one-third of all the Jews in the world. But Jews often express the belief
that to remember the Holocaust honestly, to teach and write about it, to
plead with humanity not to do anything like it ever again, is absolutely
required—in the work of justice, it is at least a place to start.

10.2 Justice as the Central Norm in the Hebrew Bible and Jewish Ethics

The Jewish commitment to justice goes beyond concerns about Holocaust memory, of course. My long experience of reading the Hebrew Bible and Jewish theology and ethics, as well as dialoguing with Jewish scholars and rabbis, leads me to the firm conclusion that justice is the central norm in Jewish ethics. This is not because love is absent from the Hebrew Bible or the sacred writings that have followed in Jewish life. But it is true that in "the law and the prophets," justice rather than love is more often centered as the central moral obligation.

Biblical and contemporary Jewish thought provided my initial path into the ethics of justice, and remains most salient for me today. I am not much attracted to the understanding of justice that came out of ancient Greece, which I consider both relatively abstract—"give to each according to his due"—and tainted by privilege—slaves and women are "due" less than free men. It was instead the Jewish tradition, beginning with the Hebrew Bible and continuing in the work of contemporary Jewish moral thinkers like Michael Walzer (see his 1985 *Exodus and Revolution* and his book from 2012, *In God's Shadow*) that became paradigmatic for me. Such themes have made their way into Christian moral philosophy and ethics, as in the work of Karen Lebacqz (*Justice in an Unjust World*, 1987) and especially Nicholas Wolterstorff (*Justice: Rights and Wrongs*, 2008). I see in these works a healthy continuity between Jewish and Christian thought, and that position tracks with my own.

Two key words for justice, **tsedeqah** and **mishpat**, constantly reappear in the Hebrew Bible. In the above passage from Deuteronomy 16, I count seven uses of variants of these two words. These two central words have overlapping and parallel meanings and usages, and yet a distinction can be drawn.

Tsedeqah happens when actions are undertaken to rescue powerless, oppressed people from the clutches of those who are harming them, and then to return them in peace to their rightful place in covenant community. *Tsedeqah* is needed because sinful human beings often succumb to the temptation to take advantage of power imbalances to exploit or harm the weak. Old Testament law, in its provisions for the establishment of covenant community, banned such injustices and commanded special attention to such vulnerable groups as "resident aliens, orphans, and widows" (Dt 14:29, 26:12–13).

The narrative backdrop for such concern in Old Testament law is clearly the grotesque injustice of slavery and the beginnings of genocide from which the Hebrew people were rescued by God, as described in the early part of the book of Exodus. But it also appears to be rooted in a sad realism about how power imbalances creep into all human societies and lead to mistreatment of those on the bottom of every social order.

Tsedeqah is sometimes translated as "righteousness" in English Bibles. Moreover, in the movement from Hebrew to Greek, *tsedeqah* was often translated as *dikaiosune*, which in turn was translated as righteousness. This would not be a problem except for the fact that most English-speaking people do not think of justice when they read the word righteousness. They instead think of personal goodness, holiness, or godliness. Indeed, in my part of the English-speaking world, the word righteousness has almost disappeared from regular use. It would be better if future English translations of the Bible used the word justice most of the time when rendering both *tsedeqah* and *dikaoisune*.

Mishpat is another term that can be translated as justice, although sometimes it shows up as "judgment" in English translations. *Mishpat* carries an even clearer judicial connotation, as when a judge makes "just decisions for the people" (Dt 16:18).

Mishpat is not about just any judgment, but specifically about judgments that advance justice, set wrongs right, vindicate those who have been mistreated, and prevent further mistreatment. When a judge renders a judgment that factories which polluted groundwater and sickened local families must pay compensation to their victims, this is both *mishpat* and *tsedeqah*. A powerful entity abused its power and harmed vulnerable people, and a judgment has been rendered on behalf of the people harmed.

Justice has multiple dimensions, the relative importance of which is often debated. These dimensions include telling the truth about specific injustices, rendering negative public judgment of the behavior, demanding restitution to those harmed, seeking reconciling encounters between victim and offender, preventing further recurrence of the unjust behavior, and punishing those who have done wrong, all for the purpose of righting the wrong and restoring peace and good order in the community.

Various approaches to law and ethics have been developed that focus on each of these aspects of justice.

Justice systems can emphasize truthtelling, because, as we have seen, injustices are usually swathed in lies which themselves harm the community. Truth matters so much that victims and survivors of injustice often want the truth told about what has happened to them as the first step, and perhaps the main step, toward making things right.

Justice efforts can emphasize public moral accountability, to teach the community the limits of morally acceptable behavior and the centrality of justice for communal well-being. Public moral accountability in this sense is mainly about communal recovery and rebuilding after injustice.

Justice work can emphasize restitution, that is, compensation for victims, attempting to even the scales by doing right to those who have been wronged. This approach recognizes that something has been taken from victims—even if it cannot be exactly replaced, some effort must be made to meet the moral debt that has been accrued.

Justice systems can bring victims and offenders together for relationship-restoring encounters that must usually begin with heartfelt apologies on the part of offenders. This is sometimes called *restorative justice*, and it has become an important strategy deployed in many criminal justice systems. This approach recognizes that acts of injustice damage interpersonal relationships, and that if reconciliation can be achieved that can be an important dimension of justice.

Justice can be about punishing wrongdoers in some manner commensurate with the offense. This is called *retributive justice*, and it tends to be the focus of most traditional criminal justice systems as well as what I would describe as authoritarian or punitive approaches in ethics.

Finally, especially when dealing with offenses that harm entire communities, the quest for justice usually involves some examination of political and legal structures and processes that might be implicated in the offense and ought to be reformed. Consider a mayor who abuses his power and harms a group of citizens, and it turns out that a lack of adequate checks and balances on mayoral power was one reason why he could do so. Justice looks like correcting that specific problem while also dealing with the mayor's misdeeds.

In the Old Testament, the office of the God-called prophets involved summoning the Jewish people back to *mishpat* and *tsedeqah*. The prophets did this by reminding the people that justice is a fundamental aspect of God's character and central to the covenant between God and Israel. A just God rescued a victimized people and called them into covenant not only with God but with each other. This covenant people was now to create a more just society than had ever been seen in human life, a society governed by God's merciful justice and not by the whims of the strongest and most powerful. Whenever Israel slipped loose from this moral vision, it was subverting the very reason for its existence.

A concern for social justice is wired into the Jewish moral tradition. The core scriptures of the Jewish community understand justice as especially about protecting and vindicating the rights of those who are "below" rather than above. The scriptures set up legal structures that attend especially to the vulnerabilities of the powerless, demand that those in judicial and political authority exercise their judgments with these vulnerabilities firmly in mind, and in general make attention to politics, law, and social justice fundamental to Jewish religion and morality.

Now I ask my readers to consider this humble question: Have these justice commitments made their way into Christian religion and morality with the same force?

The answer is clearly no.

10.3 The Erroneous Split Between Jesus and Justice

A tragic theological development in Western Christian history created a split between the undeniable Old Testament emphasis on social justice "from below," on the one hand, and our reading of the Jesus of the New Testament, on the other.

Large sections of the Christian community came to associate the concept of justice with the Old Testament only. Given the way that many Christians interpret the Hebrew Bible, this meant that justice was left behind along with most of the rest of Old Testament theology, ritual, ethics, and law.

Thus, in an effort to be "New Testament Christians," we left "Old Testament justice" behind. We were about the "Gospel," interpreted as the Good News that Jesus came to die for our sins and thus save our souls from eternal damnation.

The result was that many Christians had (and still have) little idea what to make of the concept of justice, or whether it is even relevant in light of the grace and mercy of gentle Jesus, Savior of the world. They know that justice is a word that shows up again and again on the news and in society, and they may have an opinion about it, but these Christians have not learned to think about justice in Christian theological terms. Indeed, they may have been taught to be suspicious of the term as a buzzword belonging to liberals and secularists.

This split between the purported justice message of the Old Testament and the grace message of the New Testament is yet another dangerous dualism that has sometimes emerged in Christian thought. It is woven together with a tendency to split the Old Testament from the New Testament, Jewish thought from Christian thought, law from grace, Old Covenant from New Covenant, and God the Lawgiver from Jesus the Crucified Savior.

Such a fragmentation of the canon and of the covenants is one of the church's oldest heretical tendencies, going back to Marcion. It has also produced fateful moral consequences.

Christians have learned to disregard the justice teachings of the Old Testament. Despite hundreds of references to justice and to the God of justice in the Old Testament, justice is not customarily an important part of our theology, ethics, or preaching.

We have believed that the only relevant moral teachings for us are those found in the New Testament. Having been trained to ignore the justice theme in the Bible, we have missed it when it appears in the New Testament as well. The crucial mistranslation of *dikaiosune* as "righteousness" has played a big part. Consider what would have happened if, for example, Matthew 5:6 had been translated into English as "Blessed are those who hunger and thirst for justice," and then that passage was regularly preached each year.

We have been taught to think that Jesus taught love, mercy, and grace, and to see these as the antitheses of justice. We do not know what to do when we face situations within Christian communities in which power is abused and the weak are exploited. We also do not know how our faith should inform our beliefs about gritty matters like criminal justice or prison conditions.

Often, either implicitly or explicitly, we bracket off the teachings of Jesus from any area other than our personal strivings to be holy or morally rigorous. Love, grace, and mercy, being unrealistic norms for public life, governmental affairs, and international relations, are only fit to be applied to "private life." This means that the part of the Bible that we actually use is interpreted as having nothing relevant to say about public life and the justice issues that emerge there.

This has made it extremely difficult for Christians to think coherently about public and governmental issues from within a Christian theological and ethical frame. We end up at a loss as to what to think and do about justice. We lack the resources we need to do thoughtful public ethics, at least, to do it as Christians.

Lacking any biblical norms that we think can be applied to issues in public life, a vacuum is created. We either retreat into an irresponsible privatism or borrow ideologies from outside the scriptures. In the American white evangelical context, most embrace a version of American conservative ideology as currently articulated by the Republican party, no matter who is leading that party at a given time. In the Old South, many Christians picked up a feudal agrarian aristocratic racism and saw that as just. This underwrote race-based chattel slavery and helped prepare the way for our Civil War.

In 1930s Germany, many Christians adapted quite nicely to Nazism as their political ideology, with disastrous results. Many in various settings have been attracted to less extreme but still deeply authoritarian ideologies, such as the divine right of kings. There has been a long history of Christian political authoritarianism, which privileges order over justice, rejects resistance to the state, and blesses almost any kind of ruler (especially one that believers consider to be a Christian).

While it is less frequent, sometimes left-leaning Christians have embraced Marxist understandings of justice, especially when Marxism was the hot new ideology and promised greater social justice than at any time in human history.

Too often Christians have been silent or visibly on the wrong side of the key issues of the day. The loss of the norm of justice has left us deeply vulnerable to social sins of great magnitude.

Much of the history of Western Christendom involved the aggressive export of such established Christianity in various colonizing, conquering, and enslaving ventures. This is one reason why versions of Christianity that were a part of colonizing Christianity have often had a difficult time embracing *tsedeqah* and *mishpat*, whereas versions of the faith arising from among the oppressed have often done so fully and energetically. Consider the contrast between authoritarian and liberationist versions of Catholicism in Latin America.

In relation to the absence of the ethic of justice in many Christian communities, the hope which animated Glen Stassen and me in writing *Kingdom Ethics* was that if we could show that Jesus cared about justice, then more Christians might care too. Nearly 30 years later, concern for justice has indeed spread among many Christians around the world, but there remain many tens of millions of Christians who are oblivious to it, or steeped in cultural understandings of justice having little to do with *tsedeqah* or *mishpat*.

10.4 Jesus and Justice

I described the political, social, and cultural context of Jesus' ministry when considering Howard Thurman's work. Suffice it to repeat here that Jesus was born and raised in a context of multiple overlapping oppressions, and that he is best understood as a man "from below," who led a popular movement of others in the same social location.

I have also situated Jesus in the lineage of the prophets. Like them, he emphasized the "weightier matters of the law"—like justice (Mt 23:23). It wasn't just the prophets that emphasized justice, though. Old Testament law was suffused with concrete, legislated commitment to build a just society. It was this legal and moral framework to which the prophets called the Jewish people to return. Social justice, understood as protecting and then vindicating the rights of those "below," and ensuring the moral health of the covenant community, was always one of the "weightier matters" of Jewish law. Jesus could not have been a leader in the lineage of "the law and the prophets" without a commitment to social justice. And yet many Christians have not understood this at all.

Luke 18:1–8 is a relatively overlooked passage that seems an apt partner to Deuteronomy 16:18–20 for this discussion. It also reveals much about the heart of Jesus for justice.

> Then Jesus told them a parable about their need to pray always and not to lose heart. He said, "In a certain city there was a judge who neither feared God nor had respect for people. In that city there was a widow who kept coming to him and saying, 'Grant me justice against my opponent.' For a while he refused; but later he said to himself, 'Though I have no fear of God and no respect for anyone, yet because this widow keeps bothering me, I will grant her justice, so that she may not wear

me out by continually coming.'" And the LORD said, "Listen to what the unjust judge says. And will not God grant justice to his chosen ones who cry to him day and night? Will he delay long in helping them? I tell you, he will quickly grant justice to them. And yet, when the Son of Man comes, will he find faith on earth?"

This passage is sometimes labeled in our Bibles as the "parable of the unjust judge." That's not a bad start, but I have never found it quite adequate. The judge here performs in a manner precisely the opposite of that prescribed in Deuteronomy 16. He is not pursuing justice, he is not rendering just decisions, he is not protecting the cause of the one whom we are led to assume is "in the right," and he is not looking out for the powerless—in this case, a widow. It is not hard to imagine that he is showing partiality, that he might well be taking bribes, though we do not know this. We do know that he does not fear God or have respect for people, and he is not doing his crucial job as he should.

Jesus does not have to teach, because his story assumes, that this kind of careless injustice happens all the time, even among people who should know better, and even in institutions established to prevent it. Most strikingly, he exudes an understanding that those who are deeply victimized by injustice "cry day and night" for relief to whomever will listen—whether a judge, or the God of justice. Jesus affirms that the God he knows is a God who "will grant justice" to those who cry out—and will do so "quickly." But he also knows that the experience of terrible injustice can grind down people's faith in God.

Notice how our narrator introduces this parable as being about persistence in prayer. While it is that, this prelude has misdirected many interpretations of this text. I think the parable is also a prophetic Jewish account of how God is outraged by injustice—especially that committed by those who are charged precisely with advancing justice. And it is about how God will in fact bring justice, because this is what God does and who God is.

I wonder if Jesus' promise that God will not "delay long in helping" those who "cry to him day and night" for justice is part of his understanding of his own ministry. After all, justice is one of the marks of the kingdom of God, and Jesus came proclaiming that this kingdom is now "at hand." Perhaps Jesus is not saying that on that day when he returns there will at last be justice. Perhaps he is saying that now, as the Son of Man, who *has come*, who *is preaching the reign of God*, justice is here, because that is what the kingdom of God is about.

Jesus offered consistent, though often overlooked, justice teaching and action during his brief ministry. In *Kingdom Ethics* Stassen and I show that Jesus addressed four specific kinds of injustice: mistreatment of the poor, domination of the weak by the powerful, physical violence, and exclusion of persons from community. Greed takes from the poor to add superabundance to the rich. Violence attacks physical well-being. Domination bullies the weaker, pushing them around, enabling their exploitation. Exclusion from community pushes designated individuals and groups out to the margins of community or outside of community altogether.

These four categories help make sense of events such as the Holocaust, which did not begin with gas chambers and crematoria at Auschwitz in 1941. It began with a government deciding in 1933 to dominate, exclude, steal from, and (finally) do violence against an entire group of people—actually, in the end, several such groups. Genocide was the end—before that was exclusion from employment, education, and social life, street bullying and petty violence, dehumanizing propaganda and rhetoric, economic suppression, and every kind of exploitation.

In the end, Jews and Gypsies (Sinti and Roma) were designated for total annihilation as groups, while people from many other groups were also killed in large numbers. Those who ended up in Nazi death camps were entirely stripped of their remaining possessions, relationships, dignity, and life itself, often in a matter of hours. Their possessions were shipped to Nazi Germany, their bodies were killed and burned in the name of Nazi Germany, and their memories were blotted out as far as Nazi Germany could manage it.

Injustice should not have to end up in genocide for us to care about it. Many far more routine situations in our world offer us obvious evidence of injustice involving money, domination, violence, and exclusion from community. It is far past time for Christians to care as much about justice as did Jesus, the prophets, and Jewish Law—and many of our most civic-minded neighbors, who do not call on the name of Jesus but do fight hard for justice.

Discussion Questions

1. Can you think of relevant examples in your cultural context in which accurate historical memory and truthful accounting of major injustices still has not yet occurred? What are the consequences of this problem?

2. Has justice been a significant feature of the teaching and preaching you have experienced, or offered, in church life?

3. Compare my account of the approach to social justice represented by the terms *tsedeqah* and *mishpat* with standard understandings of justice in your context.

4. If justice has been neglected in your particular Christian context, can you give an account of why that is so? How does it relate to the reasons offered above?

To watch Dr. Gushee deliver

Lecture 11: Love

Follow this link:

https://youtu.be/R3VrL94CdHk

Or scan the QR code.

To listen to the audio, follow this link:

https://qrco.de/bcOlFj

Or scan the QR code.

To scan a QR code, download a QR reader from the app store on your device, open the application, follow the directions, and point your device's camera at the code.

CHAPTER 11

Love

When the Pharisees heard that he had silenced the Sadducees, they gathered together, and one of them, a lawyer, asked him a question to test him. "Teacher, which commandment in the law is the greatest?" He said to him, "'You shall love the LORD your God with all your heart, and with all your soul, and with all your mind.' This is the greatest and first commandment. And a second is like it: 'You shall love your neighbor as yourself.' On these two commandments hang all the law and the prophets."

—Mt 22:34–40

11.1 The Centrality of Love in Christian Ethics

This great passage is known in Christian tradition as the Double Love Command or, more simply, the Great Commandment. For some Christians, it carries an authority above that of any other teaching in the Bible. After all, one can easily claim that the Great Commandment is really all that one needs to understand what it means to be a follower of Jesus. This text has been a highly motivating one for Christian moral striving. I found in my research on Christians who rescued Jews during the Holocaust that some rescuers cited this passage as the definitive reason why they rescued. That rescuers were willing to risk their own lives in this way shows how powerful was that motivation.

We find three versions of the passage in the Gospels (Mt 22:34–40, Mk 12:28–34, Lk 10:25–37). Though the texts do vary a bit, in each case Jesus enters a longstanding Jewish debate about which of the commandments of Torah is the greatest or most important. It was a hard question. To even answer the question is to risk the accusation of not taking some laws as seriously as others, as if inviting listeners to downplay or even break other parts of God's law. It would have been safest for Jesus simply to refuse to answer the question or to say that all laws carry equal weight because all come from God.

But Jesus chooses to answer. He picks two Hebrew Bible commands and weaves them together in an unprecedented way. The first is drawn from the Shema in Deuteronomy 6, a central text concerning the identity of Yahweh as the one God and the command that this God alone is the one that Israel must love, worship, and obey. The second is drawn from a much more obscure text in Leviticus 19 enjoining love of neighbor, specified in the passage as "kin" and "your people," that is, fellow Israelites.

Jesus combines them to teach whole-hearted, whole-souled, whole-minded love of Yahweh, and then, "like it," love of neighbor. He does not seem to be treating these two love commands as ranked first and second but instead as inextricably connected, and that is how his teaching, which echoes powerfully in the rest of the New Testament, was understood. Love of God is intertwined with love of neighbor, is demonstrated by love of neighbor, and is illusory without love of neighbor: "Whoever does not love does not know God, for God is love" (1 Jn 4:8).

Jesus went on to emphasize, in Luke's version of this teaching, that love of neighbor must go far beyond care for kin. It is often forgotten that Jesus' stirring parable of the Good Samaritan (Lk 10:25–37) is offered as an answer to the question "Who is my neighbor?"—which itself is triggered by Jesus' teaching that love of neighbor is essential to gaining eternal life. That parable, in my view, offers two answers to the lawyer's probing inquiry. Looking at others, one's neighbor is any person, especially anyone who is in need. Looking at oneself, a true neighbor is one who attends with care to others, especially any others in special need of it. In this way, Jesus' teaching elevates both how we look at others and the expectations we have of our own character and behavior.

Jesus' teaching in the Great Commandment, among other places, created the precondition for love rather than justice to become the central moral norm in much of Christian ethics. The fact that Jesus connected love of God with love of neighbor, radically broadened the concept of neighbor, and connected love of neighbor with eternal salvation, dramatically raised the stakes for all future generations of serious Christians when it came to love. We would need to love, expansively and mercifully, if we wanted to show our love of God and be welcomed into his eternal presence.

11.2 Four Major Christian Accounts of Love

In view of this background, the Christian moral tradition, unsurprisingly, contains a rich vein of reflection on love. Mid-20th-century Protestant ethics was filled with learned scholarship on love, and competing accounts of what it means and what it requires. This culminated in Yale ethicist Gene Outka's 1972 work *Agape: An Ethical Analysis.* Catholic theologian Edward Vacek revisited the important theological and theoretical questions in his 1994 book, *Love, Human and Divine.* Both Outka and Vacek acknowledge that the theological conversation about love has been difficult and often somewhat confused. Part of the problem has been difficulty in differentiating among various historical, linguistic, cultural, theological, and moral meanings associated with the concept of love. Attempting to discern which of these meanings Jesus had in mind in the Great Commandment has also been problematic.

In our book *Kingdom Ethics,* Glen Stassen and I suggest four primary renderings of love, also introducing some key figures who have made arguments for one or the other of them. These four definitions are ***sacrificial love, mutual love, love as equal regard,*** and ***delivering love.***

Sometimes in Christian ethics, definitions of love are tied to translations/interpretations of Greek words used in the New Testament that are all translated into English as "love." The most important of these are *agape, philia, eros,* and *storge.* What to make especially of the central New Testament term for love, *agape,* has been at the center of much conversation about the theology and ethics of love. We need to be careful about reducing the conversation about love to disputable translations/interpretations of these Greek words, though that paradigm is by now well-established in popular Bible teaching and preaching.

More practical and helpful may be to think about these issues: Whether we are to treat all neighbors with the same type and intensity of love; whether there are any limits to what Jesus asks of us when he commands us to love; whether the behavior of specific others toward us ought to have any effect on if, or how, we continue to love them; whether the obligation to love extends to the love of oneself, and, if so, what we should do when love of neighbor and love of self seem to conflict.

One way to think about the four main definitions of love considered in *Kingdom Ethics* is to think of them as overall syntheses attempting to respond to these pivotal questions. Each definition offers an account of what love *really is* in biblical terms, and therefore what Jesus is commanding us to do.

So, to say that love really is *sacrificial love*, is to say that when Jesus asks us to love, he is asking us to set aside our own interests, preferences, and needs in order to serve and care for others—even, in extreme cases, to lay our very lives down so that others might live. Love is defined by sacrifice. This is the position taken by Swedish Lutheran theologian Anders Nygren (1890–1978) in his classic 1932 book *Agape and Eros*. Nygren defined *agape*, that central New Testament Greek word for love, as sacrificial love.

To say that love is better understood as *mutual love*, is to say that healthy love involves reciprocal giving and receiving, with boundaries and limits on what love can require us to do. This emphasis on boundaried mutual love was, in part, a 1950s/1960s effort to correct the perceived dangers of defining love in terms of sacrifice. These dangers included the association of love with complete self-denial and abandonment of any self-concern. The fear was that a completely sacrificial love was either impossible or dangerously open to exploitation. Feminist ethics has been especially concerned about defining love as sacrifice, as this expectation has often been laid disproportionately on the shoulders of women.

Love as *equal regard*, the position favored by Gene Outka, is the idea that the heart of love is viewing and treating all persons equally, regardless of their proximity to us in life or any of their traits or behaviors. Love as equal regard tracks very closely with the idea of the immeasurable sacred worth of all persons. It is similarly a fixed and unalterable way of viewing other persons that creates behavioral demands on us in all human encounters.

Finally, Glen Stassen's favorite, *delivering love*, sees biblical love most clearly in concrete acts of rescuing people from oppression and setting them in places of freedom and community. Delivering love looks to liberate, rescue, and restore people. It is love exercised as compassionate action on behalf of those who most need it.

One's idea of God or Jesus and their relation to the world is very much involved in how one defines human love and understands its obligations. It is easy to find biblical narratives or teachings that can ground each one of these accounts of love, but that does not resolve the question. It turns out that one cannot think clearly about the ethics of love without doing some theological work on the nature of God's love. This is a good example of how theology and ethics are deeply interwoven.

If we zero in on Jesus, how can we miss the sacrificial love he offered during his ministry and especially in his death on the Cross? He gave up everything for humanity and the world, from his place at the throne of God to his dignity, honor, and life itself.

But Jesus also created relationships of mutual love with his disciples and called us to do the same with one another. It wasn't all sacrifice—it was also mutual giving and receiving. Recall this passage from John 15: "I do not call you servants any longer, because the servant does not know what the master is doing; but I have called you friends" (Jn 15:15). More broadly, one can look at the entirety of the biblical story as the account of a God who wants friendship with human beings, with mutual giving and receiving.

As for love as equal regard, Jesus did say that God loves the just and the unjust, showering indiscriminate blessing on all, and that those who would be like God should do the same (Mt 5:43–48). Jesus shocked those around him by how he treated every person as someone of value, including women, children, the sick, tax collectors, prostitutes, Gentiles, and so on. In a context in which religion underwrote stark status hierarchies and constant exclusion of some from the blessings of hospitality and community, Jesus constantly refused to go along.

In terms of delivering love, Jesus' ministry was indeed filled with deliverances of the sick from illness, the possessed from Satan, and the marginalized from exclusion. His death was not only sacrifice, it was deliverance of the world from sin and death into salvation. Glen Stassen argued that the two salvific high points of the Bible—the Exodus and the Cross—exemplify God's delivering love, as does the story of the Good Samaritan.

A big part of the history of Christian morality is the idea that Christians are supposed to be like Jesus, to imitate him as far as we are able. Therefore, it has been exceedingly important which way the story of Jesus' love is told, leading to various moral visions focused on sacrifice, mutuality, equality, or deliverance.

By now, I have come to believe that it is better to speak of *dimensions* of love rather than definitions, of specific *contexts* and *covenants* in which the biblical command to love requires different actions. There are indeed different dimensions, contexts, and covenants in relation to different family members, strangers, colleagues, children, elders, leaders, followers, visitors, prisoners, endangered persons, friends, enemies, and so on.

The "default love setting" for a healthy romantic relationship, such as a good marriage, will be mutual love, with constant ebbs and flows of giving and receiving and patterns of loving reciprocity.

But sometimes that very same romantic relationship will require sacrifice, as when our spouse is ill for a long period of time and we must care for her or him with little return to us. Sometimes a marriage partner needs to be delivered from oppression, such as in situations of violence or addiction. Sometimes a spouse's preferences and desires need to be left partly unmet, due to the need to care for others as persons of equal moral worth.

As for the relationship between parents and children, it goes through stages. When our children are little, we sacrifice greatly, there is little mutuality, and there is more than occasional rescuing required. As the children grow, the mutuality between parent and child grows in lovely ways, though there is always the possibility of arduous sacrifice or occasional urgent effort to deliver from disaster.

When we get old, the balance shifts, and we may be the ones who need our grown children to sacrifice for us or even to rescue us. At the very end, there can be a substantial period in which all that remains is the need for our grown children to lay themselves down for us for a time as we weaken and finally die.

Considered over the entire life span, the love between parents and children can be said to have a permanent dimension of mutuality—*you have cared for me and now I will care for you.* At any given moment, it may not feel mutual at all.

Erotic love between adults requires the capacity both to give and to receive, both to offer what the other needs and to clarify and receive what we need. Some people are selfish or oblivious, and struggle with being able to give what the other needs and wants. Others are self-effacing and sacrificial to a fault, and struggle to ask for and receive what they themselves want and need.

Feminist and womanist ethicists have stressed that the willingness and ability to offer love to self is often a problem for those who have been subjugated by the power structures of their world. Jesus did say, "love your neighbor *as yourself*" (Mt 22:39) and "Do to others *as you would have them do to you*" (Mt 7:12, italics added in both texts). These teachings acknowledge legitimate self-love and self-concern. Yet ethicist Sondra Wheeler points out in her 2007 book, *What We Were Made For: Christian Reflections on Love*, self-love has been a problem in Christian ethics, with some Christian traditions having great difficulty in accepting self-love as a legitimate moral norm.

Christian feminist ethicists, like my teacher Beverly Wildung Harrison (1932–2012), in her 2004 book *Justice in the Making*, noted that the male theologians who dominated theology for almost two thousand years defined the core of sin as pride and selfishness. But for many women under patriarchal systems, the problem is not *too much* pride but instead *not enough* pride, not too much self-concern but instead not enough self-concern.

Womanist thinkers added to this the distinctive mistreatment of many Black women under the triple interlocking oppressions of race, gender, and class, with its origins in chattel slavery. Cheryl Townsend Gilkes argued in her 1993 essay "The 'Loves' and 'Troubles' of African American Women's Bodies: The Womanist Challenge to Cultural Humiliation and Community Ambivalence," that for Black women, self-love, including bodily self-acceptance, is often a major struggle due to living in a context in which Black women's bodies frequently have been judged, disrespected, and humiliated.

From this perspective, sometimes the dimension of love that needs the most attention is not sacrificial, mutual, or delivering love but instead self-love. One could call this a *corrective* love-as-equal-regard vision, in which the one who needs to be equally regarded is one's own self.

11.3 Covenant Love

Covenant themes are important in Christian ethics. Hak Joon Lee, in his 2021 book *Christian Ethics: A New Covenant Model*, makes covenant *the* central term for Christian ethics. Covenant is a major theme, especially in Calvinist/Reformed Christian ethics, and I find in this stage of my own work the concept has also become increasingly central.

Covenants in scripture are the agreements rooted in vowed promises that bind persons in sacred, enduring relationships. The Bible's theological story is structured by a series of covenants between God, Israel, and the world, and the Bible contains depictions of many specific covenant relationships between people, or peoples—sometimes with God, sometimes witnessed by God. The theme of covenant has profound moral as well as theological significance because covenants are one major way in which the moral obligations of different types of relationships can be understood.

Generally, the paradigm for covenant ethics has been set by the example of explicit, verbalized agreements involving publicly articulated sacred vows. This certainly applies to traditional marriage relationships as well as in legal, governmental, and business settings. Explicitly articulated covenants intentionally declare the nature, structure, and boundaries of the moral obligations of the covenanting partners.

But it is possible—not unarguable, but possible—to extend the concept of covenant to *implicit* and unverbalized obligations that exist in various types of relationships. For example, when persons, or couples, become parents, as I argued in my 2004 book *Getting Marriage Right*, they now are bound in a covenant with their children. Indeed, I would argue that the covenant that binds a couple changes when they become parents because their responsibilities now extend beyond one another. Babies don't come out carrying their covenant certificates, but parents incur covenant responsibilities, nonetheless.

One way to understand love as an ethical obligation is to ask about which expressions of love best fit with the type of covenant that exists between people. The Hebrew term **hesed** is important here. It is a term with a wide range of meanings, but here I focus on **covenant love** and faithful performance of what love requires.

How one thinks about love, or the proper expression of love, depends on the nature of the covenant involved: parent-child, brother-sister, church family, spouses, lovers, employer-employee, president-people, etc. Love looks like doing what *hesed* requires, case by case. That might entail sacrifice today, self-assertion tomorrow, and deliverance the next day. This is a reminder that morality is both principle-based and also contextual. Our obligations emerge in specific relationships and moments. Love is always required. But what love requires needs discernment in the situation.

II.4 Love as the "Impossible Possibility"?

Christian theologian/ethicist Reinhold Niebuhr (1892–1971), in his 1935 book, *An Interpretation of Christian Ethics*, offered one of the most famous, though disputed, treatments of the ethics of love that exists in our tradition. Deeply affected by the assumption that love is defined by the renunciation of self-interest, Niebuhr describes "the law of love" as "an impossible ethical ideal"—always relevant to every moral decision but never fully achievable in this world. He says those who see love as a "simple possibility" are naïve, but those who see it as a remote and irrelevant ideal miss its abiding significance in all aspects of moral life. Sometimes Niebuhr settles on the paradoxical language of love as an "impossible possibility" (p. 72).

Niebuhr suggests that love is always beckoning us to transcendent heights which we can never quite reach, but to which we must continually aspire. Love constantly calls us to greater purity in our motivations and greater breadth of application in practice. We must *love*—not just a little but more—then more—then more. We must *love*—not just self, but partner, not just partner but children, not just children but neighbors, and on and on. We must *love*—with more intelligence, more effectiveness, more care, more self-giving. If we think we have arrived at love we know nothing about it.

Niebuhr's idea makes me think of our ethics highway. Love is the destination, the *telos*, the goal—but we never fully arrive. We drive in the direction of love, but our destination keeps receding further towards the horizon. Yet we dare not set our course for any other destination.

While I think Niebuhr's vision of love lacked adequate mutuality and self-regard, I do agree that love is the destination that we can never quite reach. Our love can always become purer, broader, deeper; more vivid, active, practical, universal, and unconstrained—more like the love of God for us in Jesus Christ our Lord.

11.5 On the Relationship Between Justice and Love

We close by considering the fascinating relationship between justice and love.

In intimate relationships, such as in family life, we seek and offer love, not justice. Right? I don't say to my wife, "Jeanie, I sure justice you." However, if I were ever to not treat my wife fairly, ever dominate or harm her, ever bully her or mistreat her, ever exclude her from full partnership in the economic assets of our family, she would have reason to wonder about the meaningfulness of my claim to love her. In this sense, justice is an expression of love, even if not its highest and most transcendent dimension. If we do not treat our loved ones justly, then we may not really love them, under any definition of love.

In society, we do not ask police officers to love us. We do demand that they treat us (*all of us*) justly. We do not ask governors to love us. But we do require that they advance **public justice** within the scope of their authority. We do not ask realtors to love us. But we do demand that they broker property sales without any form of discrimination.

Civil rights activist Martin Luther King was often resisted by people wielding the facile Christian claim that "the law cannot make white people love Black people, only the Gospel can do that." The intent of this claim was to tell Dr. King to abandon his efforts to change racist laws in the direction of greater justice, and instead *get back to preaching the Gospel*, which, in due time, would bring the heart change toward Christian love that was truly needed.

Dr. King would respond, time and again, with these words, which made their way into his standard stump speech: "It may be true that the law cannot make a man love me, but it can keep him from lynching me, and I think that's pretty important." King was here articulating a distinction between love and justice, in which justice is what legitimately can be required in society, while love goes beyond that. King himself spoke of the "Beloved Community" to describe his ultimate moral vision, while day-to-day he worked on justice basics like fair housing, voting rights, and nondiscrimination in employment.

Reinhold Niebuhr put it this way: "In a struggle between those who enjoy inordinate privileges and those who lack the basic essentials of the good life it is fairly clear that a religion which holds love to be the final law of life stultifies itself if it does not support equal justice as a political and economic approximation of the ideal of love" (*Interpretation of Christian Ethics*, p. 80).

Those words were written in 1935, but it is as if Niebuhr was already responding to Dr. King's interlocutors, to wit: *Anyone who claims that love is the highest moral obligation must actively support efforts to advance equal justice for all.* As American political philosopher Cornel West has often said, "justice is what love looks like in public." Exactly how much justice we create in society determines the well-being of every person in that society—all made in God's image, all regarded equally by God, all people for whom Christ died.

Discussion Questions

1. Discuss the four main definitions of love. Which was new to you? Which most resonates? Disturbs?

2. What about the idea of "covenant love" in specific relationships as providing a way forward in understanding what love requires?

3. What do you make of the idea of love as an "impossible possibility"?

4. What do you think is the relationship between justice and love?

To watch Dr. Gushee deliver

Lecture 12: Forgiveness

Follow this link:

https://youtu.be/keyLkCTEEg4

Or scan the QR code.

To listen to the audio, follow this link:

https://qrco.de/bcOlKS

Or scan the QR code.

To scan a QR code, download a QR reader from the app store on your device, open the application, follow the directions, and point your device's camera at the code.

CHAPTER 12

Forgiveness

Forgive us our debts, as we also have forgiven our debtors ... For if you forgive others their trespasses, your heavenly Father will also forgive you; but if you do not forgive others, neither will your Father forgive your trespasses.

—Mt 6:12, 14–15

12.1 Introduction: The Challenge of Forgiveness

Forgiveness is one of the most profound examples of a biblical concept that, even in secular societies, also retains currency in everyday life. Like love, and unlike, say, pneumatology (theology of the Holy Spirit), you can stop people on the street, ask them what they think about forgiveness, and have an intelligent conversation. That's because most people have some concept of forgiveness and some experience of it—and of its painful absence.

This is one reason why forgiveness is a quite important term to consider not just in internal Christian ethics conversations but also when we turn outward to engage the public. It is one place where Christian ethics and general human ethics intersect. It is also a place where the Gospel meets the world.

Once we begin to dig into it, we quickly discover that the issue of forgiveness is theoretically and theologically complicated. There is no consensus on its definition or much else about it, other than that we need it to make human life bearable.

The challenge of forgiveness is a great leveler. Whether one is good at forgiving has nothing to do with education or any other worldly status marker. It does not matter how many degrees you have or how many books you have read (or written). Forgiveness is about doing something both really hard and really liberating that Jesus commands us to do. I offer these reflections as a person who knows both the deep relief of forgiveness and the deep sorrow of unforgiveness.

12.2 The Etymology of the English Word "Forgiveness"

The English word "forgiveness" stems from an Old English term *for-giefan*. This word is traceable to the German *vergeben* and Dutch *vergeven*. The etymology of these words moves in this direction: to give, grant, allow, remit, pardon. *For-* means "completely." In its origins, then, it seems that the English word forgiveness is about giving up something and giving it up completely.

Open a standard English dictionary today and the word forgiveness is defined as follows (*New Oxford American Dictionary*):

1. stop feeling angry with someone for an offense, flaw, or mistake;

2. cancel a debt.

Notice that the "stop feeling angry" dimension of forgiveness is listed first in this modern dictionary but is not a feature of the term's etymology, which has nothing to do with feelings. This definition shows that calming angry feelings is often central to what we think forgiveness means today. If so, the meaning of the term has migrated quite a bit from where it started. This may contribute to our many contemporary confusions about it. Maybe forgiveness isn't about our feelings, which are hard to control, and instead about our actions, which we can control.

Debt cancellation, the second definition above, *is* about action, and it does connect to the original etymology. A forgiver is one who chooses to take the action of debt cancellation, in this case moral-debt cancellation. She has been wronged and is owed something, but she cancels the debt, and does so completely.

This leads to my working definition: *Forgiveness is an act in which we completely give up any claim on one who has wronged us to pay the moral debt they have incurred.* Whether forgiveness also should be defined to include giving up feeling angry at someone because of the wrong they have done to us will be considered a bit later.

The etymology may take us about this far. But this is just the beginning of our exploration.

12.3 Core Biblical Terms for Forgiveness

Let us now turn to the rich biblical vocabulary associated with forgiveness.

Biblical Hebrew has two primary terms sometimes translated as forgiveness: *Salach* means to forgive or pardon, but Old Testament scholars say that it always refers to divine forgiveness of human beings. *Nasah* means to bear, lift, carry, take, or take away. It is a common verb that can include the meaning of forgiving or pardoning.

In New Testament Greek, three primary words are translated as forgive in English. *Charizomai*, from *charis* (grace), means to bestow a favor, grace, kindness, or benevolence, which can take the form of granting forgiveness or pardon. *Apheimi* means to send away or let go, and thus can cover forgiveness as "sending away" or "letting go" of debts and sins. *Apoluo* means to release, dismiss, or set free; it sometimes is best translated as forgive or pardon.

These terms taken together speak to various issues that must be accounted for in a sound account of forgiveness. It begins with the fact that human beings can and sometimes do behave wrongly toward God and neighbor. When we are harmed by the offenses of others, we experience a compelling sense that the other has incurred a kind of moral debt to us. This debt must be addressed, through some kind of "payment" or through forgiveness.

12.4 Important New Testament Texts

The New Testament contains numerous interesting texts on forgiveness. Let's look at five especially important ones.

Matthew 6:12–15 (cited at the opening of this chapter) establishes a striking linkage between God's forgiveness of us and our forgiveness of others. In this text, Jesus makes the former conditional upon the latter. If we do not forgive others, God will not forgive us. If we are honest, this teaching should terrify most of us, to the extent we are holding back in forgiving others.

Matthew 18:21–35 begins with Peter asking Jesus how many times we are obligated to forgive a "brother." Could it be as many as seven times? Jesus says it's more like 77 times, or perhaps 490 times! Peter's jaw must have dropped. Jesus follows with the famous parable of the unforgiving servant. The key teaching is that we must have mercy on others as our master has had mercy on us. The teaching ends with another stern warning of punishment if we do not forgive, but at this point this is a reinforcement of the more positive teaching that *the posture of forgiven sinners such as ourselves should be profound gratitude that yields mercy to others.*

Luke 17:3–4 parallels this teaching in Matthew 18. But it also contains a crucial difference. Jesus says: "If another disciple sins, you must rebuke the offender, and if there is repentance, you must forgive. And if the same person sins against you seven times a day, and turns back to you seven times and says, 'I repent,' you must forgive." Here, unlike in Matthew, sin in the community is dealt with by a rebuke/repent/forgive paradigm, not just by simple forgiveness. No limit is set on the number of times a believer must forgive another, but in each case repentance is required. This feels like an amendment of the more unconditional teaching offered in Matthew 18. In any case, it reflects one of the most profound tensions in relation to forgiveness: Must we—how can we—forgive those who are not sorry?

Luke 23:34 contains that simple but unforgettable line from Jesus while on the Cross: "Father, forgive them, for they do not know what they are doing." Notably, Jesus asks God to forgive those crucifying him, even though the crucifiers do not repent. Though this sentence is not included in all New Testament manuscripts of the Gospel of Luke, and it is found only in Luke, it has been deeply influential in Christian thought. In fact, it is fair to say that these two texts from Luke help to create a permanent tension in Christianity related to the issue of a necessary link between repentance and forgiveness.

Ephesians 4:32 says this: "Be kind to one another, tenderhearted, forgiving one another, as God in Christ has forgiven you." This text prescribes forgiveness as an aspect of Christian ethics in community, making the by now familiar move of motivating our forgiveness by God's forgiveness of us. This text teaches a Christian virtue that could be called "being forgiving"— having a readiness to forgive. Theologian Greg Jones is right in emphasizing that the New Testament teaches a communal ethic of "embodying forgiveness" (the title of his classic 1995 book on the subject). Forgiveness becomes more than a principle or practice here; it becomes part of the ethos of the church.

12.5 Beyond Moral-Debt Cancellation

Part of the complexity of forgiveness is that it has more than one dimension. Though forgiveness can be defined as cancelling the moral debt incurred when someone wrongs us, there is more work that needs to be done to make things right again after serious harm has been done.

When a person sins in a significant way against another person, it creates four unhappy new realities that exist until something is done to address them:

1. The sinned-against person experiences harm that affects their well-being.

2. The offending person becomes guilty in relation to the one they have harmed, creating a moral debt.

3. The relationship between the parties is damaged.

4. The offending person brings harm upon himself by creating this moral debt, damaging a relationship, and perhaps in other ways—such as loss of inner peace and the risk of retaliation.

If we add the vertical dimension, as we must in Christian ethics, then we are reminded that all sin is sin against God, not just against neighbor. The offending person has therefore created a moral debt in relation to God and has damaged his or her relationship with God. This also must be addressed.

Forgiveness, narrowly defined as moral-debt cancellation, only deals with the second item listed above. The sinned-against person chooses to release the offender from the moral debt created by the harmful act.

That's great, of course, but perhaps now we can see more clearly that there is more work to be done even if forgiveness as moral-debt cancellation has been offered. The injured person must attempt to recover from the harm they have suffered, the lingering damage in the relationship between the parties must be addressed, and the offender may need to struggle with his or her own residual issues.

I suggest that we identify three corresponding aspects of the work that needs to be done after significant harm has been inflicted. These are all sometimes called forgiveness, but for clarity my preference here will be to confine the term forgiveness to moral debt-cancellation and name these other crucial aspects by other terms.

The offended person has *psychological* work to do. He will be far better served if he works on *releasing resentment*, choosing to no longer hold in his spirit the offense he has suffered. This psychological release of resentment is emphasized in our highly psychologized age, though, as we saw earlier, it is not fundamental to the historic meaning of the term forgiveness. It is good, indeed, to let go of grudges from within the human mind and heart. It makes us feel better and frees us to be our best selves. It is an inner psychological process helpful to mental health. It takes hard work. But I do not believe it should be defined as forgiveness.

The offender and the offended have *interpersonal* work to do—if they are willing. They will be far better served if they work on *healing their relationship*, even if the offended party has cancelled the moral debt. While any of us can choose unilaterally to cancel moral debts, interpersonal reconciliation requires both parties to work through a process that involves repentance, confession, perhaps restitution, forgiveness, and restoration of relationship.

This process matches Luke's version of Jesus' teaching on forgiveness (17:3–4). It is easy to see, from either a Christian or basic human perspective, that interpersonal reconciliation is a much more complete and satisfying outcome than just moral debt-cancellation. But they need to be distinguished clearly, because it takes two to reconcile a relationship, and we may not find (or be) a willing partner in the work of reconciliation.

Finally, the offender has *restorative* work to do. He will certainly be happier if his moral debt is cancelled through forgiveness, and if the person that he harmed is willing to walk through a process of interpersonal reconciliation. But he will be best served if he also works at his own process of restoration. He needs to acknowledge his sin without evasion, confess to God that he has done wrong, begin to undertake any needed changes of attitude and behavior, and release himself from further self-reproach and grief.

12.6 Forgiveness and Moral Reality

Thinking about the dynamics of forgiveness illuminates a few fascinating aspects of moral reality.

Humans are so profoundly relational and interdependent that we experience wrong acts as threatening our relationships as well as the inner peace of both the wronged and the wrongdoer. We really are that connected to each other. Our interpersonal bonds may be invisible, but their reality is deeply felt when things go wrong.

We have a strongly wired-in sense of justice. Even though it is distorted by sin, it still exists. There is an objective justice structure to our thinking that is so powerful that people urgently attempt to redress violations of justice—and often will hold even the most intimate relationships hostage to that redress. Justice, as we have already seen, is a crucial part of ethics. But here we see what goes wrong when a sense of justice develops in a manner that itself become oppressive. Forgiveness brings justice into contact with mercy in a way crucial to human well-being.

There is an odd kind of economic structure to human relations in our fallen world, visible in the way that wrongdoing is perceived as creating a moral debt requiring repayment. We "naturally" keep track of all such debts quite carefully when they are owed to us. How many of us still hold onto lists of wrongs done to us decades ago? There is good reason why Paul says that love "keeps no record of wrongs" (1 Cor 13:5, NIV). Keeping such lists can kill relationships and tarnish the human spirit.

Forgiveness is indispensable to human relations among flawed people, but we tend to be equally troubled both by indiscriminate forgiveness and by a total lack of forgiveness. The latter dooms human relations through its rigidity. But indiscriminate forgiveness may also doom any healthy human relationship through enabling wrong behavior. There is a perennial human struggle to balance justice and mercy. This is made even more complex for Christians by our struggle to make sense of the Cross. Christian debates over forgiveness involve both the vertical and the horizontal dimension.

12.7 Limits to Forgiveness?

Jesus' teachings on forgiveness are rigorous. As on all issues, our goal should be to obey his words, not evade them.

Life, and in some cases the texts themselves, leave us with questions to ponder. I want to ask questions about several acutely difficult situations. *Do we have to forgive someone who has wronged us and has not repented—or cannot repent, because they are dead, unreachable, or will not respond?*

Taking Luke 17:3–4 as especially relevant here, we learn that when we have been wronged, we are to communicate some form of rebuke. This is supposed to lead to repentance, which is supposed to be followed by forgiveness on our part and the beginnings of reconciliation.

Of course, this paradigm should be read against the overall background of the "forgive as you have been forgiven" narrative of the New Testament. Who of us verbally repents all our wrongs against God? How would we feel if we had our sins held against us in those cases where we do not repent explicitly?

It is indeed true that we get from the New Testament many "forgive as you have been forgiven" teachings, and "forgive if you want to be forgiven" teachings, rather than only "forgive if your brother repents" teachings.

Still, we know that forgiveness, even narrowly defined as moral-debt cancellation, is much more difficult when the other does not (or cannot) repent, apologize, and seek reconciliation.

My conclusion is that in such cases forgiveness as moral-debt cancellation is still within our power, as is the psychological release of resentment. But interpersonal reconciliation will be impossible. Meanwhile, the wrongdoer will not experience restoration because she was unwilling to begin the process. Many bear heavy burdens because of relationships permanently broken in this way.

Am I to forgive someone who wrongs someone else?

Given the general Christian calling to be forgiven forgivers, our default setting should be to forgive. But this question reminds us that an offense can be done by a person to another person and I can be witness to that harm rather than its direct recipient. Does the person owe me an apology for what he has done to someone else? Am I to forgive them for their offenses against someone else?

Consider the heinous murder of Black churchgoers by a white supremacist in South Carolina in 2015. Is it our place or responsibility to forgive him for what he did? I do not think so. That offense is between him, God, and those he harmed. No moral debt was created in relation to others, and it would be inappropriate for outsiders to offer forgiveness to that murderer.

Are there wrongs too big to be forgiven?

Imagine a murderer kills your child. Eventually he comes to full and complete repentance. He might even directly ask your forgiveness. What are your obligations?

The "forgiven forgivers" posture always remains obligatory for Christians. But in a case of this severity the difficulty level is increased to the very limits of human endurance.

Jesus forgave his murderers. We are always reminded of this when we study scripture during the Lenten season. There are Christians who have imitated their Lord even in this. We are offered no exception clauses if we take Luke 17 seriously, and especially if the wrongdoer is genuinely repentant.

I cannot imagine that I could ever be reconciled with a murderer of one of my children. Nor would I understand moral-debt cancellation to include legal-debt cancellation. I would want such a murderer to pay his legal debt, to be punished for his crime. It would require God's supernatural power for me to reach a place of moral-debt cancellation, and I would certainly also pray for God's help in releasing my excruciating resentment for the wrong done.

This reminds that forgiveness can be exceptionally hard work, sometimes requiring a long process. We are desperately in need of a spiritual power that goes far beyond our normal human abilities.

Do I have to forgive someone who keeps doing harm?

Peter seems to have been asking this exact question, and Jesus' answer was 77 times. But that was in Matthew. Luke's version requires repentance on the offender's part and then forgiveness from us, even if the process must be repeated multiple times every day. As noted earlier, this feels like an amendment, in the direction of psychological and relational realism, while still bending far in the direction of forgiveness.

While ongoing patterns of harmdoing can and should be met by moral debt-cancellation (e.g., forgiveness, narrowly defined), such behavior generally does signal a lack of deep repentance on the part of the wrongdoer. It damages relationships severely and will eventually require that we remove ourselves from the context of harm as a reasonable act of self-preservation.

Can collective groups forgive?

Can collective groups—racial, religious, political, tribal, or national—forgive? As a current resident of a country filled with unrepented intergroup sin and unreconciled group relationships, this question strikes me as an especially urgent one.

The best book on this issue is *An Ethics for Enemies* (1995), by one of my teachers, Donald Shriver. His answer is indeed, yes; collective groups can forgive, have forgiven, and must forgive if we are to live in peace. But the process is very difficult.

Part of the challenge has to do with the moral reality of collectivities. Reinhold Niebuhr had it right eight decades ago when he wrote *Moral Man and Immoral Society*. His thesis was that everyone is both sinful and has moral potential, but collectives are morally immature compared to individuals. This is so for many reasons, including the elusive nature of corporate personality, the passage of time that transcends the lifetime of any individuals, and the diffusion of responsibility in a collective group.

It is certainly true that groups can experience being wronged, through such evils as discrimination, war, enslavement, and genocide, and do experience the full range of reactions: psychological harm, the creation of a deep sense of moral debt needing to be addressed, and intergroup relational damage.

Those best positioned to begin the forgiveness process are likely to be political leaders from the offending side offering clear statements of repentance, some restitution for wrongs done, and requests for restoration of relations. But as Niebuhr noted, collectives are even more stubborn and prideful than individuals, so such transforming initiatives from the wrongdoers' side are rare. It is likewise difficult to know who is authorized or able to offer the moral-debt cancellation that is fundamental to forgiveness. Meanwhile, if there is mutual offense, and mutual repentance needed, as between nations with a history of conflict, the difficulty is compounded. This is difficult peacemaking work, which we will address again in a later chapter.

Do I always have to forgive myself?

This question speaks especially to restorative work. Sometimes a wrong that we do so offends our own conscience, or does such profound relational damage, that we find it difficult to receive forgiveness from the one we wronged, from ourselves, or from God. Those who have spiraled downward into self-loathing due to wrongs we have done may need to work through forgiveness with ourselves. Such work is made easier when a clean forgiveness and reconciliation process has happened with those we have harmed. It is made more difficult, though not impossible, when they have not been willing to forgive us.

12.8 Conclusion: Onward Toward Forgiveness

The towering witness of the New Testament drives us onward toward forgiveness, even when it is most difficult, even when we come to it kicking and screaming. We need every spiritual resource the church makes available. We need constant immersion in Christ's teaching and example. We need fellow Christians alongside us who are attempting to embody forgiveness in their own lives and in the church itself, people whose very lives call us to higher ground.

"Be kind to one another, tenderhearted, forgiving one another, as God in Christ has forgiven you" (Eph. 4:32).

Discussion Questions

1. Do you really believe that God does not forgive us if we do not forgive others?

2. Forgiveness seems to require sending away, putting away, or covering over wrongs that people do to us, and we do to others. Why is this so hard?

3. So, which is it? Do we forgive only if people repent, or do we forgive even if they don't?

4. Do you think that forgiveness should be narrowly understood as moral-debt cancellation, or also the other levels discussed in section 12.4?

5. Can you think of an example local to your context of a group needing to forgive another group?

To watch Dr. Gushee deliver

Lecture 13: Caring for God's Good Creation

Follow this link:

https://youtu.be/I0DaRKskKv4

Or scan the QR code.

To listen to the audio, follow this link:

https://qrco.de/bcOlMZ

Or scan the QR code.

To scan a QR code, download a QR reader from the app store on your device, open the application, follow the directions, and point your device's camera at the code.

Chapter 13

Caring for God's Good Creation

13.1 Introduction: A Lifecycle Approach

In ordering the chapters of this book I am attempting to take a lifecycle approach. The idea is that issues are to be taken up roughly in the order in which they are experienced in the lives of people. At this stage of my journey, my thinking has been informed by four generations of life experience—my parents, my own, my children, and their children. I have pictured these four generations inheriting the riches of Christian scripture and moral tradition, embarking on the journey of moral formation, grappling with core moral norms like truthfulness, sacredness, justice, love, and forgiveness, and now turning to the wider world to experience its gifts and its challenges.

We will begin with God's creation as our first foray into this wider world. As I write, I think of my grandchildren, now 6 and 3 years old, who spend every possible minute outside at their home in suburban Atlanta. What they know of God's creation is its wonder and its goodness. The hot sun that warms their skin, the cool breezes that ruffle their hair, the canopy of trees in their front yard where they can run and hide, the lovely flowers that their mother is growing, the dogs who were a part of the family before the children were, and the sea and land animals they get to see when they visit aquariums, zoos, and farms. It's not exactly country living, but it is still God's creation, and it is filled with a goodness that children deeply enjoy.

What my grandchildren do not yet know is that God's good creation is in significant distress.

13.2 The Profound Challenges Revealed by Creation's Distress

In the past 50 years, environmental problems have become impossible to ignore, unless we adults willfully close our eyes to them, which many of us have chosen to do.

Environmentalism in its early stages was about protecting natural beauty and wildlife, a special interest for some. Today it is about reversing grave threats to human health, species survival, and the future of life on the planet, a central concern for all of us if we are paying proper attention to reality.

Christians believe that the universe, this planet, and all life constitute God's good creation. Part of the goodness of God's creation is its resilience, its impressive ability to recover from natural disasters and human mistreatment. Human civilizations have depended on that resilience. But recent centuries have shown that such resilience is not inexhaustible. We humans are overcoming creation's rather stout defenses. We, who are supposed to take care of Earth, are despoiling it.

In ethics over the last generation, what is variously called *ecological ethics*, *environmental ethics*, and *creation care* has risen to a central place.

Unfortunately, though Christian ethicists have joined this effort, rank-and-file Christians and churches have often dragged their feet in addressing creation's distress. For various reasons, many Christians have been evading the fundamental problem that humans now face—collective human behaviors over the last 250 years, since the Industrial Revolution, have been spoiling the created order that God made.

Not everyone has been evading the problem. Creation's distress has evoked massive recent analysis and response. Societies and governments have mobilized substantial policy changes and financial resources to address environmental problems. Intellectuals have written about the moral significance of the environment, the sources of contemporary environmental problems, and the intellectual and behavioral changes that human beings need to make.

In retrospect, we can see that human beings set up an industrial capitalist world order several hundred years ago that carried the seeds of its own destruction because it did not envision long-term environmental impacts. Even once those impacts became clearly visible, the human response was sluggish. This was not just because many had self-interested reasons for delaying such response. It is also because, as ethicist Michael Northcott argued in his 1996 book, *The Environment and Christian Ethics*, secular modernity lacked an adequate sense of relationality between God, humans, and the non-human world.

We humans dwell in and depend upon God's creation like fish in the sea. For many, creation has been just the taken-for-granted context within which we pursue our many interests. We have unwisely assumed that creation itself would always be there, and would always be well, no matter what kind of society we built. We were wrong.

Fortunately, humans do have the intellectual capacity to understand the "sea" in which we all "swim." All human beings and communities need to understand creation and its distress and to care enough to rethink our entire relationship to creation. This chapter is about how that project might take shape within the church.

13.3 Modern Environmental Problems as Outcome of the Industrial Revolution

The modern environmental movement, which can be dated to the early 1960s but has longer antecedents, was a response to increasingly serious signs of environmental distress that were impacting the natural world, other species, and people. These signs included polluted water, dirty air, species losses, ruined land, sickening and dying animals and people, and the destruction of areas of great aesthetic beauty. By the late 1960s, environmental degradation moved from a boutique concern to everyone's problem, with societies around the world rapidly mobilizing to make needed changes.

Looking back on how creation had reached such a point, it became clear that the Industrial Revolution, which began in Western Europe, had proceeded without serious consideration of its environmental impact. Land had been treated merely as a commodity to buy, develop, and exploit, inert space upon which people motivated by profit were free to build productive but highly polluting factories and environmentally degraded cities for their workers to live and die in. This industrialization was happily encouraged by governments in the name of national interest.

It took a long time for societies to recognize that such economic development, while it brought various material gains, also created numerous costs. These costs were usually, at first, unforeseen. Instead of being borne by the profit-makers, these ***externalities*** (external-effect costs) were being suffered by local ecosystems, animals, and people—animals being driven from their habitats, children sickened from drinking tainted water, or adults dying early from lungs filled with soot.

It finally became clear that the reshaping of the entire world under the impact of industrial capitalism was distressing creation as a whole, and not just one locality after another. Humans had created a global economy that was testing creation's resilience, a possibility which no one had anticipated when industrialization began.

Today most ecologists believe that global climate change is the most important embodiment of the collective costs and risks that have been accruing over these 250 years. But the number of current environmental problems, some unrelated to climate change, is now truly staggering. Air, water, and land pollution/ruination, negative effects of plastics and pesticides on animal and human reproduction, alterations of our food system with negative health consequences for humans and damaging environmental impacts, freshwater shortages, habitat loss, deforestation, desertification, ozone depletion, resource depletion, overfishing, species loss, overall loss of biodiversity, urban blight and sprawl, ecosystem alteration and destruction, ocean problems like plastics pollution, acidification, and warming ... it is a catalog of horrors.

Climate change based on higher concentrations of human-released carbon dioxide in the atmosphere—released primarily through fossil fuel burning—was first anticipated by scientists Gilbert Plass (1920–2004) and Roger Revelle (1909–1991) beginning in the 1950s. Their hypothesis, which is proving itself out now, is that excess carbon dioxide could not be absorbed or dissolved and would begin to alter planetary climate conditions, mainly by an overheating dynamic with ripple effects across the world.

Some of the problems that these scientists anticipated are upon us, with systemic alterations in our weather patterns, more frequent extreme weather events like hurricanes, forest fires, monsoons, and droughts, sea level rise that threatens highly populated coastal areas, disruptions of agricultural practices dependent on temperatures remaining within a certain range, deadly heat waves, invasive species that devastate local ecosystems as they migrate with climate changes, melting polar ice caps and sea ice, and more. Human civilization is threatened by these changes, not to mention human health, political stability, economic well-being, and the health and survival of numerous other species.

13.4 Biblical Religion as the Culprit?

As scholars began to wonder about how Western culture had managed to evolve in this disastrous manner, some began pointing their fingers at the Bible and Christianity.

In a famous 1967 article called "The Historical Roots of Our Ecological Crisis," historian Lynn White (1907–1987) charged that "Christianity bears a huge burden of guilt" for the environmental problems afflicting Western society and now the whole world. White's account of this guilt is complex. The problem is not just located in the biblical story of creation but also the development of a deeply anthropocentric Christian theology, especially in the West, and then the merger of science and technology to serve a human exploitation of the Earth that continually accelerates.

Here is my own effort to summarize the problems in the way the relationship between humanity and creation has developed in Christianity.

The biblical creation story posits humanity as the pinnacle of creation, the only creatures made in the image of God (Gen 1:26). God tells humans to "fill the Earth" as well as "subdue" and "have dominion" (Gen 1:28) over Earth's creatures. The story at least plants seeds of a primal separation between God and Earth, between God and creatures, and between humans, other creatures, and creation.

The dominion mandate was gradually taken as a license for humans to conquer, dominate, and overpopulate. Human beings were elevated as kings of creation. The rivers, forests, fields, birds, fish, and land animals were viewed both as *less than* humanity in value and as existing *for* humanity's indiscriminate use. Spirit, personhood, and moral value were assigned to humans, God, and the heavenly court of angels where this was believed, but not to other creatures of Earth.

While these problems affected both Judaism and Christianity, Christianity went on to worsen the problem through theological developments that set us apart from Judaism.

The first of these is our tendency toward theological dualism, most importantly our dualism of flesh vs. spirit, or material vs. spiritual. This has encouraged in many Christians an indifference to this material world, which is seen as having limited importance compared to the spiritual realm.

Further, Christianity's redemption narrative has offered a story of human rebellion, divine judgment, and rescue at the Cross, a drama in which the created world is essentially a scenic backdrop and little more. God's relationship with humanity is what matters.

Christianity's emphasis on heaven as our ultimate destination, with Earth as a place we are just passing through, has distracted many Christians from a commitment to the well-being of the Earth.

The historic belief of Christians in a Second Coming of Jesus has shortened the time horizon in which we think of planetary affairs. This negatively affects Christian commitment to all long-term projects, including creation care.

The idea that the events at the end of time will include cataclysmic war and even the destruction of this Earth (see 2 Peter 3:10–12, though the translation and interpretation are disputed) has also contributed to environmental indifference. After all, if Christ is coming soon and the whole Earth is going to be destroyed, why should we care about polluted rivers or climate change? The intensifying of Second Coming fixations in the 1970s, around the time that creation's distress was becoming especially acute, has been striking and is perhaps another example of Christian evasion.

It is hard to deny that there are deep structural impediments to serious environmental concern within dominant Christian theological traditions. These help us understand why Western Christian leaders and people offered little resistance while industrial capitalism began undermining the conditions required for a livable planet.

We can now see that prior to the emergence of the modern environmental movement in the 1960s, most Christians had lost touch with the resources for a creation-care ethic that are, in fact, present within the Bible and our theological tradition. Western Christians joined Western culture in its unthinking drive toward modern industrial capitalism and the good life as defined by its advances. This is a cautionary tale in Christian *cultural captivity*, which happens when Christian people take their cues from culture even when their faith should teach them otherwise.

13.5 Resources for a Creation Care Ethic

Facing such criticisms over these past 50 years, and finally confronting our deepening environmental problems, many Christian thinkers recently have sought out a Christian theological-ethical posture adequate to address them. It is common to consider these approaches in terms of three categories: **theocentric** (God-centered), **anthropocentric** (human-centered), and **biocentric** (ecosystem-centered). It has been heartening to discover that both scripture and tradition offer resources relevant to all three.

13.5.1 Theocentric Approaches

Theocentric creation-care ethics begins by attempting to re-narrate Genesis 1–2 so that its interpretation by Christians can avoid the grave mistakes that critics have noted.

That re-narrating begins by paying attention to God creating a world in which an amazingly diverse array of creatures can flourish, together. God creates not just humans, and not just other creatures, but the conditions, processes, and relationships that sustain creaturely life.

The creatures are brought forth in the contexts in which they will live— sea creatures from the sea, birds that fly above the Earth, and land creatures that move along the ground. This offers a clue about the interconnection between creatures and their habitats, and the dependence of the former on the health of the latter.

It is true that Genesis says: "Let us make humankind in our image, according to our likeness; and let them have dominion" (Gen. 1:26). It is also true that only human beings are described as being made in God's image.

But theocentric ethics emphasizes that God is the center of value in the creation story, not humans. The text continually draws our attention back to God. If the text says God has graciously entrusted creation to our care, it also says that we are responsible to offer creation back to God through our careful service. Our "dominion" should be understood as stewardship.

A steward is someone who manages something for someone else. Psalm 115:16 says, strikingly: "The earth [God] has given to human beings," but this is in a management sense, not an ultimate sense. "The Earth is the Lord's" (Ps 24:1). We steward creation for the one to whom it belongs.

In his helpful 1991 book called *Earthkeeping in the '90s*, evangelical theologian Loren Wilkinson unpacks Genesis 2:15 in a profound way. He claims that according to that text humans do not own the Earth, but we do "till it and keep it." We make use of Earth while also taking care of it, so that it is "kept" for future generations. If we do not "keep it" we ultimately cannot "till it," because the fruitfulness of everything planetary depends on its health and wholeness.

For Christians, theocentric creation care also becomes Christocentric. Colossians 1:15–20 says that Christ is the one in whom, through whom, and for whom creation was made. That wonderful passage also says that "Through him God was pleased to reconcile to himself all things, whether on earth or in heaven, by making peace through the blood of his cross" (Col 1:20). This passage alone should have been sufficient in broadening our account of salvation to include *all things on earth and in heaven*, and not just human beings.

Romans 8:18–25 is another pivotal passage in this regard. It contains this line: "The creation itself will be set free from its bondage to decay and will obtain the freedom of the glory of the children of God" (Rom 8:21). Creation is part of the suffering world that Christ came to redeem. Howard Snyder and Joel Scandrett address this in their 2011 book, *Salvation Means Creation Healed*. Salvation does not only mean humans get to go to heaven.

A robust theology of the kingdom of God can also take us in this same direction. Christ came to reclaim the whole fallen, suffering world, to bring justice, peace, and wholeness to the cosmos—not just to humans. Revelation 21–22 depict, not us going up to heaven, but a "new Jerusalem" coming down from heaven to Earth. Together with the "renewal of all things" that Jesus promises in Matthew 19:28, we have plenty of hints that salvation happens right here—not *up there*, but *right here*.

Overall, theocentric and Christocentric approaches attempt to deploy classic Christian claims like the sovereignty of God and supremacy of Christ as a resource for devoted care of creation, rather than an obstacle to it.

13.5.2 Anthropocentric Approaches

Whereas theocentric creation care is motivated by a desire to honor God as Creator and obey God's commands in relation to creation, anthropocentric creation care elevates human well-being as the center of concern. There need not be any tension between a theocentric and anthropocentric approach, however. As we honor our Creator and obey God's commands, we act in ways that advance human well-being. After all, Jesus himself taught us that the highest commands are to love God and love neighbor (Mt 22:34–40), and he treated them as inextricably connected.

In ecological ethics, we need to attend to the needs of *all* human beings, with an *intergenerational* perspective, and with attention to *every* aspect of human well-being. Therefore, central norms include **environmental justice, intergenerational moral responsibility**, and **ecological sustainability**.

Environmental justice begins with the recognition of the dependence of all human beings on a healthy environment. Humans need clean air to breathe, sufficient clean water to drink, fertile and healthy soil to till, reasonably stable climate systems, and healthy neighbor-creatures. Lack of access to these imperils the physical well-being of persons, and often the most imperiled are those on the margins of power and wealth.

Loving neighbors requires loving those who are strangers to us, not just in location but also in time. A central norm for creation care must be intergenerational moral responsibility. Baptist ethicist Robert Parham (1953–2017) addresses this in his 1992 book *Loving Neighbors Across Time*. This is not instinctual for us—after all, we have trouble loving the neighbors right in front of us. But even so, we need to consider the well-being of future inhabitants of Earth. Our actions today already affect the world they will live in.

The norm of ecological sustainability means we must ask of any set of economic, ecological, or lifestyle practices whether they are sustainable in the long term within the limits of creation's well-being.

Where Christians offer anthropocentric creation-care efforts that are concerned for environmental justice, intergenerational responsibility, and ecological sustainability, such a human-centered emphasis can be both morally and strategically constructive. The history of the environmental movement clearly reveals that when human well-being is set against the well-being of other species, everyone loses. But when the well-being of all humans, the next generation of humans, and the most vulnerable humans, is stressed, environmentalism corresponds with neighbor-love in a way that anyone can appreciate.

13.5.3 Biocentric Approaches

In recent decades, a creative and forceful biocentrism has surfaced in ecological ethics, philosophy, and theology. These approaches tend to decenter humans and center Earth and our Earth neighbors. They also decenter God—at least, some traditional versions of belief in God—to draw our attention to this world and all who dwell herein.

For those who believe that biblical faith's primary error was in desacralizing nature, one option is to retrieve or create nature religions that redivinize it. Just as once the ancients worshipped the divine in the air, land, and sea, in the creatures, and in the processes of nature, today some have returned to such practices. We are witnessing a revival of nature religions in our time. Some Christians are made uncomfortable by these developments, and unfortunately associate all environmentalism with them, which has inspired books like Tony Campolo's 1992 *How to Rescue the Earth Without Worshipping Nature* by way of response.

Another move has been a retrieval of a pantheism which identifies God with creation, or a panentheism in which God pervades and interpenetrates creation in a way that goes beyond biblical claims. In some versions the Earth itself is God, or god-like, a living Being who must be reverenced and treated as divine. Earth is Mother or God, and certainly not just an object we can chop up into parcels, sell, and burn.

Some weave an eco-spirituality around evolution. One approach is to find something like a Life Force at work in the multi-billion-year process by which life has unfolded in the universe. All life is related to all other life, all life seeks to extend itself, and in engaging the development and elaboration of life forms on this planet one must respond with wonder. This is a kind of evolutionary sacredness-of-all-life religion, and ethic.

Another move involves a rethinking of community to include all creatures on Earth. If one thinks of modern history as involving a gradual recognition of the moral worth of all humans, and not just some, then the extension of this status to animals and other non-human entities can be seen as the next logical step. Robert Wennberg's (1935–2010) 2003 book *God, Human, and Animals* was a relatively early effort to argue for the recognition of animals within the community of creatures to whom humans have moral obligations. Charles Camosy's wonderful little book *For Love of Animals* (2013), offers a recent compelling and accessible account.

This move also can enlarge our understanding of Christ's command to love our neighbors to include neighbors that are not humans—and, indeed, to include the Earth itself. A Christian ethicist who has led the way in thinking out these implications has been one of my former teachers, Larry Rasmussen. His 1996 book, *Earth Community, Earth Ethics*, introduced the idea of an Earth faith, Earth community, and Earth ethic as the necessary response to creation's profound distress. His 2013 book, *Earth-Honoring Faith,* extends his argument, suggesting that this broader creation ethic requires a retrieval and recasting of some of the richest spiritual and moral resources of the world's religions. If we are to honor the Earth, we will need to dig deeply into the mysticism, sacramentalism, asceticism, prophetic practices, and wisdom teachings of the world's religions.

I join Rasmussen and others in seeing that the distress of creation that we have caused has deep spiritual roots and requires a spiritual response. Unless we intentionally develop greater understanding of, and a far deeper sense of awe, connection, and love for, God's good creation, we will never be able to break free of our bondage to a way of life that is destroying it. We just will not care enough. This is an issue of the human heart, not just theology. We value what we love.

13.6 What Do We Do Now?

Creation care begins with a renewed theological vision of God's creation and God's love for all creatures, the Earth, and the cosmos. There is so much work to be done in offering fresh teaching about creation, its place in God's heart and plans, its distress, and our creation-care responsibilities. Christian leaders must also urgently seek ways to connect to God's creation and to help our people do the same.

Creation care requires us to ask hard questions about economics and politics. We must not just ask what the economic growth rate looks like this quarter. We must instead ask whether the proper steps are being taken to evolve our fossil-fuel-based global economy toward a more sustainable paradigm and a world that our grandchildren can live in.

Creation care needs to become a local and household matter for us. We need to reduce our environmental impact by considering our buying, consuming, and discarding, our home and office energy use, our transport and travel choices, and more.

Creation care should lead us to ask new questions about our animal neighbors. Theological ethicist David Clough, in his breakthrough 2019 book *On Animals: Theological Ethics*, offers ethical analysis of how humans use animals for food, clothing, labor, research, medicine, education, sport, entertainment, and companions. U.S. ethicist Norman Wirzba focuses entirely on the ethics of food in his similarly bracing 2011 book *Food and Faith*. Clearly, we have a massive amount of moral reform to undertake in these areas.

Creation care requires that we take climate change seriously, and not join the doubters and denialists who are holding back the needed policy changes to reduce greenhouse gas emissions and global warming. We must care about climate change not just because human health and well-being are at stake, but also because of the impact on our Earth neighbors, whom God also loves and calls us to love—and because we love and seek to serve the Creator who made the world, and who made us its stewards. If the scientists who are most worried about creation care are right, we have only a little more time to transform global economic, energy, farming, and travel practices if we want to leave a bearable world to our grandchildren. Will Christians be part of the solution, or part of the problem?

Discussion Questions

1. Does creation care have a place in the theology and preaching of your church tradition?

2. To what extent would you say that you have a deep sense of connection to God's creation? If you do, what are its sources?

3. Which environmental problems or issues most deeply connect with you?

4. Do you think it is fair to place some blame on the Bible and Christianity for our ecological problems?

5. Which theological approach to creation care resonates most deeply with you?

To watch Dr. Gushee deliver

Lecture 14: Ending Patriarchy Once and For All

Follow this link:

https://youtu.be/iwsZASNXapY

Or scan the QR code.

To listen to the audio, follow this link:

https://qrco.de/bcOlNt

Or scan the QR code.

To scan a QR code, download a QR reader from the app store on your device, open the application, follow the directions, and point your device's camera at the code.

CHAPTER 14

Ending Patriarchy
Once and For All

14.1 Introduction: On Misbegotten Tradition

We continue our journey of ethics through the lifecycle with the issue of gender. Despite much that has changed in recent decades, my grandchildren, like the generations before them, have thus far encountered a world in which they have discovered two basic types of humans—males and females.

Because of the kind of Christian family in which they live, these kids have not been taught that males were created by God for leadership over females. Nor have they been taught that men are supposed to work outside the home while women are to work only at home. Nor have they been given any idea that violence against women and girls is acceptable. Nor could they conceive of a world in which boys rather than girls would be given the opportunity to go to school. Nor, finally, could they imagine a world in which males would be intrinsically valued more than females.

This is a chapter that argues that surviving Christian theologies that teach even "soft" versions of patriarchy are vestiges of misbegotten tradition that need to be abandoned as out of keeping with the moral core of Christianity. It is time to end patriarchy, once and for all.

14.2 Soft Patriarchs vs. Egalitarian Feminists

There is, unfortunately, still a "women's issue" in large portions of world Christianity. Everything about this issue is contested, including what to call it and how to frame it.

If I were to begin by framing it as follows, you likely would know where I would end up: "The problem is women rebelling against God's plan for their gracious submission to men, because feminism has confused women about their God-given roles."

If I were to begin by framing it this other way, you might also know where I would end up: "The problem is men's unwillingness to give up their historic domination and disempowering of women in the name of God."

The advocates of the first narrative today generally prefer the term **complementarian** to describe their view. They believe that God established a "complementary" ordering of male-female relations, at least in certain realms of life, in which men are to lead and women are to subordinate themselves to male leadership. Their adversaries call them advocates of **patriarchy**—systemic male power over females—even if perhaps **soft patriarchy**, compared to earlier and alternative versions that are, or were, more extreme and even cruel. There is a difference between Western soft patriarchs and the Taliban, to be sure. (I first saw the term "soft patriarchy" in sociologist Brad Wilcox's 2004 book, *Soft Patriarchs, New Men*. I think the term fits many, though not all, such evangelical patriarchs.)

The advocates of the second narrative generally prefer the term **egalitarian** or **feminist** to describe their view. They believe that God established an ordering of male-female relations in which leadership opportunities are linked to giftedness and need rather than gender. They deny any divine plan for male leadership. Their adversaries take the term feminist and use it as a pejorative, understanding feminism as a rejection of God's ordering of creation, or at least of the family and the church.

For the rest of this discussion, I will describe the conflict within the churches as being between *soft patriarchs* and *egalitarian feminists*, the two major parties in a longstanding and often bitter debate. I won't use the term "complementarian" because I believe it to be a euphemism for soft patriarchy, and euphemisms obscure truth rather than illuminate it.

In 2021, church historian Beth Allison Barr released a blockbuster book on this issue, *The Making of Biblical Womanhood: How the Subjugation of Women Became Gospel Truth*. Barr's historical research confirms what historian Margaret Lamberts Bendroth claimed in 1993 in *Fundamentalism and Gender* and what I will strongly affirm here: Female subordination, under the name "biblical womanhood," "gracious submission," or "complementarity," is a deeply flawed Christian tradition with a history that has evolved with and in cultures rather than any kind of fixed divine revelation.

Another recent blockbuster book, *Jesus and John Wayne*, by historian Kristen Kobes Du Mez (2020), makes the broader case that hardcore patriarchy and authoritarianism explain much of what has gone wrong with recent white U.S. evangelicalism. These two recent books signal that the discussion of gender in evangelical Protestantism is transitioning from a debate about what Christian women are "allowed to do" to a searching critique of toxic masculinist Christianity and its connections with the ills of American culture.

14.3 Looking Back: My Primal Engagement with This Conflict

I began my teaching career in 1993 in a setting in which the battle between soft patriarchy and egalitarian feminism played out in real time. When I began my studies at Southern Baptist Theological Seminary (SBTS) in 1984, the school had become hospitable to, if not dominated by, an egalitarian feminist vision. This was quite a change from the default patriarchy of an earlier SBTS, and of the majority of the churches of our sponsoring denomination, the Southern Baptist Convention (SBC). I was hired in spring 1993, in interviews in which I made plain my egalitarian feminist convictions.

Overturning egalitarian feminism and restoring a patriarchal vision, even if "soft," was among the first items of business on the agenda of the new president, R. Albert Mohler Jr., who began his term in summer 1993—three months after my interview with his predecessor.

The issue came to a head in 1995, when a highly qualified, self-identified biblical-inerrantist evangelical was denied appointment by the seminary president solely over his egalitarian posture on women. At a stormy faculty meeting, the president announced that henceforth no professor would ever again be hired or advanced if he or she believed that women should be allowed to be senior pastors of churches. While some faculty members tried to finesse the issue using clever verbiage, I was among many who were forced out or who left over the matter.

Ponder that: Within the span of a decade, a seminary was moved from a predominantly egalitarian vision to an enforced patriarchal vision. Presumably, God had not changed God's mind. But one group of Southern

Baptists had been forced out by another group, and when power changed hands, so did the acceptable position on this issue.

Let me now see if I can offer a reasonably fair-minded articulation of both major views.

14.4 The Soft Patriarchy Position

Soft patriarchs believe they can spot a clear male leadership theme throughout scripture.

God makes Adam first, and Eve as his "helper" (Gen 2:18). God chooses men as his covenant partners (Noah, Abraham, Moses, David, etc.). The twelve tribes of Israel are all headed by men. The kings of Israel are all men. All named biblical authors are men.

Jesus is a man. His twelve apostles are men. The qualifications of both deacons and bishops in 1 Timothy 3 include "husband of one wife," and only a man can be a husband. Paul commands women to be "silent" in church and "subordinate" in 1 Corinthians 14:34–35, and in the (disputably) Pauline text of 1 Timothy 2:12–15, the writer permits no woman to teach or have authority over a man, adding to his rationale the claims that Adam was made first, Eve sinned first, and faithful, modest women are saved through childbearing.

Paul offers an extensive theological rationale for male leadership (or **headship**) in 1 Corinthians 11:2–16. In this text, Paul asserts a hierarchy in creation that runs God—Christ—man—woman, or perhaps God—Christ—husband—wife. Because the same Greek words are used for man/husband and woman/wife, the extent of this female subordination is debated.

Paul goes on to say that man is the image and glory/reflection of God, whereas woman is the glory/reflection of man. Referring to the Genesis 2 account, Paul next says that woman was made from and for man, not man from and for woman. Though Paul later qualifies this by saying that woman and man are not independent of each other, and that man in fact also comes through woman (via birth), the woman must keep her head covered in worship as a symbol of "authority on her head, because of the angels."

Male leadership and female submission in marriage are explicitly taught in Ephesians 5:22–33 (cf. Col 3:18–19). Here again the husband is the head of the wife. Now the comparison is to Christ as head of the church, with the analogy extending to wifely submission. Husbands are to love and sacrifice for their wives as Christ loved and sacrificed for the church, with great tenderness, care, and self-sacrifice.

A major articulation of the soft patriarchy position is the "Danvers Statement," published in 1988 as the charter document of the Council on Biblical Manhood and Womanhood. This influential group is still active today.

This declaration asserts that Adam and Eve were both made in God's image, "equal before God as persons but distinct in their manhood and womanhood." God built into creation "distinctions in masculine and feminine roles." The primary distinction noted is headship. Adam was created as the head in his marriage with Eve. Human sin did not create male headship in marriage but instead distortions in that headship, in the direction either of "domination or passivity" on his part, "usurpation or servility" on her part.

While the Bible affirms both the "equally high value and dignity" of both men and women and of their respective roles, the "principle of male headship" in family and religious community is consistently affirmed. This means that "some governing and teaching roles within the church are restricted to men," and "a call to ministry should never be used to set aside Biblical criteria for particular ministries." This means that just because some women report a call to pastoral ministry, this does not negate what this declaration asserts to be clear biblical teaching against this. In church, as in family life, men are to lead, in a loving, Christ-like way, while women are to accept the God-given limitations on their roles and "use their gifts in appropriate ministries."

All composite declarations reflect power and group dynamics, involving consensus-building strategies and efforts to smooth over complex issues that might destroy the effort. But in these declarations, a seam often emerges that shows where consensus could not be reached and thus got papered over.

In the Danvers Statement, I see two of these. One is the way in which the supposedly God-given contrasting male and female roles are restricted to marriage and church life, with no reference to any other arena—such as government, business, volunteer organizations, and so on.

This leaves some important unanswered questions: Did God ordain male leadership over women in all arenas, or only in home and church? Is every woman everywhere supposed to submit graciously to every man everywhere? Did God ordain that women can work outside the home? If so, are they allowed to supervise men in such roles? Does God permit a woman to hold elective office? If so, is she allowed to supervise a man in such a role—like, for example, the way a female president would have authority over *all* men in the country?

From a review of the signatory list and awareness of other statements by some of those signatories, it is obvious that the Danvers group did not go into these questions because they would not have agreed. Perhaps also they concluded at a strategic level that it was far too late to try to persuade most women to abandon their work outside the home.

The other seam in the statement is this one: "some governing and teaching roles within the church are restricted to men." Question: Which ones? The document never clarifies exactly which roles for women would constitute "set[ting] aside Biblical criteria for particular ministries." The reason why the Danvers group could not specify further, I think, is not only that they could not agree, but also that facing the issue would have required facing the dramatic diversity of offices and leadership structures that exist in different churches.

Are we talking about churches with a team of pastors who share authority? If so, can a woman be one of them? Are we talking about a group of elders or presbyters? If so, can a woman be an elder? Can she be the leader of an elder group? Are we talking about connectional churches that have local or regional officials such as bishops? Can a woman be a bishop? Are we talking about charismatic churches in which leadership is tied to supernatural gifts? Can a woman who has such gifts assume leadership in any way? Are we talking about ordination? Can a woman be ordained to Christian ministry? If so, to what roles, and with what limits?

At Southern Seminary circa 1995, there was much discussion of whether the official limit was going to be ordination, pastoral office, or the role of senior pastor. There were arguments over whether the issue was teaching, or authority over men, or church "office." In the end, the SBC hierarchy decided to resolve it this way in their official doctrinal statement, the Baptist Faith and Message: "[The church's] scriptural officers are pastors and deacons. While both men and women are gifted for service in the church, the office of pastor is limited to men as qualified by Scripture" (BFM, 2000).

If you go back and compare the actual biblical texts cited above with the Southern Baptist declaration, or with the Danvers Statement, you notice something else: *these statements are softer and more inclusive than some of the cited biblical texts themselves.* They do not include the claim that there is a hierarchy that runs God/Christ/man/woman, that women must be silent in the churches, that women must submit to male authority because Adam was made first and Eve sinned first, that women are saved by childbearing, that women must wear head coverings as a sign of authority on their heads, that while men are the image and glory of God, women are the glory of men, and that women can never exercise authority in church life. Danvers authors cite some of these passages in parentheses (like this: 1 Tim 2:8–15) when trying to make the points they want to make, but then they do not deal with unwanted statements in these texts.

What makes this patriarchy is that, in the end, "power is held by men and withheld from women" (*KE* Glossary, p. 468). What makes this *soft* patriarchy is that, in the end, the harshest teachings of the scriptures (not to mention two millennia of Christian tradition) are omitted—which we can assume is either due to the lack of consensus of the drafters or the fact that not even many deeply conservative Christian women would be willing to accept such statements. This does raise questions as to the supposedly clear, authoritative biblical basis for the teachings offered versus those omitted.

Still, in the end, patriarchy survives, in softened form. Millions upon millions of Christians are taught some version of soft patriarchy every week, both in what is said from the pulpit and, alas, in the exclusively male humans who say it. As church historian Beth Allison Barr says, this is the ethos within which many millions of girls and women (not to mention boys and men) experience church, school, and family life.

14.5 The Egalitarian Feminist Position

The Danvers Statement was a response to the rise of egalitarian feminist thought in Christianity, which began on the mainline Protestant side in the 1960s and by the 1980s was spreading into more conservative evangelical churches and denominations. The most articulate statement of the new evangelical feminism was in a statement called "Men, Women, and Biblical Equality," released in 1989 by a group, which also still exists, called Christians for Biblical Equality (CBE). The two groups, like the positions they represent, have been locked in opposition since the 1980s.

The CBE statement opens starkly: "The Bible teaches the full equality of men and women in Creation and in Redemption." The document asserts that men and women were created in God's image, for equal partnership, with joint dominion and childrearing responsibilities. The woman's role as God designed it is as partner, not subordinate (Gen 2:18 is reinterpreted based on the Hebrew word *ezer*). Woman coming from man means unity and equality, not second-class status. Adam and Eve both sinned and share responsibility. Adam's "rulership" over Eve is an aspect of the fall, not a prescription for a "headship" which this group does not recognize as a legitimate theological category.

Redemption in Jesus Christ is for all who believe, on equal terms. The basis of service in the church is Spirit-giftedness, not gender. There is no New Testament teaching that spiritual gifts are distributed along gendered lines. In the church, ministry is offered by those gifted and empowered, period. Rather than offices, the CBE statement speaks of "prophetic, priestly, and royal functions" in ministry, and that both women and men exercise all these functions in the New Testament. All "serving and teaching ministries at all levels of involvement" must be open to women according to their spiritual gifts. Public recognition of spiritual gifts and service must be given on equal terms to both women and men.

In family life, the norm is mutual submission and responsibility, not male headship. No gender distinctions are recognized by CBE in any aspect of family life: child nurture and discipline, decision making, and leadership. Male headship is treated as a dangerous path that can lead to "wife and child abuse." Power in family life, and every kind of responsibility, must be shared.

As for all those other passages cited for the patriarchal position, these are dismissed as follows: "The few isolated texts that appear to restrict the full redemptive freedom of women must not be interpreted simplistically and in contradiction to the rest of Scripture, but their interpretation must take into account their relationship to the broader teaching of Scripture and their total context." CBE also says: "We believe that Scripture is to be interpreted holistically and thematically. We also recognize the necessity of making a distinction between inspiration and interpretation." The latter, it is clearly implied, is what the Danvers types are doing when they say they are just being "biblical." CBE conclude their document by claiming that *their* view is the one that is "true to Scripture."

From a distance of more than 30 years, the limits of this document are also visible. There is no real discussion of the substance of the texts that cut against their position. There is too much patriarchy in scripture for the texts that reflect it to be simply dismissed as "isolated." To accept this while taking an egalitarian feminist position would require acknowledging that the cultures which produced the Bible were deeply patriarchal, and it is inevitable that this patriarchy would bleed into the biblical texts. But this, in turn, would be to challenge the assumption that the biblical texts should simply be treated as divinely inspired rather than also humanly authored and culturally situated.

The CBE statement has the great virtue of *naming the issue of power*. Though the document only uses the word twice, the Danvers Statement only uses the word once and never with reference to their own position.

This is striking. I was trained with the warning that power is central in relation to every ethical issue, including family ethics, and that it is probably most central when most obscured. The fundamental distinction between the two positions we have been considering comes down to power: Soft patriarchy preserves male power, albeit described as Christ-like service; egalitarian feminism rejects exclusive male power and calls for power-sharing between women and men.

14.6 Christian Social Ethics Offers a Bigger Picture

Christians often treat every debate as a biblical faceoff. I bring my scriptures with my (right!) interpretation, you bring your scriptures with your (wrong!) interpretation, and we have it out. Christians often fail to treat either the context in which the scriptures were written, or our own context, social location, interests, biases, and so on.

I interpret the "women's issue" not only as a biblical interpretation issue but in the context of the exercise of power in human history; here, the power of men over women. A basic conviction of mine is that the implications of "power over" are *best understood from below*. Related to that is the awareness that moral-perceptual blind spots and rationalizations are especially prevalent in those who are on the top of power structures.

Patriarchy is about male power over women in social institutions, sometimes exercised through mere brute force, usually enshrined in some justifying ideology. In patriarchal societies men rule in all major spheres, including sex, marriage, family, economics, and religion. It can look as awful as the Taliban shooting young Malala Yousafzai for trying to get an education in Pakistan, or as comparatively mild as women being told they are not allowed to preach. Patriarchy is patriarchy.

Patriarchal societies have been the rule rather than the exception in human history. Rarely has this patriarchy been soft. It has involved every form of injustice—violence, domination, economic injustice, and exclusion from full participation in community. Nicholas Kristof and Sheryl WuDunn's shocking 2010 book, *Half the Sky*, offers descriptions of some of the specific miseries inflicted on women in patriarchal societies. These include sex trafficking and coerced prostitution, honor killings, child marriages, forced abortions, discrimination in education and employment, preventable maternal mortality, sexual violence, and much more. The global picture is devastating.

Feminism, in my view, is simply a resistance movement to patriarchy. It is similar to other social movements resisting other forms of structural oppression. Feminism attacks both patriarchal ideology and its various expressions. Feminism seeks to overturn patriarchy and create equality and shared power between women and men.

Frederick Douglass (1817–1895), in a famous 1857 speech, which is often called "If There is No Struggle There is No Progress," said, "Power concedes nothing without a demand. It never did and it never will." Martin Luther King Jr., writing in his 1963 "Letter from Birmingham Jail," concurred: "Freedom is never given voluntarily by the oppressor; it must be demanded by the oppressed."

Feminism demands that men give up patriarchy. Patriarchy, in turn, does what power usually does—it resists, as far as it is able, with every means it can imagine. When necessary, it takes a step or two back, conceding a bit of ground and readying for counterattack. If it loses the next battle, it retrenches, regroups, and tries again. This makes sense of something we so often see—many forms of injustice never seem to just die. They retreat a bit, maybe, and then come roaring back when given an opening.

This is how I perceive the "women's issue" in Christianity. I believe that the Bible reflects the very deep patriarchy of the cultures within which various biblical texts were written over many hundreds of years.

However, the Bible also offers countervailing resources that are even more compelling, given that the Bible emerged in patriarchal cultures. These include the powerful role of numerous women in the Bible, the role of Mary, Jesus' inclusive ministry, the radicalism of the early church, the named women leaders of these churches, the egalitarian impact of the Spirit, and a number of powerful texts pushing toward overcoming all our human hierarchies, such as Galatians 3:28 ("for all of you are one in Christ Jesus").

I seek to position Christian social ethics as an ally to egalitarian feminism. I believe that girls and women are sacred in God's sight, equal with men, typically different from men in some ways, though this varies dramatically and is always best left to women's self-definition. I believe that women reflect human diversity in their God-given gifts, personalities, skills, interests, and visions of flourishing. I believe that a just church and a just society do not accept any built-in, gender-based power-over structures.

I view the soft patriarchy position as a part of the problem of patriarchy but also an evidence of how much patriarchy has weakened in many cultures. The soft patriarchs have given up much ground, but they are still trying to hold onto patriarchy's one core commitment—male power over women as a structural feature of church and family life. In this sense, Danvers-type soft patriarchy is part of the same massive tapestry of global patriarchy that feminism has been trying to unravel for centuries. I find myself decisively on the feminist side, rather than standing with those repackaging patriarchy for modern use.

Discussion Questions

1. How would you describe the level of patriarchy in scripture? Where do you see countervailing tendencies?

2. When we see patriarchal strands in scripture, should we see these as expressions of God's will, or as cultural artifacts?

3. How would you describe the state of the contest between patriarchy and feminism in your cultural context? In your church context?

4. Who do you think makes the stronger "biblical" case: the soft patriarchs or the egalitarian feminists? Does this resolve the issue for you?

To watch Dr. Gushee deliver

Lecture 15: Repenting White Christian Supremacism

Follow this link:

https://youtu.be/ru-4UjGpvfk

Or scan the QR code.

To listen to the audio, follow this link:

https://qrco.de/bcOlQ6

Or scan the QR code.

To scan a QR code, download a QR reader from the app store on your device, open the application, follow the directions, and point your device's camera at the code.

CHAPTER 15

Repenting White Christian Supremacism

15.1 Introduction: Difference Without Judgment

Even little children notice differences in skin tone and other aspects of other kids' appearance. It is one way they differentiate between this child and that one.

But kids do not put a negative construction on those differences unless they are taught to do so. Unfortunately, we now know that such "teaching" can take many forms. It does not have to be through explicit racist instruction. It can happen through the structures and assumptions of culture.

I share the sad diagnosis that this is still where we find ourselves in every part of the world that has been shaped by European colonization. I will name the problem as "white Christian supremacism." This chapter, written by a person who identifies as white, Christian, and of European descent, explores the negative impact of white Christian supremacism as it has revealed itself in the United States. Its impact elsewhere must be judged locally.

15.2 The Social Construction of Race and the Problem of White Christian Supremacism

Racism is a harmful response to human differences through the fictional social construction of human identity as "race," usually involving a hierarchical classification system based on the invented racial categories. Racism harms people because it classifies some as *less than* and others as *more than*, justifying discriminatory attitudes and actions. As Richard Delgado and Jean Stefancic put it in their 2012 book *Critical Race Theory*:

> Races are categories that society invents, manipulates, or retires when convenient. People with common origins share certain physical traits, of course, such as skin color, physique, and hair texture. But these constitute only an extremely small portion of their genetic endowment, are dwarfed by that which we have in common, and have little or nothing to do with distinctly human, higher-order traits, such as personality, intelligence, and moral behavior (2nd edition, pp. 8–9).

White racism is the most relevant form of racism for much of the world because of the history of European colonialism. White *Christian* racism is the better descriptor, because of the fingerprints of the churches and of Christian mission.

The origins of white Christian racism are best located in Europe at the beginning of its colonial ventures. The European powers developed a vision of themselves that combined religious, moral, political, military, technological, and racial visions of their own supremacy. They were ordained by God to conquer, colonize, and thus "Christianize" large parts of the world. Their dominating power over many centuries reinforced their prideful self-confidence. This disastrous world of thought is often now described as **white supremacism**, not just racism, and that is an advance for clarity of thought. But there is yet one more step needed. Especially for a Christian audience, it is important to own up to white supremacism's religious dimension. European colonialism was in part a religious project. It left a legacy that remains with us still.

15.3 Following Katie Cannon Toward Novels by Black Authors

It is difficult for many self-identified white people of European-American backgrounds to overcome our learned helplessness in understanding our own history of racism. Inspired by a deepened sense of urgency in recent years, I have sought imaginative entry points that can pierce my own obtuseness.

Following the lead of pioneering ethicist Katie Cannon, in 2017–2018 I decided to read a host of great novels by Black authors.

Cannon was the first Christian ethicist to claim African American fictional works as authoritative for ethical reflection, blazing a trail that others have followed. In her 1988 book, *Black Womanist Ethics*, Cannon claims that "Black women's writings have paralleled Black history ... the patterns and themes in their writings are reflective of historical facts, sociological realities and religious convictions that lie behind the ethos and the ethics of the Black community ... Seldom, if ever, is their work art-for-art's sake" (p. 78). Cannon is claiming that one reason these novels are such an important source for ethics is that they have a documentary role, not merely an entertainment purpose. Another is because Black voices—women's voices in particular—so often have been shut out of recognized positions of religious authority. To hear their critical insights, especially in the past, we need to read these novels.

As an initial project in engaging these classic novels, I listened for what they had to say about white Christian people. I thought this would shed new light on the problem of white racism and teach me much that I had not known. I was scalded by their revelatory power. Cannon was right.

The rest of this chapter offers excerpts from fictional works by African Americans in search of an answer to this question: *How do these novels depict white Christian people's morality and religion?*

The novels were written in specific times and places, addressing contexts that have not remained static. Yet many of the themes, even of novels written decades ago, remain acutely relevant, at least in the U.S. setting.

My reading suggests three primary themes related to my research question: *moral debasement*, *religious powerlessness*, and *perceptual blindness*. The quotes I will offer are representative, examples that could have been reproduced many times over. I take them seriously as honest perceptions of reality from representatives of an oppressed community.

15.4 Moral Debasement

These novels depict the profound moral damage caused by societies structured and sustained by white supremacism. I see themes of greed, pride, slander, arbitrary use of power, unchecked anger and violence, and alienation from human relationship. For each, I will offer a summary statement, and then a few examples from the novels. Some of the quotes I will offer are bracing.

15.4.1 Greed

These novels suggest that white people intentionally created and still sustain a society in which whites are massively advantaged economically, in large part through the exploitation of Black people. The entire system has been set up to benefit us, we have believed these benefits to be our just desserts, and this self-serving lie is pivotal to understanding white supremacism in all periods of American history.

Alice Walker, *The Color Purple* (1982), p. 183:

> I know how they is. The key to all of 'em is money. The trouble with our people is as soon as they got out of slavery they didn't want to give the white man nothing else. But the fact is, you got to give 'em something. Either your money, your land, your woman or your ass.

Langston Hughes (1902–1967), *Not Without Laughter* (1930), p. 260:

> He understood then why many old Negroes said: Take all this world and give me Jesus! It was because they couldn't get this world anyway—it belonged to the white folks. They alone had the power to give or withhold at their back doors. Always back doors ...

Richard Wright (1908–1960), *Native Son* (1940), p. 20:

> I just can't get used to it. I swear to God I can't. I know I oughtn't think about it, but I can't help it. Every time I think about it I feel like somebody's poking a red-hot iron down my throat. ... Look! We live here and they live there. We Black and they white. They got things and we ain't. They do things and we can't. It's just like living in jail. Half the time I feel like I'm on the outside of the world peeping in through a knothole in the fence.

15.4.2 Pride

Racism is in large part about undeserved and damaging racist pride. In these novels, white people assume their superiority to Black people. The novels offer glimpses of the negative impact of this pridefulness, and not just on Black people.

Alice Walker, *The Color Purple*, p. 196:

> Ain't no way to read the bible and not think God white, she say. Then she sigh. When I found out I thought God was white, and a man, I lost interest. You mad cause he don't seem to listen to your prayers. Humph! Do the mayor listen to anything colored say? ... I know white people never listen to colored, period. If they do, they only listen long enough to be able to tell you what to do.

James Baldwin (1924–1987), *Go Tell It on the Mountain* (1952), p. 204:

> She looked out into the quiet, sunny streets, and for the first time in her life, she hated it all—the white city, the white world. She could not, that day, think of one decent white person in the whole world. She sat there, and she hoped that one day God, with tortures inconceivable, would grind them utterly into humility, and make them know that Black boys and Black girls, whom they treated with such condescension, such disdain, and such good humor, had hearts like human beings too, more human hearts than theirs.

W.E.B. DuBois (1868–1963), *The Souls of Black Folk* (1903), "Of the Coming of John" (a fictional chapter/parable), p. 172:

> The Judge sat in the dining-room amid his morning's mail, and he did not ask John to sit down. He plunged squarely into the business. 'You've come for the school, I suppose. Well, John, I want to speak to you plainly ... Now I like the colored people, and sympathize with all their reasonable aspirations; but you and I both know, John, that in this country the Negro must remain subordinate, and can never expect to be the equal

of white men. In their place, your people can be honest and respectful; and God knows, I'll do what I can to help them. But when they want to reverse nature, and rule white men, and marry white women, and sit in my parlor, then, by God! We'll hold them under if we have to lynch every N****** in the land.

15.4.3 Slander

These novels suggest that white people routinely slander the character of Black people. Yet white people are the ones whose character most clearly demonstrates degradation.

Langston Hughes, *Ways of White Folks*, p. 52:

Funny thing, though, Ma, how some white people certainly don't like colored people, do they? They go out of their way sometimes to say bad things about colored folks, putting it out that all of us are thieves and liars, or else diseased—corruption and syphilis and the like. No wonder it's hard for a Black man to get a good job with that kind of false propaganda going around.

Toni Morrison (1931–2019), *Beloved* (1987), p. 234:

Whitepeople believed that whatever the manners, under every dark skin was a jungle. Swift unnavigable waters, swinging screaming baboons, sleeping snakes, red gums ready for their sweet white blood. In a way, he thought, they were right. The more coloredpeople spent their strength trying to convince them how gentle they were, how clever and loving, how human, the more they used themselves up to persuade whites of something Negroes believed could not be questioned, the more tangled the jungle grew inside. But it wasn't the jungle Blacks brought with them to this place from the other (livable) place. It was the jungle whitefolks planted in them. And it grew. It spread. In, through and after life, it spread, until it invaded the whites who had made it. Touched them every one. Changed and altered them. Made them bloody, silly, worse than even they wanted to be, so scared were they of the jungle they had made. The screaming baboon lived under their own white skin; the red gums were their own.

15.4.4 Arbitrary Use of Power

The novels suggest that white people are capricious and abusive in using their power over Black people. This is arbitrary power, and such absolute, or near absolute power, is always morally corrupting.

Octavia Butler (1947–2006), *Kindred* (1979), p. 134:

> His father [the slavemaster] wasn't the monster he could have been with the power he held over his slaves. He wasn't a monster at all. Just an ordinary man who sometimes did the monstrous things his society said were legal and proper.

Alice Walker, *The Color Purple*, p. 87:

> [Mayor's wife] say to Sofia, All your children so clean, she say, would you like to work for me, be my maid?
>
> Sofia say, Hell no.
>
> She say, What you say?
>
> Sofia say, Hell no.
>
> Mayor look at Sofia, push his wife out the way. Stick out his chest. Girl, what you say to Miss Millie?
>
> Sofia say, I say, Hell no.
>
> He slap her.

Toni Morrison, *Beloved*, p. 90:

> Out there were whitepeople and how could you tell about them? ... Grandma Baby said there was no defense—they could prowl at will, change from one mind to another, and even when they thought they were behaving, it was a far cry from what real humans did.

15.4.5 Violence

White people created a slave system of unspeakable violence and settled into the practice of anger and violence against Black people, even long after slavery ended. Often seeming to be on a hair-trigger, in local situations white people routinely resort to violence. No one prevents it.

Zora Neale Hurston (1891–1960), *Their Eyes Were Watching God* (1937), p. 17, a scene in which a slave master's wife discovers her slave's baby looks an awful lot like her own husband [paraphrased]:

> 'What's your baby doing with gray eyes and yellow hair?' She began to slap my jaws every which way. I never felt the first ones 'cause I was too busy getting the cover back over my child. But the last lick burnt me like fire. I had too many feelings to tell which one to follow so I didn't cry and I didn't do nothing else. But then she kept asking me how come my baby look white ... So I told her, 'I don't know nothing but what I'm told to do cause I ain't nothing but a n***** and a slave.

Toni Morrison, *Beloved*, p. 212:

> Eighteen seventy-four and whitefolks were still on the loose. Whole towns wiped clean of Negroes; eighty-seven lynchings in one year alone in Kentucky; four colored schools burned to the ground; grown men whipped like children; children whipped like adults; Black women raped; property taken, necks broken. He smelled skin, skin and hot blood. The skin was one thing, but human blood cooked in a lynch fire was a whole other thing.

James Baldwin, *Go Tell it on the Mountain*, pp. 158–159:

> Blood, in all the cities through which he passed, ran down. There seemed no door, anywhere, behind which blood did not call out, unceasingly, for blood; no woman ... who had not seen her father, her brother, her lover, or her son cut down without mercy; who had not seen her sister become part of the white man's great whorehouse, who had not, all too narrowly,

escaped that house herself; no man, preaching or cursing ... who had not been made to bend his head and drink white men's muddy water; no man whose manhood had not been, at the root, sickened ... whose seed had not been scattered into oblivion and worse than oblivion, into living shame and rage, and into endless battle. Yes, their parts were all cut off, they were dishonored, their very names were nothing more than dust blown disdainfully across the field of time ... Behind them was the darkness, nothing but the darkness, and all around them destruction, and before them nothing but the fire—a bastard people, far from God, singing and crying in the wilderness!

15.4.6 Alienation

The novels depict occasions when white people seek normal, healthy human relationships with Black people, or seem to seek them. But in the end, true community is out of reach. Whites cannot release their superiority, and Black people have no particular reason to extend trust.

Butler, *Kindred*, p. 149:

Rufus [the slave master] had done exactly what I had said he would do: Gotten possession of the [slave] woman without having to bother with her husband [whom he had killed]. Now, somehow, Alice would have to accept not only the loss of her husband, but her own enslavement. Rufus had caused her trouble, and now he had been rewarded for it. It made no sense. No matter how kindly he treated her now that he had destroyed her, it made no sense.

Ernest Gaines (1933–2019), *The Autobiography of Miss Jane Pittman* (1971), p. 178. In this scene, Mary Agnes and Miss Jane are talking about the possibility of real love between her and the son of the locally dominant white man:

Jane: And you think you can handle him?

Mary Agnes: More than anything else in this world, Robert is decent.

Jane: Is this world decent, Mary Agnes?

Mary Agnes: Robert is more human being than he is white man, Miss Jane.

Jane: And how long you think this world go'n let him stay like that?

Richard Wright, *Native Son*, pp. 65–67:

He felt something in her over and above the fear she inspired in him. She responded to him as if he were human, as if he lived in the same world as she. And he had never felt that before in a white person. But why? Was this some kind of game? The guarded feeling of freedom he had while listening to her was tangled with the hard fact that she was white and rich, a part of the world of people who told him what he could and could not do.

Maybe they did not despise him? But they made him feel his Black skin by just standing there looking at him … He felt he had no physical existence at all then; he was something he hated, the badge of shame which he knew was attached to a Black skin. It was a shadowy region, a no man's land, the ground that separated the white world from the Black that he stood upon. He felt naked, transparent; he felt that this white man, having helped to put him down, having helped to deform him, held him up now to look at him and be amused.

15.5 Religious Powerlessness

There is much allusion to religion in these novels. White people's religion is always supposedly Christianity. But insightful characters wonder over this religion, which they see is powerless to correct white people's behavior despite a whole lot of churchgoing. Its main power is the ability to underwrite white hegemony and anesthetize the white Christian conscience. Like all the idols described in the Bible, white religion is most powerful in its ability to lead people away from the true God.

Gaines, *Autobiography of Miss Jane Pittman*, p. 43 (an 1865 scene when just-released slaves are wandering desperately looking for food and water):

> Don't think I love n***** just because I'm giving y'all water ... I hate y'all. Hate y'all with all my heart. Doing it because I'm a God-fearing Christian ... I hope the good white people round here kill all y'all off ... Hope they kill y'all before the night over. Now, get away from here. Get away from here before I kill y'all myself. If I wasn't a God-fearing Christian I'd kill y'all myself.

Butler, *Kindred*, p. 236:

> Some of his neighbors found out what I was doing [teaching slaves] and offered him fatherly advice. It was dangerous to educate slaves, they warned. Education made Blacks dissatisfied with slavery. It spoiled them for field work. The Methodist minister said it made them disobedient, made them want more than the Lord intended them to have.

Hughes, *Not Without Laughter*, pp. 81–82 [paraphrased]:

> White folks' religion—Lord help! Ain't no use in mentioning them ... Cause if the gate of heaven shuts in white folks' faces like the doors of their church in our faces, it'll be too bad! Yes, sir! One thing sure, the Lord ain't prejudiced.

Dorothy West (1907–1998), *The Wedding* (1995), p. 45, white "Gram" on her white friends discovering that her daughter was about to have a mixed-race baby:

> The truth about Josephine would have knocked them over like ninepins. They, like herself, had too little left in their lives to have their faith in their divinity destroyed by Josephine's apostasy.

West, *The Wedding*, pp. 74–75:

> Show me one white man who can look at a colored man without saying to himself, I see a colored man ... The only one I know of died on the cross, and the other one has not yet been

born ... Keeping us colored is one of their chief occupations. If they don't remember it every minute, they're afraid they'll forget we're not children of God.

15.6 Blindness: The Trained Ability Not to See the Obvious

One final major theme has to do with moral perception, one of the key themes in ethics, to which we have often returned. Black characters in these novels clearly see white racism for what it is, decry its injustice, and try to resist it. But white people are willfully blind to it. We choose not to or are unable to see the evil we are enforcing and the suffering we are inflicting. We live in a privileged fog, out of touch with obvious realities.

Hughes, *Not Without Laughter*, p. 82:

> I been knowin white folks all my life, an they's good as far as they can see—but when it comes to po n******, they just can't see, that's all.

Baldwin, *Go Tell It on the Mountain*, p. 75:

> In her tribulations, death, and parting, and the lash, she did not forget that deliverance was promised and would surely come. She had only to endure and trust in God. She knew that the big house, the house of pride where the white folks lived, would come down: it was written in the Word of God. They, who walked so proudly now, had not fashioned for themselves or their children so sure a foundation as was hers. They walked on the edge of a steep place *and their eyes were sightless*—God would cause them to rush down, as the herd of swine ...

Ernest Gaines, *A Gathering of Old Men* (1983), p. 108:

> Now, ain't that just like white folks? ... Black people get lynched, get drowned, get shot, guts all hanging out—and here he come up with ain't no proof who did it. The proof was them two little children laying there in them two coffins. That's proof enough they was dead.

Here I break my pattern of staying with novels and quote one of my favorite interpreters of America's racial problems, James Baldwin. This is from his famous non-fiction work, *The Fire Next Time* (1963), p. 5:

> It is not permissible that the authors of devastation should also be innocent. It is the innocence which constitutes the crime.

And then a line from contemporary writer Ta-Nehisi Coates, in his *Between the World and Me* (2015), p. 98:

> The mettle that it takes to look away from the horror of our prison system, from police forces transformed into armies, from the long war against the Black body, is not forged overnight. This is the practiced habit of jabbing out one's eyes and forgetting the work of one's hands.

15.7 When Will Repentance Come?

African American literary works offer consistent, realistic, critical description of white Christian supremacism, even when that is not their main subject. These novels trace a long arc that contains far more continuity than discontinuity over U.S. history, even if contemporary authors sometimes point to recent advances. White Christians rarely tell the story of U.S. history that way, imagining a bad but distant past—not present.

The picture these novels offer is of a criminal and abusive racist system under "the color of law," justified by an absurd ideology of white moral superiority.

White U.S. Christians have been full participants in the moral debasement, religious powerlessness, and perceptual blindness that is described in these novels. This is *our* story, not someone else's.

Black U.S. novelists, as well as essayists, sociologists, preachers, and theologians, have repeatedly warned us that much of white Christianity may be more about whiteness than about Christianity. Howard Thurman saw it—the colonizers needed a version of Christianity that would at least shield from their view the debasement embraced in choosing a white supremacist way of life.

There is no evidence that white U.S. Christians as a group have ever repented of their morally damaged faith. Whether Christians of European background have done so elsewhere is a matter of local discernment.

Without question, dealing with the continued legacy of white supremacist Christianity remains one of the pressing tasks in Christian ethics and church life today.

Discussion Questions

1. Is "race" real, or is it fictional? When you are asked to check a box with your "racial" identity, do you consider that problematic in any way?

2. The chapter claims that "white" racism is especially significant because of the history of European colonialism. See if you can restate the basis for this claim in your own words.

3. What does the concept of "white supremacism" add to the idea of "white racism"?

4. What was your reaction to the lines quoted from these novels? Did you learn something new?

5. Did the use of the novels support the claim that they are an important source for constructing Christian ethics?

To watch Dr. Gushee deliver

**Lecture 16: The Radical Economic
Ethics of Jesus**

Follow this link:

https://youtu.be/c5qkQ01n0Ls

Or scan the QR code.

To listen to the audio, follow this link:

https://qrco.de/bcOlRX

Or scan the QR code.

To scan a QR code, download a QR reader from the app store on your device, open the application, follow the directions, and point your device's camera at the code.

CHAPTER 16

The Radical Economic Ethics of Jesus

16.1 The Vast Terrain of Economic Ethics

Children encounter economic life from their birth, and the material circumstances of their parents shape their lives. It takes many years before children develop any substantial understanding of the vast economic web into which they have been born, and some never really outgrow the assumptions and experiences of their childhood.

Likewise, economic ethics is a vast arena, so vast that some ethicists specialize entirely in this one subfield. There is so much to talk about: the global economy; economic systems like capitalism, socialism, and communism; social classes; the morality of private property; income and wealth inequality; relative and absolute poverty; corporate practices and ethics; tax structures; social welfare systems; wage rates; labor-capital relations; worker's rights and unions; workplace safety and consumer protection laws; rest from work and the concept of Sabbath; the morality of the stock market; housing-related issues; the ethics of paying and earning interest; debt and debt forgiveness; advertising, luxury, and a consumer economy; the gross domestic product and alternative measures of economic and social health; the business cycle with its booms and busts; personal economic stewardship, charity, the morality of wealth, voluntary poverty ... and more.

I'm a bit biased, because I sponsored this research, but my favorite recent book on economic ethics is *Better Capitalism* (Wipf & Stock, 2021) by Mercer University graduates Paul Knowlton and Aaron Hedges. It is a comprehensive Christian treatment of economic ethics from two men with serious business, nonprofit, and legal experience, and a well-informed Christian ethical perspective.

A body of literature that is tremendously helpful in economic ethics is found in the Roman Catholic social teaching tradition, which has been wrestling with these matters seriously since the rise of modern capitalism. The wrenching challenges created by modern urban industrial capitalism, and the powerful but atheistic response offered by Marxism, were the primary impetus for the development of modern Catholic social teaching. One accessible place to find a distilled treatment of Catholic economic ethics is a 2005 sourcebook called *Compendium of the Social Doctrine of the Church*. My favorite contemporary Catholic economic ethicist is Dan Finn. See his authoritative 2013 book, *Christian Economic Ethics*.

A parallel development happened on the Protestant side at the same time, most visibly in the late 19th/early 20th century Social Gospel movement. Walter Rauschenbusch's 1907 *Christianity and the Social Crisis* remains that movement's most important work. It helped to launch what has become a global, ecumenical Protestant economic ethics tradition that remains active today.

All told, few subjects have received more attention in the history of our field than economic ethics. And yet, many Christians rarely think in Christian terms about their economic lives. Instead, they default to the practices and norms of their culture.

16.2 The Obscure Parable of the Shrewd Manager

Jesus has much to say about economic life. His teachings are both compelling and unsettling. The history of Christian economic ethics has been filled with leaders trying to soften or evade Jesus' hard words about economic life. Instead, I want to try to enter the thought-world of Jesus and to be honest about the challenge his utterly radical perspective represents.

In this chapter, I am going to offer a close reading of one especially difficult teaching of Jesus, the parable of the shrewd manager (Lk 16:1–15), using that as our entry point into his overall vision.

Here is the text:

Then Jesus said to the disciples, "There was a rich man who had a manager, and charges were brought to him that this man was squandering his property. So he summoned him and said to him, 'What is this that I hear about you? Give me an accounting of your management, because you cannot be my manager any longer.' Then the manager said to himself, 'What will I do, now that my master is taking the position away from me? I am not strong enough to dig, and I am ashamed to beg. I have decided what to do so that, when I am dismissed as manager, people may welcome me into their homes.' So, summoning his master's debtors one by one, he asked the first, 'How much do you owe my master?' He answered, 'A hundred jugs of olive oil.' He said to him, 'Take your bill, sit down quickly, and make it fifty.' Then he asked another, 'And how much do you owe?' He replied, 'A hundred containers of wheat.' He said to him, 'Take your bill and make it eighty.' And his master commended the dishonest manager because he had acted shrewdly.

—Lk 16:1–8a

Let's start off with a few basic contextual and translation notes, aided by New Testament scholar Joel Green's 1997 commentary on the Gospel of Luke.

The teaching is offered to the disciples, though we can probably assume a fluid audience that includes others. In the parable, we quickly meet a wealthy landowner, a member of the elite class in an agriculture-based economy. This rich man has hired, or deployed a slave, to manage his business. This manager is the highest-ranking employee and one with considerable autonomy over the owner's business affairs.

But he has not been handling the owner's business very well. We do not hear of dishonesty, but of "squandering," or wastefulness—though the precise meaning of the Greek word *diaskorpizo* here is debated. In any case, someone blows the whistle on him, and he is about to be dismissed, at one blow losing his job, housing, and status.

The manager quickly makes the rounds of the master's debtors and—in the name of the master but without his consent—starts offering discounted deals on their large debts. (The size of the debts helps confirm the large wealth and holdings of the rich landowner.) This part of the story is tele-scoped, leaving plenty of room for the imagination to fill in details.

In the end, what the manager has done is to reduce the master's "accounts payable" without his permission. He has done this for the self-interested purpose of creating a new kind of relationship with the master's debtors in which they now owe the manager hospitality or other service if he needs it (Green, pp. 592–593).

The surprise of the story is not that the owner finds out about the man-ager's finagling, but that instead of dismissal he offers praise to a man now described for the first time as *adikias* (unrighteous/unjust—often translated "dishonest"). His praise is because the manager has acted *phronimos*—a term usually translated as "shrewdly," but just as easily translated as sensibly, wisely, practically, or prudently.

If we cut off the text here, it seems that what we have is Jesus looking around at the world and describing one aspect of how it works. At the top of the economic pyramid (in Jesus' world) are the rich landowners. They are experts at accumulating wealth, cutting deals, and leveraging their economic power in ways that benefit themselves.

Starting there, we can perhaps see how a rich landowner *who is in the process of being cheated by his own household manager* could at the same time think him rather clever. That's because these are the kind of shrewd and borderline-dishonest moves that the rich owner has himself made from time to time in his rise to the top. The owner recognizes a "good head for business" when he sees one.

I suggest that the assumed end of this story is that the owner brings the manager back home. He gives him a stern admonition to stop wasting his money. But he also pats him on the back for his cleverness and says: "In the future, I want you to employ all that shrewdness on my behalf rather than your own. Now get back to work."

Can't you just picture a whole lot of peasant listeners—the kind of mar-ginalized people who found Jesus so attractive—all nodding their heads as they recall their own encounters with the shady economic practices of the powerful people of their world?

I want to suggest that everything from v. 8b to v. 15 in Luke 16 is Luke's attempt to make kingdom meaning out of this parable of Jesus that has been passed on to him. He makes several different tries, partly by appending free-floating sayings of Jesus to the end of this disturbing parable. These efforts reveal the difficulty of making sense out of the story but also, in my view, give glimpses of the radicalism of Jesus' economic ethics.

Interpretation #1:

> For the children of this age are more shrewd in dealing with their own generation than are the children of light. And I tell you, make friends for yourselves by means of dishonest wealth, so that when it is gone, they may welcome you into the eternal homes.

—Lk 16:8b-9

Joel Green's commentary (p. 593) helps with this obscure teaching. Green says that Jesus is drawing a distinction between two ages: "this age" and, implicitly, the "age to come," the kingdom age. The inhabitants of the age to come are called "the children of light," implicitly contrasted with the unnamed "children of darkness" of this age. Jesus is calling together a community of children of light who for now dwell in a world ruled by children of darkness. What makes the children of light distinct is that they are working alongside Jesus to give birth to a new age—the kingdom of God.

The economic ethics of the children of darkness are predictably *adikos* (unjust). Here it really helps to remember that this is the same root word we talked about earlier as having to do with justice, not just righteousness, and certainly not just honesty. Jesus is saying that in this age, dominated as it is by the children of darkness, wealth acquisition is filled with injustice.

The term the NRSV translates as "dishonest wealth" would be more literally translated as "Mammon of Injustice," and that translation has much more bite to it. Green shows that **Mammon** is an Aramaic word that means not just possessions, property, or wealth, but "an idolatrous power" (p. 593). Even the use of the word Mammon here rather than a more neutral term for money gives evidence of Jesus' perspective on the whole economic system.

Nowhere in the story has Jesus described the economic practices of the rich landowner. But Jesus seems to be implying that the landowner sits at the top of a system that is shot through with injustice, dishonesty, and the shrewdness of a corrupt age, all in the service of the endless idolatrous quest for wealth that dominates so many lives. What might be called "Mammonism" has also gotten wired into their cultural practices, so that table fellowship, friendship, generosity, and basic hospitality are tied to people's wealth, status, and indebtedness within the corrupt economic system. People who have the most resources mainly use them to accrue status, acquire "friends," compete with one another, and create various kinds of indebtedness on the part of others. Meanwhile the poor go begging.

Note the pivotal reference to friendship in verse 9: "Make friends for yourselves by means of dishonest wealth, so that when it is gone, they may welcome you into the eternal homes." The best interpretation of this obscure saying in verse 9 is that Jesus is counseling his followers, the children of the new age, to use whatever access they might have to unjust Mammon to begin demonstrating a very different kind of friendship, and building up a very different kind of treasure.

We know that Jesus reinforced central Jewish teachings about almsgiving—giving to the poor—only adding that such almsgiving should be done privately, so as not to attract attention (Mt 6:1–4). Instead of giving money publicly to fellow rich people to gain social capital, give alms privately to the poor who cannot help you at all—except for helping you store up "treasure in heaven," which is more important than any earthly treasure. Consider Luke 12:33: "Sell your possessions, and give alms. Make purses for yourselves that do not wear out, an unfailing treasure in heaven, where no thief comes near and no moth destroys." "Treasure in heaven" means reward, and entrance into eternal life.

The reciprocity game, on the other hand, involves creating social and economic indebtedness on the part of others so that they owe us something in return—in this parable, it is hospitality. But reciprocity is the game that the children of darkness play. The children of light, on the other hand, give without expecting anything in return (Lk 6:32–35), and cancel debts (Lk 4:18–19, 6:35, 7:41–42). In Joel Green's words, they demonstrate "solidarity across social lines" (p. 595). Money is used to bless, not to entrap, because for disciples the use of money has only one real value, doing the will of God, and God is keeping a different accounting system. Money can be useful, but only if disciples completely disentangle themselves from the Mammonism and injustice of this age.

Interpretation #2:

> Whoever is faithful in a very little is faithful also in much; and
> whoever is dishonest in a very little is dishonest also in much. If
> then you have not been faithful with the dishonest wealth, who

will entrust to you the true riches? And if you have not been
faithful with what belongs to another, who will give you what
is your own?

—Lk 16:10–12

The first statement could be read independently as a wise observation
about human character, the way that it reveals itself in matters small and
large. A guy who will cheat you out of a dollar in a poker game reveals plenty
about himself. Here, Jesus is turning this observation into a move something like this: Money means relatively little in the economy of the kingdom.
There are far higher and truer riches. But disciples prove their readiness to
receive the true riches by whether they learn to handle unjust Mammon in
keeping with the values of the kingdom.

Interpretation #3:

> No slave can serve two masters; for a slave will either hate the
> one and love the other, or be devoted to the one and despise the
> other. You cannot serve God and wealth.

—Lk 16:13

This text, which in Matthew is found in the Sermon on the Mount, is one
of Jesus' most memorable sayings about wealth. Joel Green surprises us in his
commentary on Luke with the news that in the Greco-Roman world, slaves
could be owned by more than one master (Green, p. 597). The issue, then, is
about "the diametrically opposed forms of service" demanded by God and
Mammon: "Since each grounds its demands in such antithetical worldviews,
one cannot serve them both" (Green, p. 597).

Interpretation #4:

> The Pharisees, who were lovers of money, heard all this, and
> they ridiculed him. So he said to them, "You are those who
> justify yourselves in the sight of others; but God knows your
> hearts; for what is prized by human beings is an abomination
> in the sight of God."

—Lk 16:14-15

Jesus has been teaching the disciples, but here come the Pharisees. They are harshly described as "lovers of money." Green suggests that in both Greco-Roman and Hellenistic Jewish circles this term (*philargoroi*) had become a stock phrase to describe self-glorifying false teachers (Green, p. 601). Perhaps here Jesus simply intends to accuse some Pharisees of participating in the money-based status games of the time rather than challenging them, which they should do as leaders of God's people.

That last line, though, sums up the section and packs quite a wallop. "What is prized by human beings is an abomination in the sight of God." Everyone desires Mammon, but Mammon is an abomination in God's sight.

Luke 16 had begun with a rich man on top of the social pyramid, fully immersed in the oligarchy of landowning wealth. Jesus' overall position on the wealthy had already been made quite clear in this statement early in the Gospel:

> But woe to you who are rich,
>> for you have received your consolation.
> Woe to you who are full now,
>> for you will be hungry.
> Woe to you who are laughing now,
>> for you will mourn and weep.
> Woe to you when all speak well of you,
>> for that is what their ancestors did to the false prophets.

—Lk 6:24-26

Here is Joel Green's overall summary of Jesus' message about those at home in this Mammonist world: "According to Luke, the rule of Wealth is manifest in theft and exploitation, hoarding, conspicuous consumption, and the more general disregard for outsiders and persons of low status and need" (Green, pp. 596–597, referencing Lk 11:39, 12:16–21, 14:12–14, 16:19–31).

Prosperous Christians in capitalist societies do not much like this message. But Joel Green is no card-carrying Marxist. He is a conservative evangelical Bible scholar reporting what is present in the text. Those at the top of the economic pyramid, for the Jesus of the Gospel of Luke, have exploited and even robbed others to get there, consume excessively, hoard wealth, demonstrate disregard for the poor, and play a reciprocity-based social game in which "wealth ha[s] value proportional to one's ability to redeem it for the currency of status honor" (Green, p. 601).

Texts pointing in this direction in Luke include the blessings and woes list of Luke 6, the parable of the rich fool in Luke 12, and the passage that follows this one, the parable of the rich man and Lazarus (16:19–31). Jesus sees the economic systems of this world as fundamentally corrupt, even idolatrous. He sees dethroning Mammon as a fundamental part of discipleship.

16.3 Applications and Implications

During the time that I was drafting this chapter, I did a guest speaking appearance at a church. The topic was "COVID, Culture, and Ethics." My task was to think about the ethical implications of the COVID epidemic after one year. Doing my research, I was struck by how much about COVID's impact, at least in the United States, was wealth- and privilege-related. COVID did not hit everyone in the same way. Basically, the higher your social-class position, the more white-collar your job, the bigger your house, the better your access to good health care, the easier your ability to miss work, the greater your savings, the deeper your investment in the stock market, and the healthier your family members, the likelier you were to be comparatively undamaged by the pandemic.

And isn't that the way it goes all the time?

In the United States, if you have no money or no bank account, you must pay to cash a check. If you have plenty of money, the bank gives you as many free checking and savings accounts as you want.

If you are poor and need to borrow money, you must pay crushing amounts of interest just to meet your monthly payment. But you don't have any money, which is why you are borrowing.

But, on the other hand, if you accrue a great deal of money and invest it, others pay you a substantial amount for using your money. For example, if you save and then invest a million dollars, in a good year you can make $100,000 while sitting around watching TV—which is more than many full-time workers make in a year.

If you come from nothing, for your kids to have a chance to succeed, they generally need especially good schools, teachers, and technology. But instead, it is the children of the rich who are more likely to enjoy such educational advantages, either because their local public schools are better funded, or because they can send their kids to expensive private schools.

If you work full time in a minimum-wage job, you remain poor in most U.S. states. But our legislatures, dominated by business interests, are reluctant to raise that minimum wage.

If a lowly laborer ends up in a workplace dispute with an unjust employer, he has no money to pay for a lawyer. The employer, though, can afford to pay $400 an hour in legal fees.

If you went to an elite university, your children are considered "legacies" and have easier admission access to the same university. If you went to Nowhere Community College, your child does not receive any such advantages.

None of these are crimes. None of these are grotesque abuses of power. They are garden-variety, everyday examples of how things work in the world, at least, the world that most of us know.

Those who make their way to the top discover immense systemic advantages. They then leverage their advantages to benefit themselves and their loved ones.

Back to that church and the COVID seminar. When I pointed out that such systemic advantages for the well-to-do even surfaced in relation to a health disaster like COVID, one of my listeners said that, while she recognized her blessings, "I worked hard to get to where I am, and I don't want to be made to feel guilty about my success."

I assured her that this was not my intention. But I wonder what Jesus would have said to her. The Jesus we meet in Luke certainly seems to join the disinherited of the Earth in looking at his world's economic system as intrinsically unjust, and even as an idol called Mammon. He looks closely at the system, and the people who prosper in it, and the culture they have created around it, and sees something that can simply be summarized as *adikos*—unjust, or unrighteous.

He asks those who would be his followers to somehow carve out a different relationship with Mammon, and to make it just money again. He calls them and us to topple Mammon and defy the culture. This means abandoning exploitation, status games, worry, pride, luxury, hoarding, and indifference to those "below." But sometimes he just says woes over the rich, and in a parable depicts a rich man who is in hell because he has ignored hungry Lazarus outside his gate (Lk 16:19–31).

Christian economic ethics is partly about attempting to correct a million unfair systemic advantages, like the ones I have mentioned. It is about cleaning up business practices so that they are not unjust. It focuses on government policies that tilt unjustly toward the affluent. It aims for a more just world for the poor. Much of historic Christian economic ethics is reformist in this way. I have joined this effort at times. It is just part of ethics work.

But Jesus' critique of the economic system of his time is not reformist. It is more radical than that. And his critique does not appear limited to Jesus' own specific economic context, deeply unjust as that was. I think Jesus looks at the world like this: In this age dominated by the children of darkness, there is no redeeming economic life. Even though this world's economic systems feed many people and organize much of culture, they are all drenched in collective human sin—sin that is especially dangerous because people take it for granted and often act as if success within this corrupt system offers evidence of their own virtue.

Jesus' economic radicalism is alarming for those who find themselves with a measure of wealth and take him at his word. (See Ron Sider's 1978 *Rich Christians in an Age of Hunger* and Sondra Wheeler's 1995 *Wealth as Peril and Obligation* as examples of serious studies that do precisely that.) But Jesus' teaching is also clarifying, because it accounts for the perennial, unreformable, never-quite-right nature of every economic system, and the limits of all economic reform efforts.

Jesus sees our vast economic structures for what they are, and with prophetic radicalism warns us about the evils that are baked into them. His teaching about the way to live in this age while participating in the economy of the next one offers a path forward. But it is a far more radical path than most Christians who have prospered in this world are willing to pursue.

Jesus never ceases to surprise us. How will we respond?

Discussion Questions

1. If someone asked you to describe the morality of capitalism, what would you say?

2. Why did Jesus speak woes over the rich?

3. Is there any hope that systemic advantages that the rich enjoy will ever be leveled out?

4. What is your main takeaway from this exposition of Luke 16:1–15?

To watch Dr. Gushee deliver

**Lecture 17: Preventing Unwanted
Pregnancy and Abortion**

Follow this link:

https://youtu.be/78tKBx08Sns

Or scan the QR code.

To listen to the audio, follow this link:

https://qrco.de/bcOlU3

Or scan the QR code.

To scan a QR code, download a QR reader from the app store on your device, open the application, follow the directions, and point your device's camera at the code.

Chapter 17

Preventing Unwanted Pregnancy and Abortion

17.1 Mature Bodies, Immature Minds

In many cultures, the onset of puberty is happening earlier and earlier while marriage is happening later and later. In the U.K., for example, the average age for the onset of puberty is 11 for girls and 12 for boys, while the average age of first marriage is 31 for women and 33 for men. The numbers are similar throughout the Western world. Together with structural economic factors frequently delaying economic self-sufficiency, our cultures face a vast and perilous gap between the procreative power of the sexually mature body and the readiness of young adults to receive and raise the next generation.

As we continue our journey through the lifecycle, and I think of my grandchildren one day becoming young adults, I must face the fact that their bodies, if healthy, will hold the power to conceive babies long before their minds and moral codes are mature, marriage is an option, or their bank accounts contain much.

At one level, this is not a new problem. There is little doubt that the procreative power of fertile young people, and the perceived need to control it for social purposes, profoundly shaped historic sexual, marital, and family ethics throughout the ancient world.

For Jews and Christians, human procreative power was met with awe, a sense of divine empowerment and blessing: "God blessed them, and God said to them, "Be fruitful and multiply, and fill the earth" (Gen 1:28). The whole Earth was to be populated by God through people. There were many divine powers which humans could only watch from a distance. But the power of bringing new life into the world would be shared between God and people.

Yet this was not a power to be trifled with. Sexual relations between men and women needed social control precisely because of their procreative potential, about which little could be done, despite primitive contraception and abortion options sometimes available in the ancient world.

In this light, the advent of modern technologies of birth control (most notably "The Pill," which was approved for contraceptive use by the United States government in 1960), must be understood as one of the most revolutionary developments in human history. A fascinating account of how this happened, and what it has meant, is found in Jonathan Eig's 2015 book, *The Birth of the Pill*.

In this chapter, I will suggest that toggling back and forth between the ancient world and our post-Pill culture can help us make sense not just of today's debate over abortion but why it takes the form that it now does.

17.2 The Ancient Context

For all human experience, which anthropologists tell us is 200,000 years, fertile men and women clearly risked making babies when they had heterosexual intercourse. The modern era saw strides in birth control, for sure. But with the Pill, a quantum leap forward was promised. The intrinsic link between intercourse and babies had been broken. Or so it seemed.

In retrospect, we can see that the legal availability of the most advanced modern technological methods of birth control draws a hard line between the context in which post-1960 humans have addressed sexual ethics, and all human history before that. That's a time span of .017% of human history.

Try to think about the circumstances facing people in the world before modern birth control and the way these circumstances shaped ancient Jewish and Christian ethics.

Almost all humans desire love and/or sex, are drawn inexorably into relationships with others and sometimes end up having sex with others. This inexorable drive is also essential for the transmission of the generations. God created humans so that when healthy fertile males and females have vaginal sexual intercourse without birth control, quite often the woman will become pregnant.

I hasten to add that under patriarchal conditions, in the past, but still also today, women routinely have been stripped of control over their bodies, their sexuality, and their childbearing. As Christian ethicist Beverly Harrison argued in her classic 1983 book, *Our Right to Choose*, gaining control of "responsible life planning in relation to her procreative power" is an essential aspect of a woman's self-determination (p. 9).

Harrison ably documented the crucial fact that complicates, even bedevils, all moral discussions of abortion. The long history of societal efforts to control sexual expression and prevent unwanted pregnancies has been inextricably intertwined with patriarchal power. This makes it difficult, when engaging issues such as sexual ethics, contraception, or abortion, to disentangle prudent efforts to structure adult sexual relations and the birth of children from oppressive efforts by men to control women and limit their choices.

A pregnancy always has been a momentous development for a woman. Harrison describes it this way:

> It is a long, complex biological process that, over time, produces a human life. In the process, a woman's body becomes the mediative vehicle for the emergence of that new life. This biological process requires a woman's cooperation. She must adjust her activities, take special care with her diet and her health, and in myriad other ways alter her lifestyle to bring the pregnancy to a successful outcome. There is always genuine physical risk involved and, in some cases actual physical danger to the pregnant woman, but we must recognize that women bear not only the biological risks but also the cultural, social, and economic consequences of pregnancy and childbearing (p. 43).

Under patriarchal conditions, visible in the Bible itself, women often had little or no choice as to whether to have sex, with whom to have sex, whether to become pregnant, when to become pregnant, how many times to become pregnant, whether their particular physical risks in pregnancy were worth bearing, and so on.

One devoutly wishes for a world in which women's moral agency in such matters played more of a role in the strict social controls that developed related to sex, courtship, marriage, and birth. Still, I suggest that even apart from damaging patriarchal assumptions, ancient societies would have created systems of social control to limit sexual contact between fertile men and women—to secure family membership, to bind men to their children and their children's mothers, and to provide a context in which the next generation could be raised to adulthood.

The social control measures that we see in the ancient world involved religious, legal, moral, and familial strategies to train the attitudes of the young, impose behavioral constraints, warn about unwanted pregnancies, and structure the relations of men and women to prevent unapproved pregnancies. The idea was that *we must keep these bodies away from each other until the approved time and context.*

Christian traditions did this, and still do this, in various ways. Many readers are, of course, intimately familiar with the strategies, good and bad, that have been attempted.

The highest sources of religious authority all banned sex between unmarried men and women, attempting to make such bans a matter of church law, moral norms, and Christian culture. Courting rituals were tightly monitored. Marriage was fixed as the organizing institution for adult life. Young people sometimes were pressed to marry as early as possible, but if not, they were still told to wait to have sex. Babies born "out of wedlock" were, for centuries, labeled with an ugly epithet to shame their parents and teach lessons to watchful young eyes. Inheritance laws were structured to discriminate against "illegitimate" children.

17.3 Ancient Christian Proscriptions on Abortion and Infanticide

Despite all social control efforts, unwanted pregnancies have always been a feature of human life, including among Christians, a crisis for women that takes place within their own bodies and in the messy, sometimes terrifying context of their actual lives.

Inevitably, given the grave crisis of an unwanted pregnancy, in the ancient world women sometimes resorted to what means were available to attempt abortion. According to Harrison, these ancient abortion methods "*endangered the life of the mother* every bit as much as it imperiled the prenatal life in her womb" (p. 124; italics in the original). Moreover, men who did not want "their" women to be pregnant sometimes attempted to induce abortions themselves, with predictably horrific results. Men also sometimes killed unwanted babies that were born, a feature noted with horror in the Roman context by Christian writers.

Harrison claims that the anti-abortion and anti-infanticide teachings that show up in early Christian documents sometimes reflect a laudable pastoral concern for women facing such terrible circumstances and risks. On the other hand, she also offers evidence that opposition to abortion was also affected by patriarchy—men seeking to retain control of women's sexuality and procreative power.

Thus, it is both certain that anti-abortion and anti-infanticide teachings appear in the early Christian tradition, and that their motives are open for some debate. Here are three widely cited texts:

"You shall not murder a child by abortion, nor kill a child at birth," says the *Didache*, one of the earliest compendiums of Christian teaching, composed in the late first century CE.

The *Epistle of Barnabas*, another early text (100 CE), concurs: "You shall love your neighbor more than your own soul. You shall not slay the child by procuring abortion; nor again, shall you destroy it after it is born" (*Ante-Nicene Fathers*, volume 1, p. 148).

Athenagoras, writing in 177 CE, argued: "We say that those women who use drugs to bring on an abortion commit murder" (*Ante-Nicene Fathers*, volume 2, p. 147).

Our ancestral Christian forebears were boxed in by nature like all the ancients. But unlike the ancient Romans, their leaders removed abortion or infanticide as morally acceptable responses to unwanted pregnancy. They did this for various reasons, including concern both for women and the children they carried, efforts to uphold Christian sexual morality, and, yes, patriarchal assumptions. Still, what resulted was a notable opposition to abortion and infanticide that set Christians apart from many of their neighbors in the Greco-Roman world.

Many learned studies have been written on the history of Christian teaching about abortion as it developed through the centuries. Harrison's pro-choice work helps us see that interpretations vary related to the reasons explicitly or implicitly supporting these anti-abortion teachings, and the interaction between premodern understandings of the process of fetal development and views about the moral significance of milestones in human development such as conception, **ensoulment** (beliefs about when the developing child gains or is given a soul), and **quickening** (the first movements of the fetus felt by the mother). With all due caveats, however, it is certainly fair to say that nothing like the current acceptance of widespread abortion was ever imaginable until very recently.

17.4 The Advent of Modern Birth Control

What changed?

We turn our gaze back to the early 1960s. It was believed that "The Pill" had broken the awesome power of nature in the arena of sexuality and put it in the hands of people, notably women, who were the ones who took it as a form of hormonal birth control. The idea has carried over to what is now an array of birth control methods.

For the first time in all human history, just 50 years ago, technology (it was claimed) was now making it possible to disconnect sexual intercourse from pregnancy—except for when pregnancy was actively sought. Human beings had invented a technology that could override nature and enhance human agency to a place of near-total control of fertility. We were no longer boxed in by nature. We could do what we wanted. If we wanted to get pregnant, we could do that. If we did not want to get pregnant, we could just as well do that. All we had to do was use the right technology in the prescribed way.

During the 1960s, a huge clash erupted between millennia of religious tradition and the possibilities created by this new technological reality. It took about ten years for the tradition to be swept away, at least in the technologically advanced democracies. Society was remade.

Regulation of young adult sexual contact weakened or disappeared. Marriage was decentered as the preferred context for adult sexual activity. Pressure on young people to marry early faded outside of conservative subcultures.

Women's sexual freedom grew dramatically, narrowing the gap that had always existed compared to men's sexual freedom. Women's ability to manage their own procreative power accompanied and helped intensify the stunning and welcome growth in their educational, economic, social, and political opportunities.

For the first time in human history, the fact that women are the ones who bear children ceased to be the most important factor in many women's lives, unless they wanted it to be. A revolution in women's social roles and social power followed wherever modern technological birth control was made available. If, as Beverly Harrison argues, feminism is about expanding the range of women's choices in general, and women's bodily self-determination and procreative control in particular, modern birth control marked a crucial advance for the feminist cause.

Men, meanwhile, now found themselves with easier sexual access to women. Most were not unhappy about this development. Indeed, a counter-history of this period could be mustered, claiming that mass distribution of modern birth control, unaccompanied by the defeat of patriarchal power, actually meant more opportunity for men to exploit women's sexuality.

17.5 But Technology's Victory Was Not Absolute

Fifty years later, we have discovered something that was not visible when this revolution began: *technology cannot entirely tame nature*. Contrary to the expectations that were birthed with the Pill and remain with us today, human fertility has never come entirely under our control.

When fertile men and women have vaginal sex, those sperm and eggs are programmed to meet, regardless of our best technology-aided efforts to prevent it.

It is true that often people use the technology wrongly or fail to use it at all in the heat of the moment.

But even when used properly, birth control does not always work. Here are some "typical-use" failure rates in the U.S.: Birth control pills: 7%. Male condoms: 13%. Spermicides: 28%. Diaphragm: 12%. Patch: 9%. Male withdrawal: 20%. (How Do You Interpret Birth Control Failure Rates? | verywellhealth.com) Today, surgical sterilization, contraceptive implants, and IUDs do reduce the failure rate to under 1%. Together, however, implants and IUDs are only used by 10% of women. (FastStats – Contraceptive Use | cdc.gov)

The bottom line is this: Both in the U.S. and around the world, the unplanned pregnancy rate is currently 45%. (Almost half of pregnancies in the U.S. are unplanned. There's a surprisingly easy way to change that. | *The*

Washington Post) The promise of technology to break the power of nature and put fertility control in the hands of people has largely failed. Human procreative power is proving beyond our technological mastery. We will certainly keep trying. There is far too much momentum in the direction of that project for humanity to stop trying. But we appear to be hitting the limits of what we can do.

17.6 The Gap Between Technological Promise and Reality Creates Our Cultural Context

During and after the 1960s, modern people loosened up millennia-old moral norms and cultural practices, many of them religion-based, partly because of *the promise that birth control offered* of breaking the link between sexual intercourse and pregnancy. It turns out that this promise was illusory. But there has been no going back on the moral and cultural changes. We have built a modern way of life based on sexual freedom and the promise of fertility control with the use of technology. The sexual freedom has continued but the technological fertility control has half-failed.

This is the peculiar context in which "beginning of life" ethical issues arise in modern cultures. Abortion, birth control, and **assisted reproduction** are available in a social context in which people expect to be able to exercise full agency either in preventing, or having, children, regardless of their sexual behavior. This was unimaginable for 200,000 years—and now taken for granted for 50 years.

The crucial weakening of the perceived link between nature and fertility opened the door to a sense of entitlement to manage human fertility and ever more expansive technological interventions in preventing, ending, or creating pregnancies. Now, on any given day on Earth, massive numbers of people are using modern technology to prevent conception, others to end pregnancies, and others to conceive children.

While it is important to see birth control, abortion, and assisted reproduction as related issues in terms of this cultural dynamic, each issue also requires separate moral evaluation. I urgently support the availability and proper use of birth control for those who are going to have sex and do not want to become pregnant. I support assisted reproduction, but only in a manner somewhat more limited and more carefully regulated than today. And, as I will elucidate in the next section, I do not consider abortion to be a form of birth control or a morally unproblematic backup plan when birth control fails or is not used.

17.7 Thinking About Abortion Today

Abortion remains by far the most morally contested bioethical issue. The debate over the morality of abortion is much clarified when we take the post-Pill context seriously. It is the *combination* of the failed promise of technological mastery over human fertility and the subsequent dramatic loosening of sexual morality that have created the massive rise in the demand for abortions. There had always been unintended pregnancies and sometimes tragic efforts to end them. But the scale and scope of both unintended pregnancies and abortion rose dramatically from the 1960s forward.

Birth control was supposed to mean that fertile people could have sex when they wanted without having to worry about pregnancy. But we have seen, 50 years after the Pill, that 45% of pregnancies every year are unintended in the U.S. and around the world. These pregnancies are resolved in various ways: Sexual partners become (or remain) couples and raise the children they have conceived; individuals (mainly women) keep and raise their children as single parents; extended families cooperate in raising the children of family members; individuals or couples give their children up for formal adoption; a miscarriage happens; finally, where it is legal and available, some portion of women and/or couples choose induced/elective abortion. In the U.S., 18% of all pregnancies end in elective abortions. (Induced Abortion in the United States | Guttmacher Institute)

It is a truism in the law that once a freedom or benefit is granted by the state it becomes exceedingly difficult to withdraw it, because people come to expect it and even depend upon it. Consider government social insurance guarantees, like senior health care or unemployment benefits.

The same thing appears to be true in the moral arena. In the advanced world especially, access to modern technologies of birth control is expected by the populace and sometimes guaranteed and even funded by the state. Access to abortion is likewise now expected and even depended upon as one option for women who find themselves facing an unwanted pregnancy. Many decades ago, the massive rise in unplanned pregnancies created a demand for abortion access that ultimately met a favorable response in law and in morality. Though this is still bitterly contested by those who believe abortion to be wrong, abortion access is not easily rolled back where once it has been offered.

Modern cultures have grown to depend upon abortion. The exact numbers may rise or fall depending on a variety of factors, but sizable demand for abortion appears to be immutable given existing cultural conditions. I believe that the modern debate over the morality of abortion has been distorted by this dependence. It is hard to think objectively about a practice much of the world cannot imagine doing without.

Given this seemingly immutable demand for abortion, any serious limitation on women's access to abortion would be entirely unenforceable, at least without draconian police-state measures against women. Especially since abortion moved into its own pill stage beginning about 20 years ago, rather than doctors' offices or abortion clinics, there does not appear to be any going back.

If and where abortion is severely restricted, women with means who seek abortions will leave their states or countries for places where they can obtain a safe abortion. Women without such means will be forced to bring an unwanted child into a high-risk situation or seek a local black-market abortion of dubious safety. In the U.S., at least, that would be the majority of women who seek abortions. Nearly 70% of all U.S. women who obtain abortions are poor.

An unenforceable law, and especially one with predictably destructive side effects, is a bad law. The law permits many things that are morally questionable or even clearly wrong in Christian terms. I would say that routine use of elective (non-emergency) abortion is one of them. As Harrison herself acknowledges, the choice of abortion "is a negative, therapeutic, or corrective act, not an act of positive moral agency at all" (p. 9). It indicates that something has gone wrong in the "wider human context" of a woman's life.

I believe that what holds true for individual women can be extended to our cultures as well. Our routine practice of abortion is a tragic consequence of cultural developments of the last half-century. It is not an expression of a society that is optimally arranging relationships between men and women or managing the successful transmission of new life. It is an expression of collective moral failure rather than moral agency.

I have essentially given up on a legislative solution to the abortion issue, especially since a negotiated solution between the opposing sides seems inconceivable, at least in the U.S. setting. Catholic ethicist Charles

Camosy's 2015 *Beyond the Abortion Wars* attempts a creative and morally serious proposal that is worth considering. His "Mother and Prenatal Child Protection Act" attempts to defend the civil rights of both mother and child and to enhance support of mothers and their children in substantial ways both during and after pregnancy. But there is no visible progress on such legislation today.

Christians often argue about abortion in casuistic, technical, political, and legal terms, with little historical context or sensitivity to the oppression facing women around the world. I hope to see the abortion discussion return to a principled, compassionate, realistic moral conversation. We can ask whether the way women are treated by men, and the widespread abortion that we find practiced all over the world, fits with the values of the kingdom of God, with love, justice, and dignity for all.

I advocate for a community of Christ-followers who arrange their lives in such a way as not to depend on abortion. That would then position us to offer a moral witness to our society in which we say that it is indeed possible to live a modern life without routine use of abortion.

We can teach pre-adolescents honest facts about the amazing God-given procreative power of their bodies. Later, we can, without shaming anyone, give good reasons for sexual self-discipline for both men and women, and the grave responsibility to use birth control properly, if having sex and not wanting to conceive. We can emphasize the gravity of adult responsibilities for the children we bring into the world. We can create family and church communities that will support women and couples of all life situations who face unwanted pregnancies and are seeking alternatives to abortion. We can do all this while also, and as a part of, seeking to end patriarchy.

We can address abortion on the demand side. That's where Christians and the church ought to really make a constructive contribution. All it really takes is for us to live out the best wisdom of our tradition. Patriarchal and anti-sex attitudes deeply damaged how this wisdom was and sometimes still is communicated. But stripped of those ills, ancient Christian wisdom about the moral responsibilities of our co-creative, procreative bodily powers looks pretty good right now in comparison with the illusions and misjudgments of our modern age.

Discussion Questions

1. Why is there a 45% unintended pregnancy rate in a technologically advanced country like the United States?

2. Discuss whether you agree that modern loosening of sexual morality standards, combined with birth control's limits and failures, created cultures that depend on abortion, with laws following accordingly.

3. Do you believe that legal limits or a ban on abortion would prove unenforceable in most societies?

4. What do you think of the perspective that modern birth-control access fundamentally changed the context for thinking about sexual ethics? Until it didn't, because birth control didn't succeed in breaking the link between sex and pregnancy?

To watch Dr. Gushee deliver

Lecture 18: Sexual Ethics after the Revolution

Follow this link:

https://youtu.be/lWMX-cMXOEo

Or scan the QR code.

To listen to the audio, follow this link:

https://qrco.de/bcOlWR

Or scan the QR code.

To scan a QR code, download a QR reader from the app store on your device, open the application, follow the directions, and point your device's camera at the code.

CHAPTER 18

Sexual Ethics After the Revolution

18.1 Introduction: Fights Over Sexual Morality Mark Our Era

While sexuality is just part of life, many cultures are torn by differences of conviction about sexual morality. Christian perspectives, even in traditionally Christian lands, no longer can claim any kind of consensus. The sexual revolution of the 1960s and gay rights movement since the 1970s have changed cultures a great deal but have not yielded a stable new order. Anyone attempting to nurture children or grandchildren today knows that the context in which they are coming of age is very different from that of prior generations.

Fights over sexuality and gender identity have now become highly politicized in many countries. Whether to approve same-sex marriage or transgender rights have become questions of cultural identity rather than merely policy issues. Ending sexual harassment and misconduct, especially toward women by men, has become an important priority in many nations. Meanwhile, great confusion reigns in practices related to sexual exploration and romantic commitment. Marriage no longer plays the role it once did as the approved destination for sexual expression; it has not disappeared, but whether it is important and what it means are up for grabs.

In this chapter and the next I will return to the focus on covenant that has threaded its way through this book. I will propose that marital-covenantal sexual morality—a concept developed in scripture and tradition and still relevant for our current cultural situation—is our best way forward. It can guide behavior constructively. And it can perhaps lower the cultural temperature a bit.

18.2 Covenant Fidelity and the Adultery Ban in Scripture

For Christian sexual ethics, a good place to begin is by focusing our attention where the Bible does—on the covenant norm of fidelity and the ban on covenant violation, most notably adultery.

There is no question that this ban on adultery is the most central biblical moral prohibition in relation to sexuality. Adultery is infidelity to a core covenant promise, and obligation, in marriage—sexual exclusivity with one's marriage partner.

The ban on adultery is, of course, one of the Ten Commandments (Ex 20:14; Dt 5:18). When Jesus teaches about sexuality in the Sermon on the Mount, it is this commandment to which he refers: "You have heard that it was said, 'Do not commit adultery'" (Mt 5:27). When a teaching shows up in both the Decalogue and the Sermon on the Mount, we can know it is important.

In choosing to name this statement of "traditional righteousness," Jesus reaches into the very heart of biblical covenant ethics. More clearly than in the Hebrew Bible, Jesus applies the ban on adultery to both men and women. He demands that men curtail their own eyes and hands, rather than blame women, in relation to their illicit sexual desire and behavior. He offers no exceptions to the ban on adultery.

I propose that the fundamental norm in any Christian sexual ethic is covenant fidelity. The first expression of that norm is the ban on adultery. It is notable that amid all the ferment about sexual morality today, hardly anyone seems to be talking about adultery, which destroys many marriages, including Christian ones.

Let's briefly review the concept of covenant.

A covenant establishes a special relationship between parties. It spells out mutual responsibilities intended to create and sustain some type of community. Covenant involves the freely given declaration of promises or even sacred oaths. Permanence is normally an aspect of covenant declarations; indeed, ensuring stability and commitment is a primary reason for making covenants. Covenants have a contractual dimension but go beyond contracts in their perceived gravity.

God is viewed as the witness and guarantor of biblical covenants, and God stipulates both blessings for covenant fidelity and curses for covenant violation (Gen 9; Ex 20; Josh 24). Biblical covenants repeatedly bind God to Israel, families and tribes to one another, and spouses to each other in marriage.

A special feature of biblical covenants is their foundation in the mercy of God. God makes covenant with Israel at Sinai, but only after having delivered the people from Egyptian slavery (Ex 1–15; 20:1–2). Grace precedes covenant, and covenant is itself an expression of God's grace. Covenant is gift before it is task, because we need covenants to flourish. But once a covenant is made, it is both gift and task. This certainly applies to marriage.

Faithfulness to covenant is a norm that applies both to our relationship with God and with others. It is clear early in the Bible that covenant faithfulness will be a fundamental requirement for any individual or people that would relate to God (cf. Ex 20:3). It is certainly how God relates to us.

The Christian tradition has from the beginning claimed that the covenant of marriage is the proper context for the pursuit of full sexual and romantic intimacy, and for the birth and nurture of children. This view sometimes has been perceived as frustrating legalism, but it should instead be treated as a gift that takes into account both human potential and human need, under conditions of sin. Our powerful sexual energies draw us outside of ourselves toward others. Our intense need to give and receive love does the same. But both drives can do a great deal of harm unless given structure. The covenant of marriage is the structure that Christian scripture and tradition have proposed, and to which centuries of human experience bear witness.

The marriage covenant's ban on sexual contact with a person other than one's spouse might seem burdensome to some marriage partners for various reasons: spousal illness, unavailability, sexual dissatisfaction, relational conflict, etc. But if God gives covenant as an expression of grace, there must be good reasons for the ban on adultery. I will name three: it deepens the set-apart nature of the bond between the spouses, permitting the highest level of trust, stability, and self-giving; it ensures that any children conceived and born clearly belong to, and are the responsibility of, the married couple, which is crucial for children's well-being; and it has demonstrably positive effects on sexual satisfaction.

This list can be distilled to three main good gifts of sexuality, all of which have received attention in Christian sexual ethics. We can alliterate these three purposes as *partnership, procreation, and pleasure*. The traditional teaching of Christian sexual ethics is that the marriage covenant, understood as a lifetime commitment, is the only one in which these three purposes of sex can be pursued without fear or harm.

18.3 The New Testament Ban on All Nonmarital Sex

The New Testament extends the Old Testament ban on adultery to a ban on easy divorce (to be addressed in the next chapter) and a ban on all nonmarital sex. This was a considerable addition to the level of rigor in sexual ethics, especially for men, who benefited from wink-and-nod laxity in all three areas, compared to the tight control of girls' and women's sexuality.

It is quite clear that both Jesus and Paul posited two acceptable options in relation to sexual intimacy—marriage or celibacy (Mt 19:1–12; 1 Cor 7). Paul's extended discussion of these matters in 1 Corinthians 7 argues that celibate singleness is a good thing, even preferable to marriage for those who can sublimate their sexual passions for kingdom work, and especially in view of eschatological and missionary urgency (1 Cor 7:1–8, 32–40). Marriage is certainly not wrong, however (7:36). If married, both spouses owe each other "conjugal rights," e.g., sexual access (7:3–5). One reason for this is that the harnessing and ordering of sexual desire is one of the major reasons to get married in the first place (7:36–38).

This combination of the linking of marriage with sex and the ban on extramarital sex helps make it clear that Paul and Jesus really did intend to teach that sexual intercourse outside marriage is not appropriate for a follower of Christ. This restriction would mainly have felt like a tight new constraint on men, who in both Jewish and Greco-Roman culture had access to prostitutes—and who, in the Greco-Roman world and if of sufficiently high wealth, had socially approved sexual access to household servants as well.

This cultural background might help us understand the justice dimension of these sexual-ethics teachings and help us separate them from mere legalism. To tell privileged men that they only have sexual access to their one wife, with whom they are in a lifetime covenant, protects wives from being abandoned for other women. It also protects others, male and female, from being sexually exploited, abused, or raped by powerful men. It lowers the risk of children being conceived outside of marriage and then being neglected, abandoned, or killed. It also protects male and female household servants from being gratuitously used and abused by sexually voracious and unconstrained masters.

18.4 Today's Vast Cultural and Normative Changes

The cultural leap from that ancient context to most current societies is a large one. Where sexual and marital decisions are genuinely the free choice of both men and women, legal and cultural norms permit sexual intimacy for adults without marriage, and marriage is optional and occurs well after puberty, the entire context for sexual ethics is altered almost beyond recognition. I hasten to add that in many parts of the world such conditions are still not in place, with women's agency very much constrained. But in modernized cultures, feminism's advances, secular values, and economic changes have indeed created vastly altered conditions. What is to become of Christian sexual ethics under these circumstances?

What has in fact happened since the 1960s has been a shattering of a single shared norm.

Generally, the conservative churches have held to the norm that sex belongs only in marriage. But as authors like Linda Kay Klein (in her 2019 book *Pure*) and Amber Cantorna (in her 2017 memoir *Refocusing My Family*) have shown, their strategies for teaching it have often produced shame as much as abstinence. Many adult adherents eventually abandon the norm altogether—sometimes leaving the church behind as well. One reason is that no matter how powerfully articulated, abstinence norms often fail to constrain sexual behavior once people are in their 20s, and the effort can breed shame, leading to considerable resentment against God.

A provisional ethic of sex-with-only-the-person-whom-one-currently-loves—kind of a serial nonmarital fidelity ethic—has become a common working sexual ethic among Western Christians. I sometimes call this the **loving relationship ethic**. It can be seen as a kind of covenantal norm, but it tends to be improvisational, provisional, and uncertain.

The advent of modern birth control and loosening of cultural sexual-morality standards has also contributed to a safe-sex-with-any-consenting-adult practice—and, in a few church contexts, a corresponding *mutual-consent/safe-sex ethic.* (I know of churches that hand out condoms in the church lobby.) One might say the only covenant here is shared mutuality and safety. This is far better than the exploitation and risk one can find out there in the wasteland of the modern world. But it is a far cry from a covenant norm.

If we think in terms of those three key purposes for sex: partnership, procreation, and pleasure, we see that our current moral confusion about sexual ethics impinges on all three.

Nonmarital or at least noncovenantal sex, when it risks pregnancy, also risks conceiving children into high-risk situations and/or abortion.

The desire for trusting intimacy, for a true partner, will always drive people toward romance novels, British period dramas, and the bedroom, but lack of clarity or shared understanding of the nature of the commitment binding the sexual partners is a recipe for heartbreak.

Merely casual, mutual-consent sex achieves nothing on the partnership side, is all-risk on the pregnancy side, and may not even bring that much pleasure on the pleasure side.

These are some main reasons why I call for the strengthening of a covenantal sexual ethic and a return of a robust theology and practice of marriage. This return to covenantal marriage would be led by Christians, with an invitation for others to consider its benefits.

18.5 LGBTQ Inclusion in Covenant Sexual Ethics and Marriage

The sexual revolution of the 1960s abandoned any idea of restricting heterosexual sex to marriage. Many Christians found these changes not just disturbing but disastrous, and found their efforts to resist them treated as laughable.

By the 1970s, a new revolution associated with sex was afoot. This revolution involved a push for acceptance, respect, and full legal rights for persons who were not heterosexual, but were instead lesbian, gay, or bisexual, and for the acceptance of the legitimacy of at least some sexual relations among such persons.

Over time the number of categories represented here has grown to include *queer* (an originally derogatory term now sometimes used within these populations for the entire category of "sexual others"), *asexual* (persons lacking sexual interest), *intersex* (persons with both male and female sexual characteristics), and *transgender* (persons deviating from standard gender-expression norms in a society). All have become part of a movement for cultural acceptance and rights. Both the categories and the language are regularly evolving—this list is not exhaustive. The magnitude and rapidity of the changes can easily evoke negative reaction among those struggling to understand it all.

It is perhaps not surprising that many Christians already nonplussed by the sexual revolution of the 1960s have treated the gay rights movement and more recent developments as further steps down a path toward moral chaos and rebellion against God. It has not helped, of course, that some very public expressions of these movements have seemed to revel in shocking traditional sensibilities. These expressions often are seen as confirming the intrinsic perversity of these sexual others. Yet marginalized people often transgress dominant norms as an expression of suffering and a cry of protest.

Still, the conservative Christian response settled into a place in which it remains: belief that the sexual revolution was bad, and that the LGBTQ movement is its most egregious expression because it is the most obviously rebellious against God, Bible, church, and tradition.

As I acknowledged in my 2014 book *Changing Our Mind*, I began my career in the early 1990s assuming that opposition to all same-sex relations was the proper Christian view. I fully understand why many Christians still hold this view. But I have changed my mind.

I have *not* changed my mind about a marriage covenant, involving two persons only, being the proper context for sex. I have *not* changed my mind about damages caused by the 1960s sexual revolution. I *have* changed my mind about whether the LGBTQ movement is just another expression of the sexual revolution. I instead see it as a human-rights movement of a marginalized population—indeed, of a population often marginalized by Christians.

I now believe that gay and lesbian people should be invited like all others to structure their sexual relationships within a sexually exclusive marital-covenantal framework, rather than being consigned to sexual chaos or no legitimate sexual expression at all. I believe this to be the proper norm not just under the law but in Christian community as well.

I now believe that to exclude gay people from such covenants is to discriminate among persons based on a category error. It would be like excluding left-handed people from holding elective office, people with freckles from being airline pilots, or red-haired people from being schoolteachers. Any such discrimination takes a variation that occurs in nature and makes it the basis for denying access to rights and opportunities available to others.

I need to say more about how I came to this dramatic paradigm shift. Here is a brief statement of my top ten reasons.

1. I have come to know and love LGBTQ Christians.

LGBTQ persons emerge as a small minority in Christian families and communities like everywhere else. Unfortunately, they are often met with rejection. I now see them as the church's own most oppressed group. My own change of mind is impossible to understand apart from knowing them, as well as listening to their talks and reading some of their books. Memoirs by Justin Lee, Jennifer Knapp, and Jeff Chu are a good place to start, as is the collection of stories in Mitchell Gold and Mindy Drucker's 2008 book, *Crisis,* and Kelly Brown Douglas's trailblazing discussion in her 1999 book, *Sexuality and the Black Church.* LGBTQ Christians (and ex-Christians) often have been grossly misunderstood and mistreated by their sisters and brothers, their parents and pastors. It is right to hear the cries of the oppressed, as God does (Ex 3:7–9).

2. I believe in the Gospel and never want to see people driven away from Jesus.

John 3:16 says, "For God so loved the world that he gave his only begotten Son, that whoever believes in him will not perish but have eternal life." The issue is not just that some Christians seem to consign all LGBTQ people straight to perdition. It is that the traditional approach is so alienating as to drive LGBTQ people away from Jesus. I take seriously any practice on the part of Christians that drives people away from Jesus.

3. In studying key biblical passages, I have concluded that the main issue comes down to creation order themes, the issue of how God set up the world.

After considerable wrestling, I have concluded that the divine creation order theme derived from Genesis 1–2 reflects the majority pattern in human life, but not the entirety of human life. People lean heavily on their imagined vision of how God created the world. But we have turned the simple and innocent vision of the primordial Garden into an immutable standard for human life, even though we do not live in the Garden of Eden, but instead in a post-fall world full of mystery, complexity, and variation. We should lean forward into what redemptive relationships look like now, for all people, instead of backward into the gauzy dream-world of the Garden of Eden.

When we integrate biblical creation themes with an honest appraisal of the world as we find it, we can hang onto concepts like all being made in the image of God, all humans as embodied sexual beings seeking interdependent relationships and "one flesh" ties, including LGBTQ persons.

4. I am aware of how often the church has gone wrong in the past in misreading the creation story.

There are past moments in history when the creation narratives were read woodenly, literally, or prejudicially. Examples include ideas that the Earth must be only 6,000 years old; that evolution must be a forbidden belief; that Earth must be the center of the universe; that women must be subordinate to men because God made Adam first; and that humans are free to dominate Earth and its creatures. Just as these other readings of Genesis have proved replaceable without abandoning Christianity, so is the idea that the world as God designed it can only consist of heterosexual people.

5. I conclude that the Genesis 3 account of human sin can be applied to everyone's equal need and difficulty in establishing faithful, fruitful covenant relationships.

We need to read Genesis 1–3, not just Genesis 1–2. Doing this shifts our focus away from the issue of why some people don't fit the male/female framework. Turning to Genesis 3 brings us to the broader human problem of how we are to address our good, yet fallen, sexuality and relationality in an imperfect world.

All of us, with the partner "suitable" to us, face the challenge of making and keeping relationships that help give structure to our lives. That then links to Jesus' own strict teaching against divorce in Matthew 19:6: "So they are no longer two, but one flesh. Therefore, what God has joined together, let no one separate." I believe covenants are crucial here. That's because even in a fallen world, even in the world as we find it, anybody can be invited to embrace a covenantal norm.

6. Close study of Romans 1 leads me to the conclusion that Paul there condemns same-sex acts as part of a rhetorical strategy that is about knocking down both Gentile and Jewish pridefulness in the divided Roman Christian communities.

I have been persuaded by biblical scholar Robert Jewett's (1933–2020) authoritative account in his massive 2006 commentary on Romans. Jewett says that what Paul was trying to do there was to knit together the fractious Roman Christian community divided along Jewish/Gentile lines. Romans 1–3 is about establishing that no group is better than any other. All are in desperate need of salvation in Christ. Romans 1 pungently describes the characteristic sins of out-of-control pagans, with many hints that it is Rome itself and the imperial court that he has in mind. Romans 2 describes the characteristic sins of Jews. Romans 3 brings everyone to the foot of the cross as equals.

Reading Romans 1 against the backdrop of Jewett's description of the omnisexual debaucheries of the emperors Caligula and Nero, and through the likelihood that some of Paul's own readers may well have been the objects of sexual abuse from upper-strata males helped me see that the text makes perfect sense in relation to that world—while being of very questionable applicability to the devout 14-year-old who discovers himself to be gay today.

7. I disentangle the 1960s sexual revolution and its problems from the LGBTQ movement.

As noted, I believe that the abandonment of a covenantal sexual ethic and marital norm has introduced considerable chaos and harm into society. But the LGBTQ movement, at least the part that I support, is not about that. It is about acceptance, dignity, and rights for marginalized people. That fits with Christian ethics as I understand it.

8. I reject the perception that LGBTQ acceptance is apostasy and instead have come to perceive it as part of a narrative of fuller participation in Gospel-shaped community.

When we look at the narrative of how the early Jewish Christian movement found its understanding of God and of Jewish Law shattered by what God was evidently doing among the Gentiles, we find an example of how the Holy Spirit could be at work within a better narrative, one of full participation in the Gospel for all people. Much of the later New Testament offers theological-exegetical wrestling with the stunning evidence that the God of Abraham, Isaac, and Jacob was now welcoming Gentiles. Peter may have said it best in his famous line in Acts 10:28: Every Jew knew that it was unlawful to associate with Gentiles, but God had shown them something new. I believe the same thing is happening today.

9. I have become convicted of my own earlier complicity with a Christian teaching that actively harms LGBTQ people.

I realize it is not enough to just be politely traditional, compassionately conservative, toward this oppressed community. Instead, I am called to full **solidarity** with suffering LGBTQ persons. I look back with sorrow and repentance on two decades of not having stood in solidarity with them, but instead was complicit with a Christian teaching that brings documented harm.

10. I believe that the broader themes of the Christian ethical tradition should lead to full inclusion of LGBTQ Christians.

Themes like the expansive kingdom of God, justice for the oppressed, love of neighbor as self and the Golden Rule, solidarity with those on the margins, and compassion for the suffering are all essential. The fact that it has taken the Christian majority so long to even hear the cries of our LGBTQ neighbors represents a profound failure to practice the Golden Rule.

We are in a transition moment and one of intense moral conflict. Society is moving on. Some Christians are unmoved, and others are deeply conflicted, but there is much movement toward full acceptance of LGBTQ persons in many places. For now, though, we face moral conflict that is simultaneously intense, inevitable, and disheartening.

While that rages, I will join a growing number of Christians who stand in solidarity with our LGBTQ fellow believers. And I will continue to call all to a covenantal and marital sexual ethic.

Discussion Questions

1. In what ways are the covenant structure and moral boundaries of marriage a "gift" to people? How are they a "task"?

2. Discuss the proposal of three central purposes or goods of sex: partnership, procreation, and pleasure. Do you agree? Is it possible to rank-order these?

3. If the three main modern sexual ethics norms are marital, loving relationship, and mutual consent, which one would you say is taught in your church? Which is practiced by the people?

4. Is it possible to teach a sexual ethic that still elevates marriage and covenant without shaming people?

5. What is the status of the LGBTQ inclusion conversation in your church context?

To watch Dr. Gushee deliver

Lecture 19: The Covenant of Marriage

Follow this link:

https://youtu.be/01BaLx5mQ4c

Or scan the QR code.

To listen to the audio, follow this link:

https://qrco.de/bcOlYF

Or scan the QR code.

To scan a QR code, download a QR reader from the app store on your device, open the application, follow the directions, and point your device's camera at the code.

CHAPTER 19

The Covenant of Marriage

Another thing you do: You flood the LORD's altar with tears. You weep and wail because he no longer looks with favor on your offerings or accepts them with pleasure from your hands. You ask, "Why?" It is because the LORD is the witness between you and the wife of your youth. You have been unfaithful to her, though she is your partner, the wife of your marriage covenant. Has not the LORD made the two of you one? You belong to him in body and spirit. And why has he made you one? Because he was seeking godly offspring. So be on your guard, and do not be unfaithful to the wife of your youth. "I hate divorce," says the LORD God of Israel, "and I hate it when people clothe themselves with injustice," says the LORD Almighty. So be on your guard, and do not be unfaithful.

—Mal 2:13–16

19.1 Introduction: A Family Lineage

One day, I certainly hope, my grandchildren will each find a spouse with whom they can make a lifetime marriage covenant.

If they do find such partners, and embark on marriage, they will be part of a lineage that takes marriage covenants seriously. Their great-grandparents, grandparents, and parents all married under Christian terms and with covenant commitments.

More than in most chapters of this book, this one will begin with narratives from my family's life, and my own.

19.2 Covenant Marriage as Delivering Love

As an oblivious young person, the marriage of my father, Dave, and mother, Janice (Jay) Gushee, was a taken-for-granted fact of my life. I had little idea what marriage was for or about until childhood gave way to adolescence for me. It was then that I discovered sexual and romantic drives in myself that I can only describe as implacable, imperious, and relentless.

I was not just a beastly adolescent male wanting sexual adventure. I was also a hopeless romantic wanting love. I sought both. It didn't take long for me to recognize that the ardency and urgency of these desires blotted out my ability to think about the well-being of others; blotted out my ability to think at all, really. I was not nearly mature enough to be left as free as I was to seek what I was looking for. I hurt people during those high-school years, and I routinely felt awful about my inability to control myself.

My later self would now tell my younger self—what you needed, boy, what you were ultimately looking for, was some structure to harness and direct those drives. If you had been living in certain other contexts, the elders simply would have married you off and sent you to work.

But that was not American culture circa 1978. Given that culture, it really would have been good if the grownups had set more limits on my mobility and privacy. But they did not.

Now I invite you to direct your eyes to my mother and father.

Dave and Jay met when he was 30 and she was 28. She was a secretary in Washington; both were working for the American Chemical Society. She was enjoying her freedom, having gotten away from western Pennsylvania and her stern mother. He was a broken-hearted man, having recently extricated himself from an unwise marriage to a cruel, adulterous young woman. By his account, he married because he was told that having sex meant you were married in God's eyes. He stayed married because he was told that marriage was for life. After seven years of this, he was shattered.

When Dave Gushee met Jay Shields, he found a woman capable of both "delivering love" and covenant marriage. Her love stitched him back together. Their marriage was nothing less than deliverance for him.

In many ways they were quite different from each other. Dad was raised by taciturn Protestant New Englanders. They were a family that had lost all their money in the Depression but carried on, because what else can you do? Dad was an MIT-trained scientist; by the time he met Mom he was not a churchgoer. Mom was of Irish Catholic origins. She was a woman with a big heart, a joyous laugh, and a working-class vibe.

Mom and Dad moved to Virginia when I was a baby. The family grew over time to six of us. It was the late 1960s and early 1970s. We teenagers were gradually surrounded by more and more kids whose parents were splitting up. But ours did not. They fought. They made up. They worked on their marriage. They matured. They made it through, to peaceful retirement years together.

It was only later, as a young scholar developing a book on marriage, that I was able to understand what was going on with the institution of marriage during my adolescence. The divorce rate doubled between 1964 and 1975, and never returned to its earlier level. In her 1997 book, *The Divorce Culture*, cultural analyst Barbara Dafoe Whitehead described how profoundly U.S. culture had changed in its normalization of divorce and called for a renewed commitment to lasting marriage. Hardly any public intellectuals even bother to make such arguments anymore.

Judith Wallerstein (1921–2012) and her team of researchers followed Whitehead's book in 2001 with a striking longitudinal study called *The Unexpected Legacy of Divorce*. This 25-year-study documented that experiencing divorce as a child takes its toll well into adulthood, in general weakening confidence that one can make a success of relationships or marriage.

Twenty years later, with marriage rates and childbearing both dropping, we can still see the fallout. Our marriage culture became a divorce culture and now appears to be on its way to a post-marriage culture. This phenomenon is not confined to the United States.

But my parents defied the trend. I went off to college in 1980. By then I was a born-again Southern Baptist, so there were some morally restraining forces that I had internalized in relation to sexuality. There was also a pro-marriage culture in that denomination that added to the influence of my parents. Sex was for marriage, and marriage was good. It was a matter of finding the right person.

After some desultory relationships and then a nearly disastrous one the next fall, Jeanie Grant from the Baptist Student Union came along. It was magic. We married right after college and before seminary. Thirty-seven years later we are still together, having raised our own three children to adulthood. Jeanie was who I had been looking for since I was 14 years old.

Now move ahead to the year 2012. My father was a white-haired 82-year-old man. My mother was 79.

My mother was in rehab from a nasty fall. So many joints had been replaced by then. She had been getting more and more wobbly. She had become afraid that, if she tried to walk again unaided, she would hurt herself even worse. Two years later, she died of cancer.

When I think about covenant, I think about the way my father related to my mother during those last years. She no longer had much energy. Her infectious laugh had largely been silenced. But Dad was always there, by her side. He sat with her. He talked with her. He took calls for her because she didn't really want to talk on the phone. Dad was doing all he could for her. And that was how it went, all the way to the end.

My father lived eight more years. He was never the same after Mom died. But the family that their marriage created remained the community in which he lived, and on which he depended, until his death.

I am who I am because they were who they were. They made and kept a lifetime marriage covenant. They sustained it by what eventually became a shared Catholic faith. Their model, and that of Jeanie's parents, built a foundation upon which both of us learned to make a lifetime marriage covenant as well. For me, as for my father, such a marriage was a kind of deliverance—from loneliness into joyful covenant community. A delivering love, indeed.

19.3 Systematizing a Christian Theology of Marriage

I learned from my parents' marriage, and my own, that marriage is intended to be for life, that the hard times are worth it, that in the end all the early effort to understand each other and make difficult decisions together pays off in a peaceful grown-up bond. The best word for the nature of that bond is covenant. Covenant is what gives structure to our sexual and romantic urges. Covenant love is what sustains the promises we make on our wedding day.

In the theology of marriage that I developed for my book *Getting Marriage Right* and that I hold to this day, covenant is the second of four key terms; the others are creation, community, and kingdom of God. It goes like this:

Creation: Marriage reflects our need for deep companionship rooted in natural attraction (Gen 2:18–25). It is not good to be alone. Truer words can hardly be found in the Bible. We were made for loving sexual-romantic partnership, and most of us feel that need deeply. There is something deeply natural about the way our sexual, emotional, and romantic urges lead us out of ourselves into the quest for a partner. Most people will end up pairing up with someone sometime. However, because what is natural about us is also damaged, even the strongest attraction to another can collapse, due to unresolved conflicts, boredom, new attractions to others, or developmental changes in ourselves or our partner. In fact, what appears to come most "naturally" to fallen human beings is one ardent relationship after another till we wear out and die.

Covenant: Marriage is designed to be a life-long sacred covenant (Mt 19:3–6; Mal 2:13–16). The Christian tradition says sexual companionship needs to go beyond a satisfying, temporary pairing up. It proposes that the couple make a binding lifetime covenant, involving sacred promises to God, each other, and the faith community. The couple become "one flesh," which means not just sexual partners, but true family to each other, kinfolk for life.

The best place to see marriage treated as a covenant in scripture is in the passage from Malachi 2 with which I opened this chapter. (Biblical scholar Gordon Hugenberger's 1994 book, *Marriage as a Covenant*, offers a substantial treatment of this text, and theme.) Elsewhere in the Hebrew Bible, God's covenantal relationship with Israel, with both its challenges and its permanence, is often compared to a marriage.

The theme carries forward into the New Testament in Ephesians 5:22–33 as the relationship between a husband and wife is compared to that between Christ and the church. That text, however, was interpreted in official Catholic doctrine as teaching the metaphysical ***indissolubility*** of the marriage relationship, because of the belief that the relationship between Christ and the church literally cannot be dissolved. Divorce between Christ and the church is not *wrong*, it is *impossible*.

I accept that. But it is deeply problematic to apply this logic to human marriages. It asks too much. Human marriages are human relationships that can be destroyed in any number of tragic human ways. The idea that marriage is a covenant intended to be permanent but able to be breached by human misconduct better captures both the potential and limits of marriage, even among Christians.

I am certainly convinced that covenant is the better approach to marriage. Natural urges get us into bed with someone else; covenant is what ensures that we stay in just that one bed and with just that one partner. Covenant takes what is natural to a place beyond what fallen nature can achieve: permanence. Covenant is why the traditional wedding service always includes some vowing ceremony in which the two make a range of oaths to God, each other, and the community. These vows state that in freedom, and in full awareness of the gravity of what is being promised, we promise to love, honor, and cherish one another under all different kinds of conditions, and to remain faithful to one another till death parts us. It is a staggering set of covenant commitments, with implications that the dewy-eyed young couple can never fully imagine.

Community: Marriage is about more than the couple. It is interesting that in Mark 10, after Jesus teaches about the permanence of marriage (10:2–12), he blesses the little children (10:13–16). In ancient culture, before modern birth control, marriage and children were tightly linked. They still are tightly linked, and any adequate Christian ethic either of sex or of marriage must always ask what way of arranging adult sexual life works out best for children. The answer is clear—loving stable permanence with a shared adult commitment to the children.

When they arrive in a marriage, children are the first additions to a growing covenant community. Historically, Christians have married in public rather than private to signal that the marriage covenant is not just a private matter. It is a community event. When two pledge to become one in marriage they are forming a new community, and one likely to lead to further expanded membership, beginning with children, and if one is truly blessed, one day extending to children's spouses, and their families, and to grandchildren, and an ever-growing web of family. The strength of the covenant that a couple makes matters deeply not just to them but to many others, beginning with any children that come along, but also extending to society, which is deeply affected by how marriages and families do.

Kingdom: Christian marriage should be considered a vehicle to advance God's reign in the world (Mt 6:33). Jesus teaches us to seek the kingdom of God in everything and through everything that we do. Christian marriage is about what God can do through us in the world—beginning with our own children. A kingdom-oriented Christian marriage will be a site of service to the world, a generator of good will, energy, and love that flows out from the couple to others who need hospitality and care. I think of how my parents took in broken souls that they met all through the years that we were under their roof. They had love enough to share. They did kingdom work together—love, justice, mercy, and inclusion in community. Marriage is not just about a happy couple turning inward, it is about a loving couple turning outward to the world with a Christian moral vision.

Many contemporary marriages, including those of Christians, have been reduced to the natural attraction dimension, with covenants likewise reduced to "as long as both shall enjoy this." There is no covenant sturdiness, no community connection, no kingdom vision. This is unbalanced and ends up contributing to unsteadiness in the relationship.

Through the years I have thought of various images for how to think about the marriage covenant. Sometimes I have seen it as guardrails. Covenant is like the guardrails that keep our car from swerving beyond where it is safe to drive. Covenant sets boundaries on our behavior *based on the promises that we ourselves chose to make.*

Sometimes I have been reminded of a hammock, one of those big stretchy but sturdy things you stretch between two trees. A strong marriage covenant is like the hammock that enfolds you and holds you on a summer day. In a good hammock, even though you are suspended above the earth, you won't fall. You are safe.

These days I would say my favorite image for the marriage covenant is a tent. Not just a little campground tent, but instead one of those great Middle Eastern time-of-Abraham-and-Sarah tents. Covenant is like a tent. You first drive your stakes into the ground and put up a tent big enough for the couple. But then you make the tent bigger as your family community gets bigger. A good tent encloses the entire family within it, while always being ready to open to offer fresh air and hospitality to weary desert travelers. Such a tent is sturdy, and yet mobile. It provides a canopy over the couple and the family.

19.4 When the Covenant Fails

Unfortunately, even carefully considered Christian marriage covenants sometimes fail. Much of the history of the Christian ethics of marriage is really a history of **casuistry** (case-by-case judgments of a quasi-legal nature) related to the permissibility of separation and/or divorce and/or remarriage. In the more legally structured Christian traditions, like Catholicism, this casuistry has binding force within what is called the **canon law** of the church.

In *Kingdom Ethics*, Glen Stassen and I offer a detailed rendering of how the Christian casuistry of divorce has developed. Biblically, it is rooted especially in what is called the *porneia* clause of Matthew 5:31–32/19:1–12 (though not present in Mark 10:2–12 in the parallel text), with an assist from Paul's discussion of separation and divorce in 1 Corinthians 7:10–16. The difficulty of interpreting the passages, together with the varied perceptual lenses brought to the texts by interpreters, has led to a stunning range of positions which have had real pastoral and human consequences.

There is a long history of Christian argumentation and indeed legislation about divorce that reflects these tensions. Roderick Phillips' 1991 book, *Untying the Knot*, tells this story. Here is my brief summary.

The Catholic Church has never been able to find a way to recognize the legitimacy of divorce, with Catholic countries always slow to legalize it. The official Roman Catholic position is that separation is permissible on certain specific grounds, but that divorce and remarriage are never permissible. However, in practice, the category of **annulment**—originally intended to cancel out invalidly contracted marriages—has been expanded dramatically by the church to respond to the pressure for some relief from disastrous marriages.

Martin Luther broke with Rome on many things, including separation and divorce. He argued that separation is permissible on broad grounds, while divorce is permitted only in cases of adultery (Mt 19), desertion, as well as impotence and refusal of conjugal rights (1 Cor 7). Also, for Luther, where divorce is legitimate, so is remarriage. Luther's basic conviction here was that sexuality is a raging fire and people need marriage and sex within marriage. Rarely have I agreed more with Luther. The Lutheran churches followed this paradigm.

The Calvinist tradition has tended to take a covenantal view and to specify covenant breaches sufficiently grave to constitute permissible grounds for divorce.

The Anglican Church for centuries taught that divorce is permissible only on grounds of adultery, with remarriage permissible and blessed only for the innocent party (that is, the one who did not commit adultery).

Many conservative evangelical Protestants have taken a similar position, perhaps adding desertion to the list, but always attempting to draw a distinction between innocent and guilty parties.

It took until the 1970s, or even much later in some churches, for domestic violence or abuse to be added to the working list of grounds for legitimate divorce. The problem was that unlike with other grounds for divorce, there was no plausible direct biblical basis for this concession to sad reality. Making the concession to deal with abuse was essential, though it helped weaken the rule-and-rare-exception paradigm operative for nearly two thousand years.

During the 1970s, as the divorce rate skyrocketed around the industrialized world, churches began to be filled with more and more divorced and remarried people. Many churches broadened their list of permissible grounds for divorce to a larger and larger number. Some simply stopped talking about the morality of divorce and remarriage, and instead decided to work at the therapeutic level. Sometimes in churches marriage was treated more like an organic entity (like a plant or a person) that can live or die and that should not be kept alive after it has lost its pulse, and less like a binding covenant. The effort to ban or stigmatize remarriage collapsed.

I believe that a covenantal paradigm is better than legalistic, metaphysical, casuistic, organic, or collapsed-to-surrender approaches. If a marriage is truly a covenant, the couple has made public vows before God, neighbor, and spouse to behave in specific ways. I believe that while God's intent for marriage is permanence, breach of the marriage vows can be fundamental and irreparable enough to destroy a marriage. Such breaches need not be confined to adultery, abuse, or desertion. If the marital vow is to love, honor, and cherish the other, and to do so in good times and bad, the negation of such vows by indifference, cruelty, dishonor, and neglect can be sufficient to bring an irreparable breach. In addition, sometimes what destroys a marriage is the moral or psychological collapse of one of the partners, which makes it impossible for that person to keep commitments to anyone.

The advantage of this breach-of-covenant standard is one that I have seen as a pastor. It offers guiding questions to ask an unhappy spouse: Has their partner breached the marriage covenant? Would a fair-minded outside observer agree that the covenant has been fundamentally and irreparably violated?

This approach avoids either legalism or anything-goes normlessness, offering boundaries but not callous indifference to human suffering. With the wisdom of tradition, it knows that in a long lifetime, a covenant marriage has good times and bad times. If there is no fundamental assault on the covenant itself, if the couple can endure the hard times, they might find a great deal of joy on the other side. Covenant love between spouses is often tried, tested, and found true. In the long run, greater human well-being is to be found in tried-but-true covenant marriages than in one fragile love affair after another.

Many can attest to this experience. Among them were my parents. And me.

Discussion Questions:

1. What was the impact of the author's narration of his family history in helping you understand his convictions about marriage and divorce? Could you see doing the same as a teacher or preacher?

2. To what extent do you believe the church has a responsibility—or even the potential—to help people who are getting married to succeed at it?

3. Does the language of covenant strike you as having the power to make a difference in whether Christian (or other) couples can stick together?

4. In your church context, do church leaders (still) attempt casuistry in relation to the legitimate grounds for separation, divorce, or remarriage? What rules do they attempt to impose? What happens to people who break them?

5. What do you think of the "fundamental and irreparable covenant breach" standard as the working norm related to the moral legitimacy of divorce?

To watch Dr. Gushee deliver

Lecture 20: Where Church Meets State

Follow this link:

https://youtu.be/7RqQc-dJfUk

Or scan the QR code.

To listen to the audio, follow this link:

https://qrco.de/bcOlZF

Or scan the QR code.

To scan a QR code, download a QR reader from the app store on your device, open the application, follow the directions, and point your device's camera at the code.

CHAPTER 20

Where Church Meets State

20.1 Introduction: The Ubiquitous State

Thus far we have said little about the state structures which direct, organize, and constrain our lives. In a peaceful, well-ordered society, the young adults whose lifecycle we are following might have little awareness, even into their 20s, of the role of the state. And yet, these young adults have lived under state authorities throughout their short lives. The state has set the rules for the recording of their births, the establishment of their identity, the question of their citizenship, the safety of their food and water, the delivery of their education, the arrangement of their health care, the conditions of their paid employment, the recognition of their marriage relationships, the regulation of their driving, drinking, and much of the rest of their behavior, and their registration or drafting into the military or other compelled public service.

If these young adults are churchgoing Christians, their churches also have operated under the terms of an arrangement with the state that sets the parameters of what both church and state can do, on their own and in relation to each other. That arrangement, often delicate and contested, shaped by centuries of history and tradition, is the focus of this chapter.

20.2 Core Convictions and Background Studies

After many forays into the religion and politics intersection, I long ago arrived at some core convictions related to the complex issue of how Christian faith should interact with public life and the state. Here is how they developed.

During my studies at a Baptist seminary in the 1980s, I was taught the standard *disestablishment* and separationist account that then prevailed among most Baptists in the U.S. That account was that the history of Western Christendom, or established state Christianity, had offered ample evidence that the official entanglement of church and state was bad for both, while a "*wall of separation*," in Thomas Jefferson's (1743–1826) words, was good for both. The U.S. First Amendment, with crucial support provided by Virginia Baptists and other dissenting Christians—not just religious skeptics—had disestablished religion while also protecting its free exercise. (See Nicholas Miller's important 2012 study, *The Religious Roots of the First Amendment*.)

The unique American experiment involved a neutral but not hostile state stance toward religious groups, with such groups entirely on their own in gaining adherents, advancing their message, and funding their work. This differentiated the U.S. approach from all Christendom paradigms but also from the hostility of the French Revolution and later the Communist Revolutions in Russia, China, and elsewhere. This friendly disestablishment approach remains a highly appealing paradigm to me, even though the exact boundaries between church and state in the U.S. are constantly a matter of argument and litigation.

My research on Nazi Germany included study of the relationship of the German churches to Hitler and the Nazi regime. It certainly seemed apparent to these American eyes that established Protestant, and in a different way, Catholic, churches proved vulnerable to the Nazi version of the German state *in part because of their legal and financial entanglements*. Ministers, theologians, and seminaries that were part of the state structure and supported with state funds were obviously vulnerable to subservience to a state turning evil in a way that seemed less likely to happen in a religious-disestablishment environment. Works on what is called the German Church Struggle became important here. See Franklin Littell's (1917–2009) and Hubert Locke's (1934–2018) 1990 edited work, *The German Church Struggle and the Holocaust* and Robert Ericksen's *Theologians Under Hitler* (1985). Dietrich

Bonhoeffer's movement from a relatively deferential posture toward the state early in his career to active conspiracy against it during World War II can only be understood—and is most striking—in this context of established German Christianity.

My critical engagement with white U.S. evangelical politics since the mid-1990s has shaped my mature view. For 20 years, I attempted to challenge white U.S. evangelicals to avoid excessive entanglement with the Republican Party, which was succeeding in enticing this demographic into their political coalition by offering cheap promises of wins on a few social issues, but at the cost of Christian independence and moral integrity on other issues. This perspective was shared widely on the evangelical center and left, as seen in works like Ronald J. Sider's *Just Politics* (2nd edition, 2012), and my own 2008 book, *The Future of Faith in American Politics*.

However, in the Trump years, U.S. white evangelicals appeared to have entirely lost their moral and political bearings, with some moving into the neighborhood of Christian neo-fascism, most apparent in the refusal to accept the results of the 2020 election and the shocking attack on the Capitol building in January 2021, in which Christians were visibly present. Notably, this Trumpian neo-fascism did not require financial or administrative entanglement with the state as in earlier Christendom contexts. It only required undue loyalty to one man, a few inducements to Christians, and a host of shared enemies.

Finally, in recent years having spent far greater attention on the history of European colonialism, it has been impossible not to notice the established Christianity entangled with these colonizing states. These were state-church, and church-state, projects. They led to some of the greatest evils in world history. It is hard to see how anyone who takes the evils of European colonialism seriously could be terribly supportive of the Christendom paradigm that fostered it.

In light of the foregoing, even though I have read with respect the learned defense of Christendom provided in the work of scholars like Oliver O'Donovan in *The Desire of the Nations* (1996), I have not been able to join this defense. While there are advantages and disadvantages for both the church and the state in most arrangements of the church-state relationship, I remain a Baptist separationist.

Overall, then, my studies in this arena lead me to a highly constrained approach to church-state relations. Church and state should be kept conceptually and institutionally separate, regardless of the religious passions of the majority population. Christians must protect their allegiance to Jesus Christ as Lord, avoiding any confusion of loyalties with other lords, notably the state, political parties, and their leaders. While Christians are members of political communities, our primary communal identity should be with the global church. Christians everywhere should seek to be caring neighbors, especially to those in need around us. Christians should have a political vision tied to the marks of the reign of God, including justice, peace, and inclusive community, as well as joining others, including state officials, in seeking the common good and human flourishing. Christians should not nurture utopian hopes for the state, nor slide into despair related to state failures, because we know that the ultimate consummation of God's intentions for this good-yet-fallen world is in God's hands.

These convictions are ultimately rooted in my theology of the church and its mission, and the state and its mission, along with an understanding of where these intersect and sometimes confront each other. Dietrich Bonhoeffer will be a primary guide in what follows.

20.3 The Church and Its Mission

The church is a living human community constituted by its covenant commitment to follow Jesus faithfully. To claim Jesus Christ as Lord is to say that he alone is the One for whom we live and, if need be, for whom we will die.

The church is the one community in the world that explicitly commits to participating in Christ's inaugurated kingdom. While there are other groups and individuals that we gratefully recognize as co-laborers in works of justice, in the words of theological ethicist H. Richard Niebuhr, the church is the "pioneering community" that goes ahead of the rest of the human family in purposefully making Christ's mission our mission (*The Gospel, the Church, and the World*, 1946).

As many have pointed out, the church is itself a political community. We certainly see this in the free-church tradition with its characteristic congregational autonomy. Such congregations are independent political communities (often, but not always, democratic), with agreed constitutions and bylaws, elected and appointed officers, rules and norms for exercising political power, voting regulations, and "town" meetings.

The church's mission goes beyond serving itself. That mission is to proclaim and embody the reign of God, inaugurated in Jesus Christ. We offer loving service to our neighbors, near and far, in pursuit of God's kingdom. We create cultural expressions like art, music, film, and literature to advance the kingdom. And yes, at times we speak to political authorities, media outlets, and the public to bear witness to kingdom values in relation to pressing contemporary issues.

Dietrich Bonhoeffer famously wrote in his posthumously published *Letters and Papers from Prison* that Jesus was "the human being for others" and likewise the church must be "for others" as he was (p. 501). Being "for others" is an excellent norm for church life—a constant reminder that we exist not only as a community for the benefit of members, but as a mission outpost for the reign of God. The kingdom of God is about the healing of God's world and reclamation of its people.

20.4 Church and State in Potential Confrontation

Arguing from Paul's image that the church is the Body of Christ, in his 1937 book *Discipleship* Bonhoeffer said that, like Jesus Christ, and like any other human body, the church "takes up physical space in the world" (p. 225). As we pursue our mission and offer our proclamation, we do so in physical worldly space, some of which is adjacent to others.

One worldly entity with which we find ourselves in frequent proximity is the nation-state, with its laws and the government officials who enforce them. When we preach about the poor and serve them, when we speak about the sacred worth of refugees and migrants, when we organize to protect the legal and human rights of the imprisoned, we find ourselves in a neighborhood which the state also inhabits.

In a free and democratic society, the church will be left unhindered when our mission overlaps in shared civic space with the state's work. Certainly, we should be free to proclaim our understanding of Christian values, even if these values are not shared by the state. This is true even when our kingdom work involves protesting state actions.

Sometimes our mission might lead us to the question of whether we must directly contravene the will of the state. We might, for example, find it morally obligatory to offer aid to refugees or migrants that the state is attempting to deport because they have arrived illegally. This has happened in the United States for decades, with various sanctuary movements directly disobeying state laws. Not every Christian agrees that this situation—or, indeed, any situation—merits disobedience to the state, but the majority witness of both the early church and the modern church is that such disobedience at times may be required of Christians who are attempting to follow Jesus.

In more radical situations, the state may directly turn against the church. It may attempt to hinder, block, ban, or even destroy the church. From prison, Bonhoeffer describes this as a situation in which the Body of Christ is first pushed to the margins of the world and then, in extremis, "pushed out of the world and onto the Cross," like our Savior (*Letters and Papers from Prison*, p. 479). It should never come to this, but when it does, says Bonhoeffer, our response must be to do what Jesus warned us that discipleship requires—to take up our Cross and follow him. Even though sometimes Christians cry persecution when they are merely being inconvenienced or losing cultural clout, there are indeed real situations of persecution.

20.5 A Christian Vision of the Mission of the State

For two millennia, Christian theologians have attempted to offer our own account of what the state is commissioned by God to do in this world. We believe that if the state rightly understands the nature and limits of its mission, situations of extreme conflict with the church should not arise. Here is my vision of the state's mission.

Drawing from Romans 13:1–7, most Christians have accepted the need for political order, provided by state structures, led by legitimate government authorities. Indeed, that passage treats government as established by God for human well-being, with a special mandate to deter wrongdoers from harming others, using "the sword" if necessary (Rom 13:4).

It is fair to say that political theologies leaning most heavily on Romans 13 have tended to support authoritarian, rather than democratic or egalitarian, political visions. We will revisit the problems with Romans 13 in the next chapter. But the constructive contribution of this text is in its recognition that all forms of human community need to be ordered, they must be led by recognized authorities in various offices, and that these authorities must threaten and use coercion to deal with recalcitrant forces in human nature.

Genesis 1–2 is another text that bears some weight in political theology—perhaps undue weight, sometimes tied to literalist readings. Still, that primal passage's dreamlike glimpse into a pre-sin world has invited speculation as to whether any form of governance would have been needed in a world without sin. Imagine a Garden of Eden full of little naked families living the dream for, say, a thousand years. In such an idyllic condition, no coercion would be needed because there would be no sin in human nature. But these primal humans would still need to get some things done, like organizing sufficient food, shelter, education, and childcare for the little ones. Even a sinless world would need some governing structure.

It was a modern Calvinist vision, as presented especially by political philosopher James Skillen in works such as his 1994 book *Recharging the American Experiment*, that solidified for me this conviction that some of the most important functions of government are not related to the darkness of sin but instead to the hopeful work of organizing communities for the common good. Many things that governments do are not related to fighting crime and waging war, but instead are happier tasks like organizing education, libraries, and the arts.

Still, in a world sick with sin, authority structures not only organize human communities for the common good, but also motivate, coerce, and even punish those who refuse to cooperate. Whether in a first-grade classroom, a family, a sports league, the highway, or a court, governing authorities both attempt to advance the common enterprise and deploy coercive power to keep unruly human beings in line.

But what happens when governing structures themselves become abusive? The book of Revelation almost certainly uses its coded images to depict and condemn the Roman Empire at a time of intense persecution against the church. A careful reading of this book reveals an intense critique of the idolatry and violence of Rome. Those Christian theologians most concerned about states overreaching and misusing their power have drawn Christian attention to this reading of Revelation. This can be a helpful corrective to an authoritarian reading of Romans.

Christian political theology long has understood that various sectors or spheres of human life exist in every society, each making its own unique contribution to human well-being, each doing what only it can do, each semi-independent of others, each a good gift from God and a good expression of human creativity and agency.

These sectors have been named in various ways, but an expansive understanding would include families, religious communities, voluntary associations like clubs, educational institutions, cultural, sport, and entertainment organizations, professional organizations and unions, and various levels of state authority. Jim Skillen's *"**principled pluralism**"* approach helps clarify that the autonomy of each of these sectors must be protected from takeover by others. The opposite happens in totalitarian societies like Nazi Germany or the Soviet Union, where the state attempts to control all other sectors.

Government has plenty to do in advancing the common good and public justice, but its mandate has definite limits. Government must not usurp other spheres; for example, it must not tell seminaries how to educate students or tell parents that they must (or must not) read certain holy books to their children. In democracies, governments must adhere to their own constitutions and laws and the limits on their powers set there. Governments must protect everyone's human rights.

Governments must not understand themselves as responsible in any way for advancing the religious mission of the church, which is a task belonging only to the church. This is the core conviction behind the idea of separation of church and state, and for the legal disestablishment of religion. Baptists, among others, have tended to believe this arrangement is healthier for both the church and the state.

The church declares to the state our understanding of the state's proper purpose and limits. We remind the state that the Earth belongs to God and that no state's power is absolute. We affirm the sacred worth of each person and ask the state to respect that worth in its actions. We acknowledge that the state has unique responsibilities to preserve order, and justice, and to advance the common good. Examples of the services that modern states must provide include national defense, a criminal justice system, and a social safety net for the sick, aged, and disabled.

The church does not ask the state to preach the Gospel—but we do ask the state not to hinder our preaching of the Gospel. We tell the state that we are fully aware of the intrinsic danger of its vast powers, that we are always monitoring the state in this regard, and that we will be willing to resist the state directly if it abuses its powers. Finally, we remember and proclaim that the state is a provisional instrument of this world and this age, and that one day, all states and governments, rulers, powers, and authorities, will give way to Jesus Christ.

20.6 A Test Case: When the U.S. Started Torturing People

During my career as a Christian ethicist, I have had a handful of significant forays into the public square. To close this chapter, I would like to tell you about the most intense of these.

In Fall 2005, I got an email from the main editor at *Christianity Today*, the flagship magazine of American evangelicalism. He was wondering if I would be willing to write a moral analysis of the issue of torture. He said that they were getting inquiries from evangelical Christians in the U.S. armed forces and intelligence services who were troubled by the sudden initiation of cruel, even torturous, treatment of prisoners in the "war on terror." They needed moral guidance. Should they participate in and support this behavior, or should they dissent?

In February 2006, my article came out with *Christianity Today*, titled "Five Reasons Torture Is Always Wrong." Here is my argument:

1. Torture violates the dignity of the human being, made in the image of God.

2. Torture mistreats the vulnerable and violates the demands of justice.

3. Authorizing torture trusts government too much.

4. Torture dehumanizes the torturer.

5. Torture erodes the character of the nation that tortures.

In conclusion, I said this:

> It is past time for evangelical Christians to remind our government and our society of perennial moral values, which also happen to be international and domestic laws. As Christians we care about moral values, and we seek to vote on the basis of such values. We care deeply about human rights violations around the world. Now it is time to raise our voices and say an unequivocal no to torture, a practice which has no place in our society and violates our most cherished moral convictions.

The criticism I received for this article was ferocious, and mainly from fellow Christians. I was attacked for my purported partisanship, lack of patriotism, overly emotive moral analysis, and betrayal of Christian values.

But meanwhile over the next several years I got catapulted into a community of Christians, Jews, Muslims, secularists, retired military, retired judges, and others who deeply appreciated the article, even when they did not share its religious premises, and were themselves engaged in fierce anti-torture efforts.

I ended up leading an evangelical organization we called Evangelicals for Human Rights. We drafted a lengthy "Evangelical Declaration Against Torture" that gained a 39-to-1 favorable vote of the board of the National Association of Evangelicals. This was a shocking development for those who knew the political leanings of that very conservative organization. I submitted testimony before the Senate Judiciary Committee at their request. The Bush Administration quietly backed away from torture beginning in 2007. I got to ask candidate Barack Obama on CNN in 2008 about his position on torture. The oppositionist stance he articulated became official government policy in January 2009. As far as I know, the U.S. military and intelligence services have never again resorted to torture.

I tell you this story because I think it connects to some of the core convictions I have mentioned in this chapter.

The *Christianity Today* essay began as an effort to serve serious Christians who were attempting to follow Jesus, but who sensed that their government was asking them to do evil. While they were loyal enough to the U.S. to have joined the military or intelligence branches, they perceived that even such profound loyalty must be constrained by their higher loyalty to Jesus Christ.

These women and men recognized that the state has the legitimate mandate to provide for the defense of its citizens. They were so committed to this belief that they had made national defense their careers. But they doubted whether cruelty, abuse, or torture were an appropriate expression of the goal of national defense. Something within them was also stirred by the contrast between such brutality—even against suspected terrorists—and the sacred worth of all persons.

In writing to assist Christians with their personal and vocational struggles, I unintentionally (at first) found myself contributing to a national public debate about the morality of torture. Once I saw that this was happening, I decided to join with others in intentionally challenging the state where we believed it was breaking the law and violating its God-given mandate. The non-Christian activists chose different language than I did, but their purpose was similar. Out of love for their country, but also belief in values that transcended their country, they were demanding a halt of practices that earlier American leaders had explicitly banned, by law and treaty, and that the civilized world had long ago condemned.

You might say that the beliefs and practices of some earnestly Christian and American soldiers and intelligence officers became the point of intersection—and confrontation—between Christ's kingdom and the U.S. government. These men and women were simultaneously seeking to be faithful Christians and responsible national security professionals. They found torture to be irreconcilable with the former, they asked for help, they protested in their agencies, some went public with their concern, and in the end, torture was rolled back.

I was willing to address this controversial issue because regular engagement with public policy issues of substantial moral significance is part of what the church, and its ethicists, must do. As Stephen Mott helpfully points out in his 2011 *Biblical Ethics and Social Change*, advocacy for "creative reform through politics" is one aspect of a holistic Christian engagement with the world. We share the Gospel, form a faithful church, refuse to cooperate with evil, and seek political reform when needed. In the end, opposing torture involved all four of these aspects of Christian mission.

20.7 The Value of a Transcendent Vision

As I look back, I can see that in that particular moment in U.S. history, religious and moral voices played a unique and indispensable role. We brought a transcendent vision that was desperately needed.

When our country was enduring a public moral debate about torture, the most often asked question was not "is it right?" but instead "does it work?"

Think about it. "Does it work?" is a utilitarian question. It tries to determine the morality of torture by asking whether it is "effective." This assumes that if the answer is yes, then torture is the "right" thing to do. I knew a lot of people who were not Christians, indeed not religious at all, who were deeply disturbed by how this major moral issue got reduced to a crass utilitarian question.

Among those terribly uneasy with this were military officers and lawyers who knew that soldiers who torture violate their training, the Geneva Conventions, and the Uniform Code of Military Justice. It also included policymakers who drafted our felony bans on torture, diplomats who negotiated international treaties against torture, constitutionalists seeking to protect the rule of law, and human rights activists seeking to protect both vulnerable people and vulnerable public support of human rights.

Still, in my experience, it was frequently religious people who most strongly resisted merely utilitarian thinking. That is because in our very relativistic, utilitarian society these are the largest group of people who still believe there is such a thing as an absolute right or wrong and who still believe they are obligated to live accordingly. *Sometimes it seems that only stubbornly held religious convictions hold the power to resist the passions of the moment, the demagogues of the hour, and the hatreds of the majority.*

Those who deploy religious language and values in the public square are often treated as misguided, intolerant zealots. Of course, that is sometimes what they are. But sometimes it is also true that only people of transcendent religious vision can help societies avoid driving off the moral cliff.

Discussion Questions

1. Do you believe it is ever permissible for the church to bless, organize, or participate in disobeying the laws of the state?

2. Is the church a political community? If so, how does this affect the way we think about church/state relations?

3. A refrain of this chapter is that the state exists to serve public justice and the common good. But many Christians argue more narrowly from Romans 13 that the state exists simply to deter and punish wrongdoers. What do you think?

4. In your cultural context, has the state more often been a friend or enemy of the church and its mission?

5. Do you support the disestablishment of the church and the separation of church and state? Why or why not?

6. What are the lessons you derive from the torture issue in the U.S. as described here?

To watch Dr. Gushee deliver

**Lecture 21: Policing Crime—
        and the Criminal Justice System**

Follow this link:

https://youtu.be/tp2fbna6INs

Or scan the QR code.

To listen to the audio, follow this link:

https://qrco.de/bcOlaO

Or scan the QR code.

To scan a QR code, download a QR reader from the app store on your device, open the application, follow the directions, and point your device's camera at the code.

CHAPTER 21

Policing Crime—and the Criminal Justice System

Let every person be subject to the governing authorities; for there is no authority except from God, and those authorities that exist have been instituted by God. Therefore whoever resists authority resists what God has appointed, and those who resist will incur judgment. For rulers are not a terror to good conduct, but to bad. Do you wish to have no fear of the authority? Then do what is good, and you will receive its approval; for it is God's servant for your good. But if you do what is wrong, you should be afraid, for the authority does not bear the sword in vain! It is the servant of God to execute wrath on the wrongdoer. Therefore one must be subject, not only because of wrath but also because of conscience. For the same reason you also pay taxes, for the authorities are God's servants, busy with this very thing. Pay to all what is due them—taxes to whom taxes are due, revenue to whom revenue is due, respect to whom respect is due, honor to whom honor is due.

—*Rom 13:1-7*

21.1 On Social Location and Romans 13

One of the striking things about long experience in a biblically oriented religious community is that one learns over time which parts of the Bible seem to carry disproportionate weight.

In conservative Christianity, Romans 13 has tended to be the starting point for thinking about criminal justice. This comes from a long Christian tradition of considering Romans 13 the foundational text for thinking about the state. It is the most extensive New Testament discourse on the subject, and it is easy to conclude that here the New Testament is offering an authoritative doctrine of the state.

Unfortunately, Romans 13 offers no account of government wrongdoing or even its possibility. It offers an entirely top-down flow of political authority from God to the state and then to the subject. The text is incompatible with democratic understandings of political authority, offers no provision for protest, let alone disobedience, and explicitly authorizes state violence without any provision for accountability or countervailing checks and balances. Whatever rhetorical strategy Paul might have been employing, and for whatever reasons, the text as it stands is ready-made for adoption by authoritarian Christian rulers.

Challenges to Romans 13 as the authoritative text on state power and violence have tended to come from "below" rather than above—from communities, groups, and individuals over the centuries who have found themselves on the receiving end of unjust state power. In the United States, those Christian groups who are developing alternative accounts of state violence, and are protesting its actual use in everyday life, tend to be people of color and of lower economic strata.

This may also provide a clue why Romans 13 is popular with many conservative Christians. Where such people are in the upper echelons of society, with the preferred skin color and social location, they live at a convenient distance from most negative, especially life-threatening, encounters with police, courts, prosecutors, and jailers. They are likely to read the authoritarian warnings in Romans 13 as good news for themselves, assuring them that the state is their protector from *those bad people out there*.

This chapter attempts to offer a Christian ethical account of the criminal justice function within society. I will argue that every society needs policing, but also that the police itself need policing—a level of scrutiny, accountability, and citizen control that could never be envisioned from Romans 13 alone.

21.2 Three Encounters with the Criminal Justice System

I have never written autobiographically about my experiences with the criminal justice system. This seems like as good a time as any to break my silence.

In 1984, I was driving to Kentucky to begin seminary. At the time I had a wheezy old Ford, whose most remarkable characteristic was its inability to move faster than 57 miles per hour. When I crossed the state line from West Virginia to Kentucky, I was pulled over. I was charged with going 73 mph in a 55-mph zone. My 22-year-old self indignantly told the police officer that said speed was quite impossible for that car. He threatened me with a trip to the county jail if I kept complaining. I believe I was targeted because of my out-of-state license plate. The state of Kentucky unjustly stole some of my money, under the color of law, because I was vulnerable to it as a young Virginia driver just passing through.

In 2017 there were many awful incidents of unjustified police violence against Black people in America. Every Black person who was paying attention was angry and afraid. One day during this time I went out for lunch in my Lexus. I was pulled over in a residential neighborhood by a police officer. When he approached the car, he told me I was stopped for driving without insurance. This was a mistake, but apparently a common one at the time, as a computer system change was causing many missing records.

While the police officer was back in his car figuring out what he should do next, I reached my insurance office by phone. I was able to get someone who was ready to verify that I did have insurance. Holding my dark phone in my upraised hand, I started walking back to the police car to put the officer on the phone with the insurance guy. The officer threw open his door and yelled sharply that I must return to my car immediately. When he finally came back to me, I put him on the phone and my insurance was verified. My Black students told me later that *getting out of a car in the city of Atlanta during a traffic stop while holding in an upraised hand a shiny metal object pointed in the direction of a police officer* is a really good way to die—and that they would never have considered doing it.

About a year later I was riding as the passenger in a car driven by one of my favorite Atlanta seminarians, a burly Black pastor named Steven. We were driving along, talking animatedly, when the blue police lights appeared behind us. Steven immediately pulled over. When the police officer, who was also Black, came up to the car, the encounter took a tense turn right away. Though Steven was following all the steps that Black drivers learn to take—rolling his windows down, keeping both hands visible on the steering wheel, talking courteously with plentiful "Sirs"—at one point he sighed audibly. The officer immediately became combative—"Do you have some kind of problem?" Steven then became angry that even though he was doing his best to follow all the unwritten rules involved in deescalating encounters with the police, his tension, oozed out in a sigh, itself became a problem. They exchanged some uncomfortable words before Steven was written his ticket and allowed to drive away.

Steven and I believe that the fact that I was in the car that day may well have helped prevent something bad from happening. But we both knew that I would rarely be in his car with him. I would return to my freedom from undue fear of the blue lights, while he would not.

21.3 The Bible's Striking Sympathy with State Victims

If some of us privileged ones could read the Bible afresh, we might just discover that it views the situation of prisoners far more frequently from "below" than from "above." Rather than containing only a Romans 13 lens, in which the seemingly trustworthy and innocent state deters, captures, and kills criminals, the Bible also includes numerous cases of unjust and corrupt states detaining, imprisoning, and killing innocents.

We would notice the Egyptian government enslaving and murdering its Hebrew minority, until God acts to set the oppressed free in the Exodus.

We would notice the Assyrian and Babylonian governments defeating Israel and Judah in war, killing multitudes, and capturing, imprisoning, and deporting multitudes more into exile.

We would notice that pretty much the entire books of Daniel and Esther are about Babylonian, Mede, and Persian kings threatening to use their absolute power over life and death to destroy Jews and other subjects.

We would notice King Herod attempting to find and kill baby Jesus (Mt 2), and in the effort slaughtering the "holy innocent" babies; and a later King Herod imprisoning John the Baptist and ordering his execution to fulfill a drunken oath to his stepdaughter (Mt 14)—as well as imprisoning and killing the Apostle James (Acts 12).

We would notice early apostles like Peter, Paul, and John being imprisoned and often beaten and abused by local and Roman officials during the early missionary days of the church. We would not forget that both Peter and Paul were later murdered by Rome, notwithstanding the rather quiescent counsel of both apostles to submit to governing authorities (Rom 13/1 Pt 2:13–17).

We would notice the death of Jesus in some new ways. We might see, just as Howard Thurman saw, that Jesus was in human terms a powerless noncitizen, a mere object of Roman imperial power, arrested on false charges, given a sham overnight trial, beaten and cruelly abused, and subjected to the cruel Roman torture-execution known as crucifixion. We would not take his story as grounds to support the death penalty, as some Christians do.

We would notice the numerous biblical texts expressing sympathy with those imprisoned by states, echoing their yearning for freedom, and calling on us to do our part:

> Father of orphans and protector of widows
> > is God in his holy habitation.
> God gives the desolate a home to live in;
> > he leads out the prisoners to prosperity,
> > but the rebellious live in a parched land.

—Psalm 68:5–6

> Happy are those whose help is the God of Jacob,
> > whose hope is in the LORD their God,
> who made heaven and earth,
> > the sea, and all that is in them;
> who keeps faith forever;
> who executes justice for the oppressed;
> > who gives food to the hungry.
> The LORD sets the prisoners free;
> > the LORD opens the eyes of the blind.
> The LORD lifts up those who are bowed down;
> > the LORD loves the righteous.
> The LORD watches over the strangers;
> > he upholds the orphan and the widow,
> > but the way of the wicked he brings to ruin.

—Psalm 146:5–9

> Is not this the fast that I choose:
> > to loose the bonds of injustice,
> > to undo the thongs of the yoke,
> to let the oppressed go free,
> > and to break every yoke?
> Is it not to share your bread with the hungry,
> > and bring the homeless poor into your house;
> when you see the naked, to cover them,
> > and not to hide yourself from your own kin?

—Isa 58:6-7

The spirit of the LORD God is upon me,
  because the LORD has anointed me;
he has sent me to bring good news to the oppressed,
  to bind up the brokenhearted,
to proclaim liberty to the captives,
  and release to the prisoners;
to proclaim the year of the LORD's favor,
  and the day of vengeance of our God;

—*Isa 61:1-2*

With all these biblical texts ringing in our ears we might be ready to revisit more recent history and remember the tens of millions of prisoners who disappeared, mainly to death, in the prisons of Communist China, the USSR, Nazi Germany, Cuba, South Africa, and oppressive regimes everywhere. Not to mention those prisoners languishing in the "prison-industrial complex" of the United States. The U.S. has the highest rate of imprisonment among democratic nations, and it is disproportionately experienced by the poor and the non-white. The authoritative recent work on this problem, Michelle Alexander's 2010 *The New Jim Crow*, argues that the modern criminal justice system in the U.S. fully participates in the centuries-old abuse of state authority perpetrated against Black people.

The United States is also alone among democratic countries in retaining the death penalty, both at the federal level and in 28 states. Fortunately, its use even in the U.S. is now declining, and growing religious opposition to the death penalty is one reason. James Megivern's magisterial 1997 book, *The Death Penalty*, offers the best Christian theological and historical account of the death penalty's use and growing rejection, even as of the date of that book. Surely, a human family that had adequately absorbed the lessons of the 20th century—and earlier centuries—would have abolished the power of any nation-state to kill its own citizens. So many millions, killed by statute, killed by the state for political crimes—or for no reason at all other than the offense of their existence!

As Howard Thurman rightly saw, massive parts of the Bible (at least) were clearly written from "below" to those "below." The Jewish people, so often dispossessed, attacked, imprisoned, and murdered, produced sacred literature telling us that God is on the side of those whom governments deprive of freedom, dignity, and life.

Jesus embodied the experience of the dominated and dispossessed of the Earth. Both Jesus and the prophets before him included the liberation of the imprisoned and their return to their homes and communities as part of the new age of salvation. Both Jesus and the prophets set the liberation of prisoners as a moral task for the people of God participating in the kingdom of God. For Christians to overlook for centuries all these passages to fixate on Romans 13:1–7 has been a grotesque, privilege-driven misreading of the Bible.

21.4 Kingdom Marks and Core Moral Norms Related to Criminal Justice

I remember one time applying for a job at a radical evangelical magazine. I was brought up short by two things they told me. One was that my wife and I would be welcome to join them in picking through dumpsters to help make ends meet, as this group, on principle, paid only poverty-line wages. The other was that part of their moral agenda was abolishing prisons and setting all prisoners free. I said no, thanks anyway, as I could not agree to either position.

It might seem from what I said earlier that I would have sympathy with the prison-abolition agenda. The problem, however, is one that is relevant to all moral issues we address in this book: Even as we lean into the kingdom of God, even as we work to participate in its dawning, it is not yet here in all its fullness. This is the time after the solution to humanity's sin problem has been offered, but before that solution has been fully accepted by humanity.

The marks of the kingdom of God are always authoritative as Christians seek to address social-ethical issues and existing human institutions. But in facing all ethical issues, Christians must take the abiding problem of human sinfulness seriously, *always remembering the prevalence of social sin and not just individual sin.* If we want to build a world order as much like the kingdom of God as possible, we will lean hard into a vision of that kingdom—while remembering that the greatest obstacles to it are more likely to be the sins of social structures (like criminal justice systems) than the sins of individuals.

21.5 Elements of a Christian Moral Vision for Criminal Justice

Let me attempt to sketch out some basic elements of a Christian moral vision for criminal justice systems in any society.

Societies do need an apparatus of laws and their enforcement for preventing the very real harm that we humans in our sinfulness sometimes inflict on one another and our communities. These laws should be made democratically, by representatives elected freely and fairly, who are a part of the community, and accountable to the community. The laws should define and punish crimes in proportion to their real threat to public safety, with attention to whether laws fall with undue harshness on one or another population in the society.

All neighborhoods need policing, and all people in all neighborhoods need to be able to live without fearing the police. The police need to be compensated properly and to function within a culture free of bribery and corruption. On patrol, they need adequate weaponry but should be trained in nonviolence, de-escalation, and citizen rights—and need not be armed and trained like soldiers at war. The police must strictly avoid harassment and brutality.

All people must be treated equally under the law—a principle that is daily violated in my own society as much as anywhere else. Fighting for human equality before the law must always be on the agenda of Christians.

Every actor in the criminal justice system must be carefully monitored—lawmakers, police, prosecutors, court officials, judges, prison wardens, floor-level jailers, parole officers, and so on. Who watches the watchmen? Who polices the police? This question will never go away.

The basic rights long enshrined in democratic societies need to be protected for all. These include limits on police searches, the right to know the charges against one and not to be held indefinitely without trial, the right to a qualified, skilled attorney, the right to remain silent under questioning, the right to a translator if needed, the right to a fair trial, and so on.

Because it is the case that once citizens are detained, they lose their freedom and are out of public sight, systems of oversight and accountability of the opaque prison sub-world must be developed and enforced with special care. People are never more vulnerable than when they disappear from public view and are within the maw of the state. Policymakers, civil agencies, and religious leaders need to be permitted regular and routine access to prisons for surprise inspections, policy reviews, and interviews with the imprisoned. They must ensure that prisons are not overcrowded, that brutality is not permitted, that all have enough to eat and dwell in decent living conditions. Prisoners must never be treated as if they have lost their status as human beings or their basic human rights. For-profit prisons should be abolished because they have proven to be misgoverned due to the profit motive.

Those who have served their sentences should be reintegrated into society with care and should be restored to all the rights and privileges of other citizens, notably fair opportunity to work, fair access to housing, restoration to their families, and all political rights, including the right to vote. People who have been charged with various offenses, but then have had the charges dropped, should have their records expunged without having to ask or pay for the privilege.

The bias of the entire criminal justice system must be to limit the power of the state over its citizens, as far as this is possible while protecting public safety. State officials must never lose a sense of the grave dangers of their power and must be committed to interfere with the lives of citizens as little and as respectfully as possible. In a free society innocent people should be left alone by the criminal justice system, suspects should be presumed innocent until proven guilty, and punishments for crimes should be as limited as possible. Fines violate citizen freedom less than probation; probation less than prison; short prison terms less than long ones; long prison terms less than the ultimate penalty of death, which should simply be abolished. No society should practice mass incarceration.

The moral environment of prisons must be a matter of concern for morally alert Christians. Perhaps one reason why Jesus makes visiting those in prison a matter of eternal judgment (Mt 25:31–46) is because hardly anybody and hardly any place needs visitors more than a prisoner and a prison.

My visits to U.S. prisons have taught me that they are a world unto themselves and dangerously susceptible to abuse. Never is one more aware of the vast power of the state than when stepping through layers of security to get access to a prison. A remote location, numerous metal detectors, razor wire all around, heavily armed guards everywhere—no wonder prisoners are some of the most wretched of the Earth; no wonder so many biblical texts dream of prisoners being set free; no wonder Jesus says that to visit those in prison is akin to visiting him.

Yes, I do believe that some people are such a danger to society that they must be imprisoned. This is evidence of our sin and brokenness, both at the individual and societal level, when one considers every factor that leads a life to such a horrible end. But there should be *as little imprisoning as possible, and as much citizen freedom as possible.* The entire society must remember this: While a bad individual can do substantial harm to a small number of people, a corrupt criminal justice system can do substantial harm to massive numbers of people. For this reason the criminal justice system needs to be vigilantly constrained.

From the evidence of history, no political community appears capable of creating a criminal justice system that can adjudicate its cases with consistency and impartial justice. Indeed, such systems have been rife with abuse, prejudice, and the shedding of innocent blood. Yet no political community appears to be able to do without such a system. This is the paradox in which we find ourselves. Our best solution is to retain a criminal justice system, but sharply limit its power, and never allow its exercise without careful citizen oversight.

Discussion Questions

1. How should Christians think theologically about the criminal justice system in relation to the kingdom of God?

2. Discuss the significance of very different social locations ("embodied contexts") in relation to the criminal justice system.

3. Consider the personal accounts the author offers of encounters with the criminal justice system. Which one resonates most or raises the most questions for you?

4. How is the death penalty as a moral issue similar to or different from other aspects of criminal justice? Do you believe it is "biblical"?

5. How have criminal justice concerns been important in your local church context?

To watch Dr. Gushee deliver

**Lecture 22: Sacred Violence and Nonviolence:
The Ethics of Peace and War**

Follow this link:

https://youtu.be/HyVEsKNADNk

Or scan the QR code.

To listen to the audio, follow this link:

https://qrco.de/bcOlbo

Or scan the QR code.

To scan a QR code, download a QR reader from the app store on your device, open the application, follow the directions, and point your device's camera at the code.

Chapter 22

Sacred Violence and Nonviolence: The Ethics of Peace and War

22.1 Christian Ethics on War: The Standard Account

Christian ethics was born under the leadership of Jesus Christ, who, within an oppressive and revolutionary context, forswore personal violence, taught peacemaking and enemy-love, and went to the cross without resistance. His earliest followers imitated and obeyed him, building a nonviolent community. They did not participate in the Jewish revolt against Rome in 66–73.

Writings from church leaders during the first three Christian centuries reveal consistent teaching against Christian participation in any kind of violence or killing—including war. Believers were taught that a central mark of conversion was the abandonment of violence: "So we no longer take up the sword against nations, nor do we learn war anymore, since we have become children of peace, for the sake of Jesus" ("Origen Contra Celsus," *Ante-Nicene Fathers*, volume 4, p. 558). In the face of outsider criticism, Christian leaders defended this posture of *pacifism* as the best contribution Christians could make to the peace of Rome and of the world.

A pacifist tradition has remained present in Christianity since this early period. All competent overviews of Christian tradition on war and peace, such as Roland Bainton's (1894–1984) classic *Christian Attitudes Toward War and Peace* (1960) and Lisa Sowle Cahill's recent *Blessed Are the Peacemakers* (2019), describe Christian pacifism in some detail. The dramatic increase in the technological killing capacity of humanity in the 20th century, most notably nuclear weapons, created new interest in the pacifist tradition, as it became clear that full-scale war now had the capacity to mutilate or destroy humanity.

Newly confident and comprehensive defenses of pacifism were offered from various quarters, including Anabaptists, who have always espoused pacifism. Mennonite ethicist John Howard Yoder (1927–1997), in a number of works, most notably *The Politics of Jesus* (1972) and *Nevertheless* (1992), for decades became the most significant defender of pacifism within Christian ethics. (His works remain lucid, though his personal credibility was damaged by credible allegations of sexual abuse.)

When the Emperor Constantine became Christian, and Christianity transitioned from a persecuted sect to the official religion of the Empire, most Christian leaders did not retain pacifism. There were exceptions, but the Christian moral tradition made a decisive transition from being largely pacifist to supporting violence in order to defend or advance the Christian emperor and the Christian empire. The power of Jesus' example did not disappear, but it was sequestered to the religious vocations rather than understood as a demand for all Christians.

In the late fourth and early fifth centuries, as the Roman Empire began to weaken in the West under violent assaults by external enemies, church leaders Ambrose (340–397) and then Augustine (354–430) reworked older Stoic approaches to develop what became known as Christian *just war theory*. This theory was continually refined in succeeding centuries and remains the dominant Christian approach to the ethics of war.

However, as ethicist Kevin Carnahan points out in his 2017 book *From Presumption to Prudence in Just-War Rationality*, for decades there have been two main ways to argue for just-war theory, and they have tended to yield quite different analyses. Beginning in the late 1960s with Ralph Potter (1931–2021), these have been summarized as *presumption against war* (or against harm) vs. *presumption against injustice*. I was taught the presumption against war approach by Potter's student Glen Stassen. It is visible in the U.S. Catholic Bishops' 1983 pastoral letter *The Challenge of Peace* and other church documents from the Cold War era.

This approach begins with the claim that war is a grave evil, a deep and tragic reflection of human sinfulness, with predictably grave costs in lives and treasure. The proper stance toward such a reality is to begin with a presumption against it. The burden of proof rests with anyone who would justify war.

Those who would advocate a war must meet every one of a lengthy set of criteria to make entry into war morally justifiable. These *jus ad bellum criteria* include the following: just cause, last resort, just authority, just intention, probability of success, *proportionality* of benefit in relation to cost, and, in some lists, clear warning. These sum up in this way: Only the legitimate sovereign may make war, only as a last resort and with a just cause, only with the intention of restoring a just peace, only if there is a legitimate chance of winning, only if the costs in blood and treasure are not too great, and only if the adversary has been warned that war is imminent unless they change their course of action. This sets a high bar against war; most wars in history would not qualify. This is fitting in light of war's dangers and damages.

The other side, supported by three generations of ethicists including Paul Ramsey (1913–1988), James Turner Johnson (*Morality and Contemporary Warfare*, 1999), and Nigel Biggar (in his influential 2013 work, *In Defence of War*), says that the better place to start is with a presumption against injustice, acknowledgment of the urgent need to defend innocent people from aggression, and a recognition of the legitimate role of the state in prosecuting war. War is recognized as an evil, certainly, but so is an unchecked aggressor. A robust readiness to deter and combat unjust aggressors in the interest of justice is seen as appropriate in a fallen world, a legitimate task of the state, and viewed as an expression of love of neighbor. Often the ethicists who take this starting point also interpret the inherited criteria of just war theory with somewhat less strictness, making the bar against war easier to meet.

It is too simple, but still largely accurate, to say that more politically liberal ethicists take the presumption against war approach while more politically conservative scholars embrace the presumption against injustice view.

Just war theory goes on to propose two core criteria to constrain warfighting once it has begun. These are called *jus in bello* criteria. Proportionality carries forward as a continual testing of the good to be achieved by the war, versus the growing cost over time. *Discrimination*, sometimes also called *noncombatant immunity*, requires that civilians be distinguished from and treated differently than soldiers and that disarmed and wounded fighters be treated humanely. Soldiers cannot intentionally kill civilians, civilian population centers cannot be targeted, and surrendering soldiers or prisoners of war cannot be tortured, starved, or killed. However, it is recognized that civilians can be harmed by becoming **collateral damage** of legitimate warfighting. Indeed, they often are.

22.2 Crusades vs. Just Peacemaking

The mainstream Christian ethics tradition treats the development of just war theory as a breakthrough in limiting and rationalizing warfare, bringing restraint, reason, and a measure of mercy into the waging of war. Even today, just war theory is a routine part of military training in many nations, and it is the foundation of the laws of war recognized around the world. Nations and militaries trained in and accountable to just war norms certainly act with much more restraint than those that are not.

Many accounts of the ethics of war stop here, proposing two options for the ethics of war—pacifism, the church's original position, and just war theory, the church's revised position.

However, there are two other options.

The first of these is sometimes called **holy war** and sometimes called **crusade**. Two important scholarly works on holy war are offered by Christian ethicists James Turner Johnson in his 1997 book *The Holy War Idea in Western and Islamic Traditions* and Lloyd Steffen in his 2007 book *Holy War, Just War*. Steffen treats any holy war idea as a deeply unholy and even demonic form of religiously inspired violence, tending toward atrocity precisely because of its explicit religious motives. Johnson, though, sees holy war as a "subcategory within just war tradition" (p. 43), and not necessarily more savage than other wars.

A holy war is a war believed to be commanded by God, fought on God's behalf, led by God's authorized representatives, with specially empowered and even anointed holy warriors. Holy wars often have been fought to protect or advance religion itself against the adherents of another religion, heretics, or schismatics. A holy war is a sacred event in the eyes of its participants, an act of service to God that relates directly to God's redemptive purposes. The danger of holy war is that it can be seen as a positive good, not a necessary evil, and that its divine sanction can mean the relaxation of moral restraint both on entering into it and how it is conducted.

The holy war idea has biblical roots, most visibly in the Joshua narratives, and a long and deep historical record for Christians, most notably in the Crusades of the Middle Ages. Holy war appears as a part of other religious traditions as well, including Judaism and Islam.

I was taught a version of Christian tradition in which holy war was viewed as an aberrant moral descent, long ago repudiated by Christianity. That 'repudiation' turns out not to be the case.

Instead, as the real third option for the Christian ethics of war and peace, we find *just peacemaking theory*, pioneered by Glen Stassen in several works under that name. I prefer his 2008 edited collection, *Just Peacemaking: The New Paradigm for the Ethics of Peace and War*.

The core biblical insight of just peacemaking theory is that Jesus did not merely ban violence, he commanded peacemaking. Nonviolence is a negative—*we do not kill*. Peacemaking is a positive—*we make peace*. Nonviolence can be practiced by doing nothing, while peacemaking requires active efforts to bridge gaps, bring reconciliation, transform conflict. Just peacemaking can be viewed as fulfilling the "last resort" criterion of just war theory. It can also be viewed as transcending just war theory's own tendency to focus on when it is legitimate to make war with the better question of how to make peace.

Stassen, over time, standardized a list of ten peacemaking practices. Each of these deserves intensive consideration, and I refer you to his works on the subject. I will distill them here in this way.

1. Support nonviolent direct-action strategies that address injustice without the use of force;

2. Take independent initiatives in conflictual situation to break logjams, invite reciprocation from the other side, and offer a path to deescalation and peace;

3. Use recognized cooperative conflict resolution strategies to "get to yes," rather than pursue fruitless win/lose scorched-earth battles;

4. Acknowledge our side's share in responsibility for the conflict, confess wrongdoing, invite the same from the other side;

5. Promote democracy and human rights so that oppressed people don't feel the need to turn to violence;

6. Foster just and sustainable development so that hungry people have hope that their economic needs will be met without revolution;

7. Work with emerging cooperative forces in the international system such as global trade flows that knit nations and peoples together and make war destructive for all;

8. Strengthen the United Nations and international organizations which exist for the peaceful adjudication of international disputes;

9. Reduce the trade in offensive weapons, the spread of which makes the quick resort to massive violence, even in the poorest lands, and the fear of being pummeled by the other side, such a dangerous factor in intergroup conflicts;

10. Encourage grassroots peacemakers and peacemaker groups who pioneer local strategies and serve as salt and light in conflictual situations.

Just peacemaking practices do not guarantee that war will be prevented but they do have a proven track record of conflict resolution. Getting Christians trained in these practices directs our attention to proactive steps that we and our governments can take, and it moves the conversation in conflict situations away from the slippery-slope question of when it might be okay to start killing. Just peacemaking was Glen Stassen's most important contribution to Christian ethics, and I honor him as I bring the tradition forward to you here.

22.3 Sacred (Non)Violence and Sacred Texts

I have just offered you the old-school account of the Christian ethics of peace and war, then added holy war and just peacemaking. Now I want to complicate the issue further, in this way: It is clearer to me than ever that people, including Christians, can come to believe that either violence or peacemaking, either violence or nonviolence, are sacred. Not just permissible, but *sacred*.

Just war theory has not tamed the sinful human tendency to turn the shedding of blood into a sacred act. Just war theory, some days, looks like a puny restraint indeed compared to the tidal wave of zeal that moves men and women toward war.

At a *psychological level*, humans, including Christian humans, have sacralized killing in our bones. Most of us could never consider killing another human being unless we believed it was somehow right, even sacred, to do so. In other words, it is not only in the holy war tradition that violence is treated as sacred. It is more central to human psychology than that.

I am also saying at an *empirical level* that the specifically Christian crusade tradition is alive and well, not dead and buried. Europeans killed

Native Americans in its name and spirit; so did Nazi-era Germans (and other Europeans) kill Jews; and so did Orthodox Serbs kill Bosnian Muslims during the 1990s genocide there. Studying genocide—especially James Waller's troubling 2007 book, *Becoming Evil*, on the social psychology of genocide—makes it abundantly clear that the genocidal violence that erupted in the 20th century was supported by sacralizing rhetoric, including Christian crusade motifs.

When a mob of many thousands attacked the U.S. Capitol Building on January 6, 2021, among them were people flying "Jesus Saves" banners, and otherwise reflecting their explicit Christian convictions and identity. Holy-war thinking was present at the U.S. Capitol siege that day.

We must face the fact that the Bible and Christian tradition still contain active resources that can fund violence in the name of Jesus, alongside other resources that can fund pacifism or peacemaking in his name. It is the grave responsibility of leaders and Christians in every time and place to draw only from those resources that do not make violence sacred.

I want us to consider three biblical texts which I believe still actively support, respectively, nonviolent suffering, sacred killing, and peacemaking. These are 1 Peter 2:18–25, Genesis 9:5–6, and Matthew 5:38–48.

22.4 Sacred Endurance: Suffering Injustice Like Jesus Did: 1 Peter 2:18–25

Jesus suffered a cruel torture-execution on a Roman cross. His brutal execution will never be irrelevant to Christian thinking about violence. It is imperative that the Cross be understood as a resource for nonviolence, not for violence. First Peter offers a prime case of a New Testament attempt to exhort nonviolent endurance based on the example of Christ.

Probably a late first-century document intended for churches in Asia Minor, this circular letter addressed the oppressive situation facing small Gentile Christian communities dealing with increasing marginalization, rejection, and abuse from their neighbors.

The letter is filled with an oppression/exaltation dynamic: You are God's chosen people (1:2), exiled in diaspora (1:1), reborn, protected by God's power, ready for a glorious salvation coming "in the last time" (1:5). You will soon be exalted with Christ. But now is a time of great suffering and abuse. This trial by fire is preparation for greater glory "when Jesus Christ is revealed" (1:7).

After various comforting reminders of their salvation and demands for a way of life proper for "a chosen race, a royal priesthood, a holy nation" (2:9), the author calls his readers toward submission to human political institutions, even when these institutions do not act with kindness or justice (2:13–18). This passage begins with a disturbing and often abused call to slaves to accept the authority even of harsh masters. The theological rationale is this: "if you endure when you do right and suffer for it, you have God's approval" (2:20). Unjust suffering met with patient endurance is pleasing to God.

Jesus himself is the model. Clearly thinking about the events of Jesus' arrest, trial, and crucifixion, the author notes: "When he was abused, he did not return abuse; when he suffered, he did not threaten; but he entrusted himself to the one who judges justly" (2:23). This is submission to unjust violence, without retaliation, empowered by Christ's trust in a just divine judge.

The author of 1 Peter makes one final move which only deepens the power of the moral instruction. "He himself bore our sins in his body on the cross, so that, free from sins, we might live for righteousness; by his wounds you are healed" (2:24). In what is clearly a reflection on the Suffering Servant passage of Isaiah 53, Jesus is seen as one whose suffering is vicarious; he bears the weight of our sins on the cross. We who are not innocent, but forgiven, must learn to endure unjust suffering, and in so doing we participate in the redemptive work of Jesus Christ.

This moral instruction to the suffering Christian community demands nonviolent endurance under persecution, rather than any kind of violence. Indeed, the violence in this scene is directed at Christians and absorbed by them—never the other way around. Just as the unjust violence Christ endured won our salvation, so the unjust suffering we absorb wins God's blessing (3:14). Indeed, it draws us closer to Christ because in a mysterious way we come to "share Christ's sufferings" as we will later share in his glory (4:13). In this way, our unearned suffering can become sacred.

This is instruction offered to victimized people, giving them a way to think about how to deal with unjust abuse and violence directed at them. It had a powerful effect, equipping martyrs for heroic nonviolent endurance. It permanently affected the pacifist strand of the Christian tradition.

22.5 A Sacred Reckoning for Human Life: Genesis 9:5–6

I have mentioned that the Joshua texts are especially important in grounding the holy war tradition. But I want to turn here to a single text I believe to be even more significant than Joshua in leading to sacred violence: Genesis 9:5–6.

The peace of the primordial Garden has been disrupted by foolish human rebellion (Gen 3). Disobedience to God deepens into fratricide with the Cain and Abel story (Gen 4). Fratricide broadens to become a comprehensive pattern: "Now the earth was corrupt in God's sight, and the earth was filled with violence" (6:11). God's heartbreak over Earth is centered on the human descent into systemic violence (cf. 6:13). The Creator of Genesis 1 becomes the uncreator of Genesis 7, with the Flood. Human violence is met by divine violence-as-judgment. When the saved remnant of Noah and his family begin the reconstruction of the earthly community, the text presents God as saying:

> I will require a reckoning for human life.
> Whoever sheds the blood of a human,
> by a human shall that person's blood be shed;
> for in his own image, God made humankind.

> *—Gen 9:5b-6*

Human violence had triggered God's judgment, and now such violence is expressly forbidden. Because human beings are made in God's image, we must refrain from murdering each other. Murder is the ultimate desecration, the ultimate crime against God and neighbor.

And yet (or, *and so*): Genesis 9:6 couples the ban on murder with the command that those who shed blood will have their blood spilled in return. The depth of the sacred worth of human life is revealed by the ultimacy of the penalty for those who murder. Blood for blood. Life for life.

This text has long been pivotal in debates over the morality of the death penalty. If it is articulating a command of God to all humanity as part of the covenant with Noah, that is a potent argument for the death penalty. *Life for life because life is so sacred* is the logic. It is a logic—or perhaps, an instinct—that runs so deep in the human heart that we see it still today. It underlies much of the passion animating the criminal justice system, interpersonal vengeance, warfare, and even genocide. You killed my beloved ones, who were sacred to me; the only appropriate recompense is that you too should die. A fine is not enough. Prison is not enough. Victory is not enough. You must die.

Anyone reckoning with the issue of violence must deal with its odd, and dangerous, connection to a human sense of the sacred value of human life.

22.6 Sacred Peacemaking: Matthew 5

But Jesus does not agree with retributive violence. In Matthew 5, Jesus offers three teaching triads on the issue of violence and enemies. In the first one, Matthew 5:21–26, Jesus notes the Old Testament ban on murder, diagnoses an escalating pattern of anger that leads to violence, and teaches a transforming initiative of dropping what you are doing to go and make peace with your adversary. Peacemaking is sacred.

In Matthew 5:43–48, Jesus says that traditional righteousness recognizes an ethic of love of friends and hatred of enemies. But Jesus implies that this itself is a sinful pattern because it does not resemble God's love for both those who love God and those who do not. Therefore, the transforming initiative is to act in love toward one's enemies. In no case are we to harm them. Enemy-love is sacred.

In Matthew 5:38–42, Jesus quotes a version of the law of retaliation that we have just been discussing. Even in referring to this tradition, Jesus omitted saying "life for life" and "shall be put to death," as if the sacred logic of retribution needed no reinforcement.

Jesus instead commanded transforming initiatives. The three relevant ones here are turning the other cheek when struck, thus surprising the violent attacker by inviting him to shame himself by striking you a second time; giving up your cloak as well as coat when unjustly sued in court by an economic predator; and volunteering to go a second mile carrying a pack for a Roman soldier, beyond the required first mile. Jesus counsels those who would please God to resist the Romans only using nonviolent means, that could transform the dynamics of oppression.

Into the situation of oppression and seething violence, Jesus comes saying: Do not murder, but find ways to make peace. Do no "eye for eye" vengeance, but instead resist violence without inflicting it. Do not hate enemies but instead pray for them and seek to love them. Why? Because this is the will of God, this is the way God relates to enemies, and if you really want to be God's people you must be perfect in your mercy to enemies as God is perfect (cf. Lk 6:36). In other words, peacemaking is sacred, like God is. Peacemaking reflects how God looks at all of us—as sacred. Even the ones we think of as enemies.

For Jesus, there can be no sacred violence. There can only be sacred nonviolence. "Nonviolence" is not an adequate term, because it does not quite capture the creative, dynamic, surprising, transforming initiatives that Jesus commands here. And it does not quite capture Jesus' striking picture of the merciful, loving heavenly Father whose character is honored by such creative peacemaking. Sacred violence here gives way to *sacred peacemaking*.

22.7 Conclusion

An honest reading of history shows that, for Christians, violence has been sometimes abhorred and sometimes embraced, sometimes seen as sacred and sometimes as profane. Sacred texts have been read as providing instruction for crusades and pogroms, for just wars and preemptive wars, for nuclear wars and wars on terror, for death penalties and tortures. But other texts have been read for creative peacemaking, nonviolent resistance, and patient martyrdom. It is hard to center Jesus in Matthew 5 and get crusades, insurrections, or even just wars. It is much easier if we center Genesis 9 or the holy war texts in the book of Joshua. Much really does depend on where we center our reading of the Bible. As Christians, we are, after all, pledged to follow Jesus, not Joshua.

I teach an ethic featuring examples of courageous nonviolent resistance to injustice and violence. I invite Christians to withdraw to a critical distance from anyone who asks or entices us to go off to battle. While we have not yet attained the kingdom of God, Jesus shows us two paths in that direction. Sometimes we will have the opportunity to make peace. And sometimes we will be required to endure injustice and absorb its sting without retaliation—like Jesus did.

Discussion Questions

1. What do you think of the idea that the holy war tradition has proved to be alive and well in Christianity even to this day?

2. Which version of just war theory makes the most sense to you—presumption against war or presumption against injustice? Discuss.

3. Do you believe that sacred violence is, as the author describes, a deeply imbedded human instinct?

4. Have you ever participated in a peacemaking initiative that yielded good fruit? Discuss.

5. Do you resonate with the teaching in 1 Peter about suffering unjustly being a form of participation in the sufferings of Christ?

To watch Dr. Gushee deliver

Lecture 23: Christian Ethics at the End of Life

Follow this link:

https://youtu.be/lF3eGehkS6U

Or scan the QR code.

To listen to the audio, follow this link:

https://qrco.de/bcOld0

Or scan the QR code.

To scan a QR code, download a QR reader from the app store on your device, open the application, follow the directions, and point your device's camera at the code.

CHAPTER 23

Christian Ethics at the End of Life

23.1 Introduction: When Death Comes Near

Every living thing eventually dies. It is not just the inevitability of death but the nature of our awareness of it that determine the meaning of human existence. We live toward our own death. We live knowing that everyone we love will also eventually die.

This staggering information is not fully assimilable. Much of the time we try not to think about it. That becomes more difficult as we age, not just because we know we are moving toward death but also because death comes nearer to us in the loss of our family members and friends.

Moral questions that emerge at the end of life challenge all ministers, and all ethicists. Any Christian ethics textbook must deal with these concerns, and there are a massive number of excellent treatments of the subject. I found Harvard ethicist Arthur Dyck's treatment of assisted suicide (*Life's Worth*, 2002) influential at an early stage of my journey, along with resources provided by the Center for Bioethics and Human Dignity, including a fine 1996 compilation called *Dignity and Dying*.

While my views have altered on several issues, my conservative convictions on bioethical issues, including assisted suicide, have remained immovable. It is true, though, that as I look back on my bit of early writing on end-of-life issues, I see a youthful distance from death. The first edition of our Stassen/

Gushee *Kingdom Ethics* text came out in 2003. I wrote the discussion of
end-of-life issues in that volume. Today, that chapter feels abstract and theoretical. That younger me offers the relevant terms and concepts but has little
feel for the agony of the dying, and the agony of their families.

This chapter is written from a different place. I have now buried my
mother, father-in-law, mentor, sister, and father. I am beyond grateful that
I did not also bury a child, two of whom have had near-misses. Death has
come much nearer to me since 2003.

I aim to offer a treatment of end-of-life ethics that speaks out of these
experiences and avoids academic abstractions. Indeed, I cannot unsee what I
have seen, unlearn what I have learned.

23.2 Society, Medicine, Technology, and Death

Technological advances have fundamentally altered the context in which
moderns think about sex and consequent moral issues arising at the beginning of life, including birth control, abortion, and reproductive technology.
But technology has proven only partially successful in giving human beings
control over the procreative power of the human body. Our thinking, including our values, and thus our behavior, has changed more than the technology
warranted, and in that painful gap is where we find ourselves.

Something similar—though not identical—can be said about the end of
life. Especially in the industrialized nations, dramatic advances in nutrition,
lifestyle, medical care, pharmaceuticals, public safety, hospital practices, and
other factors have extended the life span considerably. Likewise, medical and
technological advances constantly gain victories for life against death, sometimes even defeating scourges like cancer, often extending human living, and
human dying, far longer than our ancestors could have imagined.

These advances have changed the context in which most people in modern societies live their final days. In the United States, despite 80% of people
expressing a preference to die at home, only 20% do so. Of the rest, 60% die
in hospitals and 20% in nursing homes. (Source: Where do Americans die? |
stanford.edu) The dying process has been medicalized, and so the context of
dying has changed from home to institution. I can say from experience that
when a family member dies in an institutional setting the family can often
experience a profound loss of privacy and control. Strangers intrude during
some of the most important, intimate, and painful moments in a person's

and family's entire life. The dying person and the family are swept up in a system that dwarfs and overwhelms them.

These losses are accepted as part of the price of fighting death with the best means available. But it is still true that death eventually wins, one hundred percent of the time. Medicine and technology have proven only partially successful in defeating disease and giving human beings longer lives. Medicine and technology have been, and presumably always will be, completely unsuccessful in defeating death, until Christ wins the final victory over death as promised in scripture (1 Cor 15).

What modern medicine *has* been able to do, however, is to take over the dying process for most people. This includes offering treatment options for conditions that would once have been considered irremediable. Medicine can keep people alive who, in the past, would have died far earlier. But also: Medicine can go in the opposite direction to offer options for hastening or directly causing death, if that is what is sought. What we ask medicine to do for us at the end of life—if anything—is entirely a human choice. And that is where ethics comes in.

23.3 The First Ethical Issue: Is It Who Decides or Who Accompanies?

Secular Western medical ethics tends to be **principlist** and procedural. Two crucial core principles in medical ethics are **autonomy** and **informed consent.** The affected persons (often shorthanded as "patients," although we must remember the dangers of reducing persons to patients) must be the ones to make the decisions related to their care. Their autonomy, or self-rule, must govern. In order to make sound autonomous decisions, patients must be offered truthful, relevant information related to the choices that they face, to which they respond by offering informed consent as they choose among treatment options.

This is hard enough in the best of circumstances. That's because average patients are not medical experts, they are injured or ill, and they often feel overwhelmed by the choices placed before them—sometimes by medical professionals who have lost the ability to speak comprehensibly to regular people. Often, patients face the most difficult choices at the very moments in which they are most dependent, their decision-making powers greatly weakened or even nonexistent—when they are medicated, severely injured, ill, semi-conscious or unconscious, or gradually losing their intellectual strength and abilities due to conditions associated with extreme old age.

Anyone with much hospital experience, as patient, health care provider, or both, can easily attest to how imperfect are the processes for protecting patient autonomy and informed consent. The problem, it seems to me, is with the autonomy paradigm itself. Western ethics wants to focus on autonomy, even at the end of life, when the reality of most human experiences of decline and death is great dependency on others. In her 2017 book *Human Dependency and Christian Ethics*, Sandra Sullivan-Dunbar is on target in elevating dependency as a moral reality and in seeking to develop an ethic of dependent care.

Medical practice, ratified by law in many nations, has responded to obvious patient difficulty in exercising autonomy at the end of life mainly by offering procedures for declaring one's choices in advance. In the U.S. these were first called ***living wills*** and then ***advance directives***. These have moved into the realm of standard documents that states provide, and hospitals, doctors, or lawyers deploy, to help individuals make medical decisions in advance. These documents generally are framed today as offering a spectrum of choices concerning how aggressive people want health care providers to be in sustaining their lives under such extreme conditions as severe brain damage, or permanent dependence on a breathing machine.

There are three fundamental problems with such documents. First, they assume a continuity of preference between, for example, a healthy 55-year-old person filling out some papers and a gravely ill 85-year-old in a medical crisis. Second, these documents are, and can only be, vague and generic, whereas medical situations are detailed and specific. Third, the whole advance directive paradigm fails to take account of the fact that when most people head to the hospital, they bring not just a document (if they even do that) but also loved ones who will almost always become the central decision-makers regardless of what a document says.

This is why the move to supplement or replace advance directives with a document that we call in the U.S. ***durable power of attorney for health care*** has been wise. Rather than vague direction specified years in advance by an individual, that same individual names a power of attorney for health care (sometimes called a ***health-care surrogate*** or ***proxy decision-maker***), a trusted person to make decisions in their best interests.

Health care surrogacy is grounded in the concept of **substituted judgment**. The proxy substitutes his or her judgment for the disabled patient, either by attempting to do just what the patient said in advance they would have wanted, or by altering or overriding that advance judgment based on the proxy's determination of what is best for the patient in the precise situation. Even with a proxy, patient autonomy is being respected at a legal/moral level because the patient is the one who has designated the proxy for just such a moment. The proxy supplements, aids, or even substitutes his or her judgment for that of the patient, who is no longer able to function autonomously.

This is a fearsome responsibility. Anyone who has ever been a health care surrogate knows this to their core. The role has its profound moral complexities, including the issue of whether the proxy must do what the sick person attempted to specify in advance or whether to make a different decision based on relevant factors in the current health crisis.

Complicating matters is that the interests of the proxy are not necessarily identical with that of the gravely ill patient. Perhaps we are talking about a proxy watching a small inheritance draining away day by day through expensive end-of-life care of their parent, thus creating a financial incentive to discontinue treatments. Plus, a loving proxy is dealing with his or her own emotional trauma as they watch a loved one suffer and perhaps move toward death, so the proxy's own functioning is somewhat impaired. Or perhaps the proxy has unresolved issues with the loved one and cannot bear to make a decision that might lead to a quicker end because they desire time for reconciliation.

My own end-of-life experiences with dying loved ones lead me to the conclusion that the autonomy/informed consent/substituted judgment ethical proceduralism does not at all capture what bedside decision-making is like when a dying person is surrounded by people who actually love them. What a sterile formula—Patient A fills out a form in 2005 and the decision-making of their loved ones by the bedside is supposedly irrelevant compared to this old form! It does not happen that way in real life, and it should not happen that way in real life. That's because what is really going on in that hospital room or nursing home involves a *community* (a family, usually) not just a once-autonomous patient.

I submit that the first ethical issue is therefore not so much who *decides*, but who *accompanies*.

In the best case, a dying person is accompanied by people who love them fiercely and will do everything they can—in their grieving, addled, imperfect way—to love their person faithfully to the very end. The covenants that have bound the dying person to family and dear friends are tested and revealed at the bedside. What we should all want is to have people with us when we are fading who love us dearly and who will do their best for us as we meet our death.

When one experiences the total vulnerability of dying persons, and the ineffable comfort they feel when surrounded by love, knowing that the decisions being made for them come solely out of love, it becomes utterly clear that it is covenant love far more than legal documentation that ensures the proper care of the dying.

My father had as his decision-making and caregiving community his children and their spouses. We were there, in large part, because of the marriage covenant he and Mom had made and kept with each other, and the covenant he had made and kept with his children, over six decades.

In a society like the contemporary U.S., finding and keeping such love seems comparatively rare. This raises profound questions as to what health care at the end of life is going to look like going forward. It certainly seems that more and more people will die alone, utterly dependent on the good will of health care professionals, who will be the last ones to accompany them on their earthly journey. Most health care professionals are at least implicitly aware of their own covenant responsibilities to patients. (See William F. May's important 2000 book *The Physician's Covenant*, on this theme.) But doctors, nurses, and aides are not family members, and they cannot be expected to offer what families do.

23.4 The Ultimate Ethical Issue: Whether We Wait for Death

The ultimate ethical issue at the end of life is whether we wait for death or instead hasten it. A massive and sometimes confusing vocabulary in ethics, law, and health care has developed around this distinction. Let me see if I can simplify it.

Modern living conditions in advanced societies have extended the average human lifespan considerably, as we have noted. Diseases and conditions that would once have killed people have proven beatable. People are living far longer. But eventually minds and bodies wear out and death comes to everyone.

In my experience, the *examination/diagnosis/treatment* paradigm rules to the end in modern health care. Doctors look for what is "wrong" with the patient, come up with a diagnosis, and offer treatment options. What modern people have gradually discovered is that after a while these treatments may no longer be worth the trouble. Indeed, examination/diagnosis/treatment may no longer even be the right paradigm.

Here is a person who is very old and their body is wearing out. His condition is bodily breakdown or system shutdown due to extreme old age. There is no treatment for extreme old age. In such cases, it is sometimes best to discontinue various largely futile treatments and shift to a posture of helping the person prepare to die. The patient might die a bit sooner because, for example, their cancer is no longer being treated with chemotherapy. But he was going to die soon anyway, and the treatment is causing more suffering than it is preventing.

The decision to discontinue treatment when more could be attempted used to be called **passive euthanasia**. This is most certainly not a helpful term to use. Perhaps the old-fashioned phrase *letting nature take its course* remains the simplest and most accurate description. The decision to no longer intervene with high-end medicine is often the best one and is in most cases not morally objectionable at all. It recognizes that death comes to all of us. Stopping the fight against an insurmountable diagnosed condition is often a step in the direction of dignity, humanity, and easing of suffering.

Let's say we do let nature take its course and the person begins to move toward death. In most circumstances this process takes a while. Even an ill or extremely aged body does not give up immediately. There is a dying process. It can take months, weeks, or days. While details and timing vary, these last weeks or days are always difficult and at times awful, both for the dying person and for the family members supporting them.

The ancient Jewish and Christian traditions have forbidden any hastening of this process because of the belief that God does not permit us to be the ones to end a human life. I will say more about this but for now I want to note the remarkable restraint that this tradition creates. A person that we love is dying in our presence. Her mind and body are shutting down. She loses interest in eating. Eventually she loses interest in drinking. Her body begins to change markedly and disturbingly. She can experience times of great distress and agitation. Sometimes mental or physical pain can become acute. For family there are moments of great sadness, fear, and maybe even horror. The last week or two can seem like it takes months.

Though everyone is suffering, though there is little or no quality of life remaining for the dying person, though she becomes completely unable to defend herself or even express an opinion, what the rest of us decide to do is … basically, wait. We keep vigil. We wait. We pray. We rub their backs. We give them palliative medication. We sing to them. We stay up nights. We wait some more. With an excessive dose of pain medicine or a hand over the mouth and nose she could be gone. But we do *not* do that. We wait still further. Finally, when she dies, on her own, and only then, it is over.

Active euthanasia is one term that has been given for refusing to wait—for actively hastening death at the end of life. When active euthanasia is what the patient desires, it is sometimes called *voluntary active euthanasia*. *Physician-assisted suicide* is the term for when a doctor helps someone hasten death—if death is sought by the patient and the state permits it. Some approaches to physician-assisted suicide allow doctors to administer lethal drugs directly, while others limit doctors to prescribing drugs that patients or families administer. Either way, if what the person dies of is the drug intended to cause death, this is assisted suicide.

Now that some societies have begun to abandon it, the remarkable nature of our former moral restraint becomes clearer. We have believed that it is not right for any human being to intervene to bring death, even to a dying person. Our human task, we have believed, is to bear the dying through that last dark night, to accompany them until they take their last breath, without us doing anything to hasten it.

It is this restraint that is now under question or has been abandoned in law and/or ethics, in certain localities. Where I write, in the state of Georgia, in the United States, actively causing the death of a dying person is still treated as murder. But in a number of nations, and now nine U.S. states, this legal norm has been partly or wholly abandoned. Whether that should happen is the ultimate end-of-life ethical issue. I believe the embrace of active euthanasia is a great mistake. But it takes a bit more Christian ethics to show you why I believe this.

23.5 Which Moral Vision Shall Govern?
Nietzsche vs. Bonhoeffer

In his 1878 book *Human, All Too Human*, German philosopher Friedrich Nietzsche (1844–1900) had this to say about the end of life:

> Why, aside from the demands of religion, [is it] more praiseworthy for a man grown old, who feels his powers decrease, to await his slow exhaustion and disintegration, rather than to put a term to his life with complete consciousness? In this case, suicide is quite natural, obvious, and should by right awaken respect for the triumph of reason (p. 60).

And this, from his 1889 book *Twilight of the Idols*:

> To die proudly when it is no longer possible to live proudly. Death of one's own free choice, death at the proper time, with a clear head and joyfulness, consummated in the midst of children and witnesses: so that an actual leave-taking is possible while he who is leaving is still there, likewise an actual evaluation of what has been desired and achieved in life, an adding-up of life—all of this in contrast to the pitiable and horrible comedy Christianity has made of the hour of death (Section 36, p. 88).

Contrast Nietzsche's moral vision about the end of life with that of Dietrich Bonhoeffer. Bonhoeffer wrote his secret book *Ethics* in awareness of the Nazi "euthanasia" campaign against those people the Nazis called "unworthy of life":

> If we nevertheless must say that self-murder is reprehensible, we can do so not before the forum of morality or of humanity, but only before the forum of God. The self-murderer is guilty before God alone, the creator and lord of the person's life ... Unbelief hides from people in a disastrous way the fact that even self-murder does not deliver them out of the hand of God, who has prepared their destiny. Unbelief does not recognize, beyond the gift of bodily life, the Creator and Lord who alone

has the right to dispose over creation … The right to self-murder breaks down only before the living God (pp. 198, 202).

At one level these two Germans—the 19th century Nietzsche and the 20th century Bonhoeffer—could hardly seem more different in their moral visions. Nietzsche favors suicide as a proud act of self-assertion before one falls into "exhaustion and disintegration," evocative terms which aptly describe many people's dying process. Bonhoeffer says precisely the opposite, that "self-murder is reprehensible."

But at another level they appear to agree. It is only "the demands of religion" (Nietzsche) and "only … the living God" (Bonhoeffer) that bans self-murder. Still today, it is true: A main reason for banning the hastening of death is the belief that "the Creator and Lord … alone has the right to dispose over creation." Where that belief fades, the moral norm against hastening death also fades.

There are, in fact, other good reasons not to give ground here. It should certainly be sobering that Nietzsche went on to argue that physicians have a duty to participate in "the ruthless suppression and sequestration of degenerating life," including the dying. Physicians indeed took the lead in engineering an *involuntary euthanasia* campaign in Nazi Germany that took over 100,000 lives, which is the main reason Bonhoeffer took up the subject, and which he fiercely opposed. Sometimes today one runs into accounts of medical personnel believing it to be their heroic responsibility to end the lives of patients they consider to be suffering too much or otherwise living on too long. Many medical ethicists believe that it is not good for the medical profession to integrate killing into their work under any circumstances—both we and they need to know that their job is to be *for life*, period. Here the ancient Greek Hippocratic Oath combines with the biblical tradition to set a moral boundary that most medical professionals still find to be impermeable. Physicians heal and comfort, never kill.

I was glad for that clear boundary as we undertook at-home hospice care for my father during his last 10 days of life. Everyone involved—our doctor, a hospice nurse, aides whom we paid to keep us and Dad company overnight, and all family members—understood that we were going to keep vigil with Dad until he drew his last breath.

Some of these moments were excruciating, grievous, and even horrifying. Dad himself, in some of his last lucid comments, wondered why it was "taking so long" for him to die. He was ready to die. Yet he too understood that no one caring for him was going to hasten his death, and as a loyal Catholic Christian he supported this decision.

Control over the exact moment when David Elwood Gushee was to die belonged to the same God who had sent him into the world in January 1930 and had sustained his life through many perils over nine decades.

Dad went when God deemed it was his time. Not a moment before.

Discussion Questions

1. Have you developed a written document that names your health care surrogate or offers advance directives as to your care? Why or why not?

2. What are the laws concerning assisted suicide in your state or nation? What is your opinion of them?

3. Are there lessons you can share from your experience of the dying process, either in your family or in ministry, that help inform your moral thinking?

4. See if you can restate the distinction between waiting for death and hastening it. How is that distinction clarified (or not) by terms like passive vs. active euthanasia?

5. What do you think are a minister's most significant responsibilities with dying persons and their families?

To watch Dr. Gushee deliver

**Lecture 24: The Moral Dimension
of the Ministerial Vocation**

Follow this link:

https://youtu.be/AIqkDQRG9LQ

Or scan the QR code.

To listen to the audio, follow this link:

https://qrco.de/bcOleP

Or scan the QR code.

To scan a QR code, download a QR reader from the app store on your device, open the application, follow the directions, and point your device's camera at the code.

CHAPTER 24

The Moral Dimension of the Ministerial Vocation

Remember your leaders, those who spoke the word of God to you; consider the outcome of their way of life, and imitate their faith ... Obey your leaders and submit to them, for they are keeping watch over your souls and will give an account. Let them do this with joy and not with sighing—for that would be harmful to you.

—*Heb 13:7, 17*

24.1 Ethics for Christian Ministers

As we make our way toward the end of this book, in view of my intended audience I believe that we need to devote some attention to the special moral obligations of Christian ministers. Clergy members accompany their congregants through life from infancy to the deathbed and beyond. Ministers are not just called to be good human beings or faithful disciples of Jesus. We are called to something more, to responsibilities that are unique to this ministerial vocation.

There is a meaningful body of literature that has been developed in the last generation under the heading of *ministerial ethics*. Works such as Gaylord Noyce's (1926–2009) *Pastoral Ethics* (1988), Walter Wiest (1920–2017) and Elwyn Smith's 1990 *Ethics in Ministry*, and Joe Trull and James Carter's *Ministerial Ethics* (2nd edition, 2004) have attempted to articulate the specialized moral responsibilities of clergy.

Noyce organizes his discussion around the primary tasks of the minister: leadership, preaching and teaching, pastoral care, financing ministry, relating to other clergy, community outreach and service, public relations, evangelism, church growth, and management of personal life.

Wiest and Smith focus on issues of truth, authority, character, and relationships. Joe Trull and James Carter address ministerial vocation, moral choices, personal life, congregational, collegial, and community relations, and the issue of clergy sexual abuse. Trull and Carter also suggest that ministers draft a code of ethics to govern their ministry, and share it with their congregations.

Most ministerial-ethics books address the issue of whether ministers should be considered "professionals," and whether ministerial ethics is a form of *professional ethics*. The answer tends to be that ministry is a profession, while also being more than a profession, and that it is important for ministers to think systematically about their professional ethics. Karen Lebacqz, noted earlier for her work on justice, helped bring the professional ethics discussion into contact with ministerial ethics through her 1985 book *Professional Ethics*. But it took some time before ministerial ethics began to be treated routinely as a species of professional ethics, and even today the idea is an unfamiliar one in many Christian settings.

But professionalizing the ethics of ministers is indeed needed, At least in many U.S. church settings, many churches do not adequately prepare, educate, examine, guide, or regulate the ministers who serve them. In a time in which most professions are making significant efforts in professional ethics, ministerial professional-ethics standards are often nebulous and woefully inadequate, and ministers too often drift or rush headlong into moral disaster. Abuse of power, financial misconduct, sexual abuse and immorality, violations of confidentiality, spiritual manipulation, and other forms of misconduct are reported routinely and create grave problems for those who are affected.

Ministerial ethics is not just about developing a code of ethics, informing clergy about their legal responsibilities, and providing a structure of oversight for the work of ministers. While all this needs to happen, ministerial ethics is also about two prior questions: whether churches can still provide a context in which spiritually and morally mature persons sense a call to ministry, and whether ministerial training, in seminaries or elsewhere, will refine these budding ministers to become persons of sustained integrity and faithful service.

There is another dimension of ministerial ethics: the role of the minister in shepherding Christians toward faithful discipleship.

24.2 Sondra Wheeler on *The Minister as Moral Theologian*

On this theme, we turn to *The Minister as Moral Theologian*, a 2017 work by Methodist ethicist Sondra Wheeler. This book reminds us that ministers are not just responsible for developing strong personal morality and professional ethics, but are also, as Hebrews 13 reminds us, charged with looking after the moral well-being of our flocks.

Ministers study ethics, not just so we can become better Christians but so that we can become more competent guides on the discipleship journey of those we serve. It is a major viewpoint shift when we move from considering what all this material means for *me* to what it means for *them*—all those we will serve in ministry, all those for whom we bear sacred responsibility.

Sondra Wheeler was trained at Yale University and served until 2021 at Wesley Seminary. She has offered throughout her career a version of Christian ethics oriented toward the formation of morally serious Christian disciples—and morally serious Christian ministers to serve them. Her love for the church has motivated her work in Christian ethics. That is very much how I understand my own vocation as a Christian ethicist. I do Christian ethics as an expression of my prior call to Christian ministry.

24.3 Wheeler's Central Claims

The central claim of *The Minister as Moral Theologian* is that all ministers are moral theologians (another term for Christian ethicist). While Wheeler seems especially to be thinking of pastors and other congregational ministers, she does not exempt those serving in other ministerial posts, such as pastoral counselors or chaplains, from the same moral responsibility. I fear that the proliferation of ministerial vocations outside of the churches, with professional formation and ethical expectations that likewise come from outside the churches, to some extent threatens the clarity of ministerial identity and ethics.

Wheeler knows the idea that ministers are moral theologians for those whom they serve is not universally shared among ministers. That is not just because of weaknesses in ministerial formation. It is also because not all ministers—or Christians—understand the church to be "a body that must be a moral community if it is to retain its identity as the church" (p. xiii). In practice, some churches are not communities of serious moral purpose as an expression of discipleship. But, for Wheeler, when that is the case the church has fundamentally lost its way.

Wheeler argues that "a church must be a moral community in the deepest sense in order to retain its identity as a witness to the gospel and a sign of the reign of God" (p. 7). If the church is not a community that seeks to follow Jesus faithfully, we are not the church—regardless of what the sign on our building might say.

Moreover, if we are not a community serious about following Jesus, we also fail our mission in a core aspect, because we do not give any evidence to the world that the claims of the Gospel are true. I imagine many of you can think of sad cases of churches in which this is exactly what has happened—a public moral scandal or collapse, leading to massive credibility loss, resulting in derision toward our claims about Jesus.

But if the church is a serious moral community seeking to follow Jesus, this has implications for what ministers must be and do. We occupy the pastoral office, which is consecrated to serve the church in its quest for faithfulness to Christ. One aspect of this office is that we must be the in-house moral theologians for our people. We must have the knowledge, character, and skills to perform this role. Wheeler further specifies that our goal should be to encourage the church to be a community of moral discernment, formation, conversation, reform, and reconciliation. We must seek this through all aspects of our work, including preaching, teaching, and counseling, and in our personal conduct, especially amid difficult congregational relationships and power dynamics.

24.4 Morally Responsible Preaching

Wheeler argues that quality Christian preaching requires us skillfully to interpret the text, the current moment, and the listening community. Good preaching is not just a matter of developing excellent exegetical skills in relation to scripture, though these are, of course, essential. It is also a matter of being able to read the moment and the audience, to have a sense for what a timely word looks like in the precise context of these people—this text—this moment. Preaching is so deeply contextual in terms of both moment and audience that few sermons can just be picked up and reused without alteration in different times and contexts. While your exegetical work on a text may be able to cross over, everything else will probably require reworking.

Dealing with the most difficult biblical passages and contemporary moral issues requires trust between congregation and preacher. Trust is built up over time, earned through our caring performance in countless pastoral situations, and ultimately rooted in the congregation's sense of our character, vocation, and love for God and the church. Many fiery young ministers forget this. They run directly from seminary to a congregation, say something perhaps true but also incendiary in the first month, and end up selling shoes or cookies a few months after that.

This is not an excuse, though, for failing forever to address hard texts or issues. Perhaps you have experienced preachers who never seem to get around to morally significant texts or morally important contemporary issues. They offer pablum week after week because they think it will help keep their people happy and the minister's family in food and diapers. Wheeler is right that this approach is an abdication of the minister's vocation as moral theologian. She is also correct in saying that silence itself teaches, and that sometimes things happen in the world, nation, neighborhood, or congregation to which the morally responsible minister must respond. There are also central texts—such as the Sermon on the Mount—that raise crucial moral issues and must be addressed periodically in the preaching program of the minister. We are not free to "edit the Word" (p. 34), says Wheeler; we must address what is there and we must do so honestly, though with great sensitivity to our audience and moment.

Here is a suggestion drawn from my experiences as an interim pastor: Develop a preaching program that offers a balanced diet of scriptures, themes, and issues. If you are concerned that people will think you are likely to overdo the "ethics stuff," surprise them with the breadth of your theological and biblical interests. In one long-term interim I did a sermon series on the Cross, the Gospel of John, the Holy Spirit, the parables of Jesus, Christian practices, and several rounds of Advent. Even though I am a Christian ethicist, I did not load up my sermon time on Christian ethics.

There were times when I had to address divisive social-ethical-political issues in a politically diverse congregation. I was able to do that successfully because I had not worn out my people with constant preaching on contested topics. In Wheeler's terms, I had earned their trust, partly by my regular pastoral-care attentions, but also by regular theological sermons. When it was time to go hard on the ethical issues, I was able to do so and keep the congregation with me.

24.5 Morally Responsible Teaching

Wheeler distinguishes between preaching and teaching about moral issues. She sees both as exercises of the minister-as-moral-theologian but as involving different processes and skills. As a Baptist minister, I think of the distinction between the 20-minute Sunday morning sermon and the long-form teaching opportunities that might happen in educational programming or retreats.

When speaking of the teaching role, Wheeler emphasizes that teaching competently about moral issues involves thoughtful use of scripture, tradition, reason, and experience. Moral teaching, says Wheeler, requires not just tossing off opinions about moral issues, but showing the sources from which those views come, giving clear reasons for your position based on those sources, and demonstrating awareness of counterarguments that, in the end, you choose to reject. Wheeler is arguing for ministers demonstrating both moral arguments and their process for developing them. This approach has the virtue of showing the congregation *how* to think, not just *what* to think. It also can invite the community into a rigorous deliberation process on contested issues.

24.6 Morally Responsible Counseling

In *Minister as Moral Theologian*, Wheeler pleads with Christian ministers to reject value-neutral approaches in counseling and instead to offer Christian moral counsel fit for a community that is serious about discipleship. Wheeler knows that her approach cuts against common approaches in secular counseling, some of which have migrated to Christian counseling and pastoral care.

When you go to a secular counselor, probably they have been trained to ask you what your goals and values are and to align their counseling accordingly. The counselor is not to impose her goals and values but instead help you achieve yours.

But, says Wheeler, the Christian minister represents the Christian community. He or she is the bearer of the tradition and the holder of an office with a distinctive responsibility—to keep watch over the souls of the flock. This means that the minister cannot be value-neutral in counseling, but instead aims to help the professed Christian follow Jesus. Wheeler writes:

> A minister cannot simply accept uncritically whatever life goal or strategy parishioners offer and neutrally set about helping them to achieve the proffered aims by whatever means come to hand. Rather, the minister must engage with the counselee in the work of discernment, of coming to moral clarity and judgment, and must call the person to faithfulness in this work as an aspect of discipleship (pp. 4–5).

This does not mean that the minister starts preaching at the counselee. Wheeler offers strategy tips like asking questions, listening, offering general care and support, and engaging the imagination. But Wheeler firmly says that Christian counseling falls into the tradition of *aided Christian moral discernment*. If a congregant is on a path that clearly violates the way of Jesus, and if she cannot or will not see that for herself, eventually she will need to be challenged and admonished, perhaps called to repentance and reminded of God's forgiveness for those who repent. Even in a context of love and support, of faithful journeying together with the congregant, the goal is to help believers follow Christ faithfully. Ministers may not always find congregants willing to be guided toward that goal, but we are certainly not free to abandon the goal ourselves.

I remember a situation from decades ago in which a young man active in our church decided to have an affair while his wife was pregnant, and then left her for the other woman. This man later went to our pastor and looked for his support in a quick second marriage. The pastor offered that support and in fact performed the wedding himself. In several tense conversations within the church about this matter, the pastor said that "who am I to judge?" was his philosophy in such situations.

I am confident that Wheeler would say this is both a misunderstanding of what the New Testament teaches about "judging" and a gross abdication of pastoral moral responsibility. I agree, even though I know that attempting to do anything more corrective or confrontational in such a situation can be vocationally risky—especially when the member holds substantial power in the congregation. Ministers need to keep their suitcases metaphorically (or literally) packed, aware that moments such as these can arise at any time.

24.7 The Minister's Moral Example

Wheeler acknowledges that ministers face "constant scrutiny" (p. 111) and are expected to be moral exemplars. This pressure is remarked upon by most ministers and often deeply resented. Wheeler recognizes that life in the ministerial "fishbowl" is highly stressful, and that ministers can be the objects of judgment and gossip quite undeservedly.

However, says Wheeler, it is certainly clear that glaring moral failure in ministry is disastrous for all concerned. Indeed, that is what most ministerial ethics textbooks focus on: the most egregious instances of clergy misconduct, often related to sex. But, she adds, even moral "mediocrity" (p. 112) on the part of ministers is problematic. Congregants and society in general look to us as models, judging our words by the quality of our lives. If our office is to shepherd communities whose calling is to follow Christ faithfully, not obvious failure alone but also lazy mediocrity presents an obvious vocational problem.

Wheeler writes with great sensitivity about how, if ministers are moral models, we are "models made of clay" (p. 115)—and we must be the very first to acknowledge this. The journey of Christian discipleship is a vulnerable one, empowered by God's grace, a long process of growth in love, humility, and maturity. We are not capable in our own power of becoming "signs that point to the possibility of goodness overcoming evil" (p. 118), but by God's grace we can become this. We must constantly recenter spiritually, take our bearings from our deepest sense of call, remain honest with ourselves, keep in communication with our own trusted counselors, maintain appropriate transparency about our human struggles, be sure to take "time out of the bowl" on a regular basis, and never forget that we are on a journey toward holiness (pp. 129–247).

24.8 Accountability, Community, and Freedom

Some readers of this book serve (or will serve) in church contexts in which the very idea that a minister might challenge the actions of a congregant is entirely beyond the pale. Such churches assume or emphasize maximal personal freedom, including the freedom to affiliate quite loosely with the congregation or to move readily from one church to another if anything becomes uncomfortable or displeasing. Sometimes, in Baptist settings, such a maximalist freedom position is explicitly grounded in doctrines like the priesthood of all believers. This core Baptist belief can tend to weaken the role of church authorities and heighten the responsibility of individual believers in their walk with Jesus.

I would suggest that even within a Baptist framework that emphasizes the priesthood of all believers, congregations need a covenantal dimension to their identity, and ministers have a covenant-guarding responsibility. A church is not a church if it is just a loose, temporary affiliation of people who currently find the congregation a pleasing religious product. That is more of a consumerist model than anything like a covenant, in which members enter a disciplined community with shared commitment to a serious journey of Christian discipleship.

I find it impossible to read the New Testament seriously and accept that the minister is just a provider of religious products, with no obligation to care for the souls of the flock, including by providing directive, sometimes corrective, moral counsel. Sondra Wheeler agrees, which is one of the reasons why I find the work of this Methodist ethicist an important contribution to our conversation in this book. We are called to be moral guides to those Christians whom we serve, and we will be held to account by the God who called us.

Discussion Questions

1. Do you believe that ministers are called to keep watch over the souls of their flock and will be held to account for our conduct of this role?

2. Can you think of a time in your ministry or church experience in which you, or a minister you witnessed, spoke a brave, timely, ethical word in a tough situation?

3. Similarly, can you think of such a time in which you, or a minister you witnessed, missed the opportunity to speak such a word?

4. Are you more concerned about ministers intervening too little or too much in the moral lives of those they serve?

5. Do you believe that church membership should be understood as covenantal in the way discussed at the end of this chapter?

To watch Dr. Gushee deliver

Lecture 25: Why Following Jesus Is So Hard

Follow this link:

https://youtu.be/-4nCeN1_cDE

Or scan the QR code.

To listen to the audio, follow this link:

https://qrco.de/bcOllv

Or scan the QR code.

To scan a QR code, download a QR reader from the app store on your device, open the application, follow the directions, and point your device's camera at the code.

CHAPTER 25

Why Following Jesus Is So Hard

*Enter through the narrow gate; for the gate is wide and the road is easy
that leads to destruction, and there are many who take it. For the gate is
narrow and the road is hard that leads to life, and there are few who find it.*

—Mt 7:13-14

25.1 On Facing Christian Moral Failure

In retrospect, I can see that during my long career as a Christian ethicist
I have rotated between hopefulness and disappointment about the moral
performance of Christians. Happy talk about Christian moral goodness
certainly is attractive to Christian audiences and makes us feel good about
ourselves. But it can also be quite misleading and untrue regarding what
happens among real Christian people.

In *The Righteous Gentiles of the Holocaust*, I offered stories and an analysis of the thousands of Christians who rescued Jews during the Holocaust.
Hearing about individuals and groups who risked their lives to save people
targeted for death is intrinsically inspiring. These are indeed stories of *When
Light Pierced the Darkness*, the title of Holocaust survivor Nechama Tec's
1987 book on the rescuers.

Yet the rescuers were a tiny minority—certainly well under 1% of the
Christian population of Europe. The official statistics of the State of Israel
at the time of this writing have documented 27,725 rescuers. Even if there
had been ten times that many rescuers, they would have been a small group.

The vast majority of European Christians were **bystanders**; they neither
helped nor directly harmed their Jewish neighbors. The best study of this
group is a 2000 book by Victoria Barnett called *Bystanders: Conscience and*

Complicity During the Holocaust. In most situations where a group is being harmed, most people in the non-targeted groups choose to be bystanders. They are not directly involved as participants in the evil, but they are not doing anything to help the victims. Bystanders aid perpetrators by their silence, noninvolvement, or indifference.

Finally, another small minority of the European population during the Holocaust were perpetrators in the mass murder of their neighbors. Most of these perpetrators, too, were Christians, by any standard measure—baptism, self-identification, theology, or church membership. It wasn't just "bad old Nazis" who murdered Jews. It was people you might meet in church.

While my first book was about Christian rescuers, a projected upcoming book will be about Christian Nazis. This move represents my work coming full circle. I began my career by wondering what went so right in the moral formation and behavior of a few Christians. Thirty years later, I plan to circle back and ask what went so wrong with many others.

Isn't Christian moral failure a most urgent question? Why is it that Christians so often fail?

It must be that following Jesus is hard. This concluding chapter explores why this is so. In *Kingdom Ethics*, second edition, p. 173, we use a chart known to generations of anguished students as "The Four-Box Diagram." I include a version of it on the next page. The rest of this chapter will deploy it to help us understand why following Jesus is so hard.

25.2 Why Is Following Jesus So Hard?
Because Our Moral Reasoning Is the Tip of the Iceberg

The entire proud history of moral theory emphasizes the great capacities of human reason. Human beings are more than creatures of instinct. We have minds! And not just minds—tremendous, multifaceted, ever-evolving cognitive abilities. We have used our minds to figure out how to fly to the moon, and a fortunate few have done it. What a species to be able to do things like this!

Our rational capacity is one of the most extraordinary things about humanity. It has often been viewed as one of the key markers of our deservedly elevated status, demonstrating that we have been made in the image of God.

Moral philosophers have conceived sublime visions of the human good. They have offered grand theories as to the goals that humans should seek,

Four Dimensions of Character

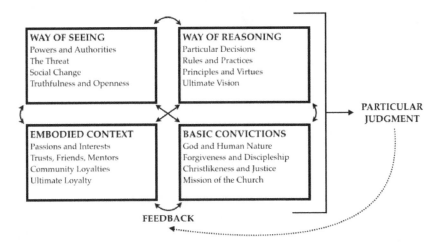

and the rules we should apply to our moral lives. They have offered detailed methods for making sound moral decisions.

All such efforts have tended to operate from the assumption that a human being is something like an airplane, with Reason as the pilot. While some Christian moral theorists may have offered greater attention to other factors that affect moral decision-making, pretty much all Christian ethics assumes a substantial role for high-functioning rational efforts for those who are capable of them.

It is most unfortunate, then, that human beings turn out to be an often-chaotic mess of instincts, impulses, loyalties, emotions, relationships, ideologies, biases, perceptions and misperceptions, interests, fears, and mixed motives. You know how the area behind most people's desks does not look like one strong cord running in a straight line from a computer to the wall, but instead a tangled mass of cords, and you have no idea why some of them are there or what they do? It turns out that human mental functioning is much more like that than we have wanted to admit.

In both editions of *Kingdom Ethics*, Glen Stassen and I put "Way of Reasoning" in the upper-right-box of our diagram in part to signal that what we humans *think we have thought*—what we *reason that we have reasoned*—is deeply affected by other factors that are somehow underneath, or more basic, than reason itself. If we even want to be honest with ourselves, let alone if we want to be faithful followers of Jesus, we must go behind the desk and find out what the tangled mass of cords down there are, and what they are contributing to our supposed reasoning.

There is a word that must be in the working vocabulary of any ethics student—that word is **rationalization**, defined in the *Kingdom Ethics* Glossary as "The mistaken use of reason to justify what should not be justified, or to ascribe reasonable and proper motives for actions motivated by less noble considerations" (p. 470). Human beings use their God-given rational capacities not only to think through problems but also to justify the unjustifiable. Rationalization should be paired with another term, **self-deception**, to remind us that the human capacity to deceive even ourselves seems pretty much infinite.

Think about that complexity for just a minute—a human being is complicated enough that one part of the self often feels the need to try to deceive another part of the self about what the first part is doing, and why. Our very selfhood is often deeply divided, and not just in cases of mental illness. Romans 7:19 gets at this with painful acuteness: "For I do not do the good I want, but the evil I do not want is what I do." Who is the "I" here? How many "I's" are there in one person?

The use of reason for rationalization and self-deception reflects both reason's great power and its corruption under the effects of sin. When we rationalize, we use our fine minds to call evil good and good evil, or to lie about why we are doing what we are doing, whether to someone else or to ourselves. Rationalization takes one of the most sublime capacities of the human being and turns it into a grubby, degraded, and sometimes deadly weapon.

Every time I read another book about Nazi Germany, I am given fresh examples of government rationalization of evil. But you don't have to look to the Nazi government to see governments doing this, or even look to government at all—because we all do it.

One great example in the public policy realm is how wealthy people rarely think that high taxes on the rich are a good government policy. But when they make their arguments against higher taxes on the rich, it is almost never by saying that they just want to keep more of their money. Instead, their argument usually focuses on some rationalization that imposing higher taxes on the rich saps the national work ethic, or costs lower-level workers their jobs. Self-interest distorts our reasoning—you can count on it—unless conscious actions are undertaken to counter its impact, but, even then, it rarely seems that self-interest is entirely overcome.

One reason why following Jesus is so hard is because the very minds we use to discern what Jesus wants from us are corrupted by sin. Our efforts to reason our way through situations, to interpret the Bible, or to apply a moral theory in real life, are affected by forces of which we may not even be aware. Watch out for those who are unaware of their own capacity for rationalization, for these are the most dangerous people of all.

25.3 Why Is Following Jesus So Hard? Because Our Perceptions Are So Easily Distorted

If we have functioning eyesight, we look at the world through our eyes— eyes which are such remarkable instruments that they are often still used as evidence of divine creation of this world.

But some people do not perceive color at all, or some colors, or very well. My father was so poor at perceiving and matching colors that my mother took over his outfit selections early in their marriage, and grateful co-workers were the lifetime beneficiaries. Other people do not see well at night. Some people have difficulty reading because the words on the page appear backwards to them. Hardly anyone has 20/20 vision, and almost no one has perfect vision over the entirety of their lives.

Vision has another level. Some people just seem to "see better" than others. Poets and painters, for example, seem to see more clearly, more fully, more acutely, than regular people do. Some people seem to see more details than others do. I know that I would make for a lousy witness in court because I miss a lot of details. I think it may be because I am so often distracted by whatever I am thinking about. Or maybe I just never trained myself to be very observant.

The word **discernment** is used in relation to both ethics and sight. The term "blind spot" is also used in this manner. Ethicists have never been able to avoid metaphors involving sight. Everything about ethics involves sight, discernment, and vision. Ethics is deeply implicated in what exactly we "see" when the pregnant teenager comes to us for advice, or what we "see" when we glimpse a police officer, or what we "see" when we look at a dying person in the hospital. Then there is moral discernment—what we discern when an extremist politician begins gathering large crowds, or when a homeless person asks us for money, or when government bails out failing banks during a financial crisis.

Moral vision is a useful term in ethics to describe our big-picture lens for looking at people, the world, or the future. Martin Luther King's most famous big-picture moral vision was of the "Beloved Community," and it resonates to this day. Purity has often been a moral vision, as have holiness, patriotism, honor, and strict obedience to God's law. Concepts we have already considered, like the sacredness of life, can be described as a moral vision, for when we really think of every person as sacred, it can deeply affect how we treat people.

Likewise, if our corrupted moral vision is of a racial hierarchy based on color, or an intelligence hierarchy based on IQ, or a sexual hierarchy based on gender, that is what we will see when we look at people. One amazing thing about human life is that *we* get to make the basic life decision as to how we will view the world. Sometimes the decisions we make are beautiful and give life. Other times they are hateful and harm life. This is entirely up to us.

Kingdom Ethics emphasizes three specific arenas in which moral perception is important and often distorted—how we perceive this world's powers and authorities, how we view the site of the most important threats to our well-being, and what we see as the best paths to social change. Because our perceptions are *always* prone to distortion, we must be committed to truth and constantly open to self-correction. Repentance should be a regular and expected part of following Jesus, and a big part of it is repenting of bad ways of seeing moral reality.

This, then, is the second reason why following Jesus is so hard—because our moral perceptions are commonly damaged, and we have abundant moral blind spots, sometimes from factors inside us and sometimes from factors outside us.

While we have plenty of resources for attempting to align our vision with that of Jesus, we are also beset by many possible vision-distorting powers. It is no surprise that Jesus so often spoke of sight, with striking comments like this: "The eye is the lamp of the body. So, if your eye is healthy, your whole body will be full of light; but if your eye is unhealthy, your whole body will be full of darkness" (Mt 6:22–23). Jesus was not speaking about ocular nerves, but moral perception.

25.4 Why Is Following Jesus So Hard? Because We Are Bodies in Context

Of the many contributions of Glen Stassen's ethics, I personally have found his ideas now covered under the label **embodied context** in *Kingdom Ethics* to be among the most illuminating. Let me try a fresh approach to presenting it here.

Let's start by taking a hammer to the fantasy that human beings are, or can be, piloted strictly by Reason. We are not disembodied minds. Instead, we are embodied spirits. Our reasoning capacity is tied to organic matter, to physicality and nature, not just to our brain but to our entire human body.

Moreover, human bodies exist in specific places, in relationship to specific persons, living in a certain manner. These bodies, situated in particular contexts, over time become sites of memories, which exist not only in our brains but in our entire selves. I think of how the long scar on my right leg is a site of memory of a horrific accident of my childhood.

Our embodied selves also are associated with practices that we do with our bodies. These could range to loading trucks each week with food for the poor, to bulimia, to rummaging through dumpsters to find something to eat during a time of poverty, to swimming at the country club, to cradling a child, to shouting out our lungs at a football game, to going hunting with Grandpa.

The relationships we have experienced in our bodies shape us, as do the memories most powerfully inscribed, and the practices most often undertaken, in our bodies. If we are asked to "reason" or "discern" about something, we will be affected by the experiences we have had in our bodies and the beloved people with whom we have had them. Likely we will be loyal, perhaps unduly loyal, to those individuals and communities we bodily associate with our happiest experiences. We will find it difficult to reason, perceive, or choose in a way that directly or indirectly repudiates them.

Where we have trusted ourselves most deeply to others, including groups, we will find it difficult to admit that this trust could have been misplaced. Because we have a stake in feeling good about ourselves, our memories, and our loved ones, we will have difficulty making new moral choices that demonstrate that our former good feelings were inappropriate. We are more likely to misperceive current situations, to rationalize potential wrong courses of action, or to remain loyal to persons unworthy of it.

Someone suggests hunting is wrong, but (consciously or not) your embodied self is loyal to good times with Grandpa. Someone asks whether Christians really should support war, but you feel the tug connecting you to your parents in the military. Someone wonders whether Christians should buy memberships at exclusive country clubs, but some of your best times were spent there when you were a kid. Someone says boxing clearly causes brain injuries, but you were a great fighter and never felt better about yourself than during those golden days.

So: Why is following Jesus so hard? Because we dwell in embodied contexts that quite easily misdirect us from Jesus' way to other ways due to the relationships, passions, trusts, loyalties, memories, and hurts that are inscribed upon us. There is little we can do about these other than to name them, own their power, and submit them to Jesus, even to the point of renunciation.

25.5 Why Is Following Jesus So Hard? Because We Worship Idols Rather Than Jesus

You shall have no other gods before me.

—*Ex 20:3*

Now large crowds were traveling with him; and he turned and said to them, "Whoever comes to me and does not hate father and mother, wife and children, brothers and sisters, yes, and even life itself, cannot be my disciple. Whoever does not carry the cross and follow me cannot be my disciple."

—*Lk 14:25–27*

In *Kingdom Ethics*, the lower right box of the four-box diagram is called "Basic Convictions." It lists convictions about God and human nature, forgiveness and discipleship, Christlikeness and justice, and the mission of the church.

Recall that convictions provide the ultimate foundation for principles, from which we derive rules, which ultimately lead to our judgments in specific situations.

Basic theological convictions could hardly be more important in grounding the moral discernment process that is supposed to lead Christians toward faithful following of Jesus Christ. This is one good reason for the strong emphasis on doctrinal clarity, even purity, in many Christian circles.

Theology certainly matters. But the challenging part is that there have been various versions of even orthodox, traditional Christian theology, and huge disputes over which theological approaches best understand Jesus and contribute to faithful discipleship. There is a contrast, for example, between the theological tradition that mainly runs through Christ crucified in Paul's writings, to Augustine, and then to Luther, over against another that mainly runs from the prophets, to the teachings of Jesus, to the early church, to the Anabaptists, to the Social Gospel, to liberationism.

Even if we do get some solid theology going among a group of Christians, it may not produce Jesus-following moral convictions. There are lots of Christians who are all theology, little ethics.

And then, even if we somehow manage to get both good theology and good moral convictions in place, we may not be good at practicing them in real life. That could be because we never learned how, or because we got distracted—or even because we got seduced away from following Jesus.

The seduction away from Jesus could have happened when someone (a friend, role model, lover, pastor, or politician perhaps) or something (wealth, power, sex, attention) ended up taking the role of our ultimate loyalty when it should have been Jesus.

But even worse, it might have happened when we were no longer able to discern the difference between Jesus and the Idol, and thought we were following Jesus when we were actually following the Idol. When we lose the ability to tell the difference between Yahweh and Baal, or Jesus and [fill in your idol here], then we are well and truly lost, deep in the land of idolatry.

In the very worst case, everything can go wrong, even for devout Christian people. Our basic convictions can fall short of good Christian theology, or even get twisted beyond recognition. Our embodied context, teeming with loyalties other than to Jesus, can set us far off course. Our way of seeing reality and of discerning our responsibilities as Christ-followers can become hopelessly confused—all blind spots, no clear vision. When all of that is going on, our reasoning, logic, and arguments can become nothing more than making excuses for the demonic.

This is indeed what happened among far too many Christians in a Germany that became Nazi overnight in January 1933. Loyalty to nation, race, lost sons in WWI, and Hitler characterized the embodied context. Theology became Germanized and racialized, often quite explicitly. Some Christians literally wanted to cut the Old Testament and some of the New Testament out of the Bible because these parts were seen as too Jewish. Perceptions got distorted—Christians could not discern that Nazi violence and tyranny violated basic justice and must therefore be resisted. And some of Germany's finest theologians, biblical scholars, lawyers, and other specialists used their exquisite reasoning skills to call good evil, and evil good, often in the name of Jesus.

Why is it so hard to follow Jesus? Because we are easily led into idolatry. John Calvin (1509–1564) was right in saying that the human heart is a veritable factory of idols. Or to use a modern image, idolatry may be the default setting of the human heart. Even God's chosen and beloved people—even those who have every reason to know better—are susceptible to idolatry. Truly the gate is wide and the road is easy that leads to destruction.

Education doesn't protect us from idolatry. Churchgoing doesn't protect us. Awesome worship services don't protect us. Knowing Greek and Hebrew doesn't protect us.

Christian ethics as a discipline attempts to help Christians understand what following Jesus looks like. During our study we have encountered many tools that can help. But, ultimately, following Jesus is about far more than the knowledge of ethics or any other discipline. It is about keeping our hearts free of any idol that would displace Jesus Christ as Lord. That, in turn, is spiritual work, undertaken through the quiet disciplines of daily prayer, Bible reading, and theological and ethical study. Also indispensable is participation in a community of Christians who journey with us on the narrow road of covenant fidelity to Christ. The way is hard, but the journey's end is everlasting life in the kingdom of God.

Discussion Questions

1. Try to think of other examples of gross moral failure on the part of Christians that you have read about or known. What went wrong?

2. Can you think of a situation in which you now recognize that you misperceived or wrongly discerned what was going on, or what you were supposed to do?

3. What do you think of the idea that moral reasoning is just the tip of the iceberg of how we actually make decisions? Can you think of any examples of major rationalizations that you have seen being offered?

4. Try to come up with at least one example per person of a loyalty, memory, or practice that might affect your moral discernment today.

5. Discuss the idea that idolatry may be the human default setting, and that following Jesus faithfully is what is exceptional.

Works Cited

Alexander, Michelle. *The New Jim Crow*. New York: The New Press, 2010.

Athenagoras. "A Plea for the Christians." In *Ante-Nicene Fathers*, Volume 2, edited by Alexander Roberts and James Donaldson. Peabody, MA: Hendrickson Publishers, 2004: 123–148.

Bainton, Roland. *Christian Attitudes Toward War and Peace*. Nashville: Abingdon Press, 1960.

Baldwin, James. *The Fire Next Time*. In *James Baldwin: Collected Essays*, edited by Toni Morrison. New York: Library of America, [1963] 1998.

Baldwin, James. *Go Tell It on the Mountain*. New York: Dell, [1952] 1980.

Barnett, Victoria J. *Bystanders: Conscience and Complicity During the Holocaust*. Westport, CT: Praeger, 2000.

Barr, Beth Allison. *The Making of Biblical Womanhood: How the Subjugation of Women Became Gospel Truth*. Grand Rapids, MI: Brazos, 2021.

Bendroth, Margaret Lamberts. *Fundamentalism and Gender*. New Haven and London: Yale University Press, 1993.

Biggar, Nigel. *In Defence of War*. Oxford: Oxford University Press, 2013.

Birch, Bruce C., and Larry L. Rasmussen. *Bible and Ethics in the Christian Life*, revised and expanded edition. Minneapolis: Augsburg Fortress, 1989.

Bonhoeffer, Dietrich. *Discipleship*. Dietrich Bonhoeffer Works, Vol. 4. English edition edited by Geffrey B. Kelly and John D. Godsey. Minneapolis: Fortress Press, 2001.

Bonhoeffer, Dietrich. *Ethics*. Dietrich Bonhoeffer Works, Vol. 6. English edition edited by Clifford J. Green. Minneapolis: Fortress Press, 2005.

Bonhoeffer, Dietrich. *Letters and Papers from Prison*. Dietrich Bonhoeffer Works, Vol. 8. English edition edited by John W. de Gruchy. Minneapolis: Fortress Press, 2010.

Bonhoeffer, Dietrich. "What Is Meant By 'Telling the Truth'" In *Ethics*. New York: Simon & Schuster, 1995: 358–367.

Butler, Octavia. *Kindred*. Boston: Beacon Press, 1979.

Cahill, Lisa Sowle. *Blessed Are the Peacemakers*. Minneapolis: Fortress Press, 2019.

Camosy, Charles. *Beyond the Abortion Wars*. Grand Rapids, MI: Eerdmans Publishing Company, 2015.

Camosy, Charles. *For Love of Animals*. Cincinnati: Franciscan Media, 2013.

Campolo, Tony. *How to Rescue the Earth without Worshipping Nature*. Nashville: Thomas Nelson,1992.

Cannon, Katie Geneva. *Black Womanist Ethics*. Atlanta: Scholars Press, 1988.

Cannon, Katie Geneva, Emilie M. Townes, and Angela D. Sims, editors. *Black Womanist Ethics*. Louisville: Westminster John Knox Press, 2011.

Cantorna, Amber. *Refocusing My Family*. Minneapolis: Fortress Press, 2017.

Carnahan, Keven. *From Presumption to Prudence in Just-War Rationality*. London: Routledge, 2017.

Catechism of the Catholic Church, 2nd edition. New York: Doubleday, 1995.

Chilton, Bruce. *Pure Kingdom*. Grand Rapids, MI: Eerdmans Publishing Company, 1996.

Christians for Biblical Equality. "Men, Women, and Biblical Equality." 1989. cbeinternational.org | https://www.cbeinternational.org/sites/default/files/english_0.pdf

Chu, Jeff. *Does Jesus Really Love Me?* New York: HarperCollins, 2013.

Clough, David. *On Animals: Volume 2: Theological Ethics*. London: T &T Clark, 2019.

Coates, Ta-Nehisi, *Between the World and Me*. New York: Spiegel & Grau, 2015.

Cone, James H. *God of the Oppressed*. New York: HarperSanFrancisco, 1975.

Cone, James H. *A Black Theology of Liberation*. New York: J.B. Lippincott, 1970.

The Council on Biblical Manhood and Womanhood. "The Danvers Statement." 1988. The Danvers Statement – CBMW: https://cbmw.org/about/danvers-statement/

Davies, W.D. *The Setting of the Sermon on the Mount*. Cambridge: Cambridge University Press, 1964.

De La Torre, Miguel A. *Embracing Hopelessness*. Minneapolis: Fortress Press, 2017.

De La Torre, Miguel A, editor. *Ethics: A Liberative Approach*. Minneapolis: Fortress Press, 2013.

Delgado, Richard, and Jean Stefancic. *Critical Race Theory*. New York: NYU Press, 2012.

"Didache." Didache: The Teaching of the Twelve Apostles https:// legacyicons.com/content/didache.pdf.

Douglas, Kelly Brown. *Sexuality and the Black Church*. Maryknoll, NY: Orbis Books, 1999.

Douglass, Frederick. "If There is No Struggle There is No Progress." (1857) Frederick Douglass, "If There Is No Struggle, There Is No Progress" | Blackpast.org https://www.blackpast.org/african-american-history/1857-frederick-douglass-if-there-no-struggle-there-no-progress/

Du Mez, Kristen Kobes. *Jesus and John Wayne*. New York: Liveright Publishing, 2020.

DuBois, W.E.B. *The Souls of Black Folk*. New York: Barnes & Noble Classics, [1903] 2003.

Dyck, Arthur C. *Life's Worth*. Grand Rapids: Eerdmans Publishing Company, 2002.

Eig, Jonathan. *The Birth of the Pill*. New York: W.W. Norton & Company, 2015.

Ellsberg, Robert, editor. *Gandhi on Christianity*. Maryknoll, NY: Orbis Books, 1991.

"The Epistle of Barnabas." In Roberts, Alexander, and James Donaldson, editors. *Ante-Nicene Fathers*, Volume 1. Peabody, MA: Hendrickson Publishers, 2004:133–150.

Ericksen, Robert. *Theologians Under Hitler*. New Haven and London: Yale University Press, 1985.

"An Evangelical Declaration against Torture." Reprinted in David P. Gushee, *The Future of Faith in American Politics*. Waco, TX: Baylor University Press, 2008: 253–270.

Finn, Daniel K. *Christian Economic Ethics*. Minneapolis: Fortress Press, 2013.

Fletcher, Joseph. *Situation Ethics*. Louisville: Westminster John Knox Press, [1966] 1998.

Frei, Hans. *The Eclipse of Biblical Narrative*. New Haven and London: Yale University Press, 1974.

Gaines, Ernest. *The Autobiography of Miss Jane Pittman*. New York: Bantam Books, 1971.

Gaines, Ernest. *A Gathering of Old Men*. New York: Vintage, 1983.

Gilkes, Cheryl Townsend. "The 'Loves' and 'Troubles' of African American Women's Bodies: The Womanist Challenge to Cultural Humiliation and Community Ambivalence." In Katie Geneva Cannon, et. al., editors. *Womanist Theological Ethics*. Louisville: Westminster John Knox Press, 201: 81-97.

Gilligan, Carol. *In a Different Voice*. Cambridge, MA: Harvard University Press, 1982.

Gold, Mitchell, with Mindy Drucker. *Crisis*. Austin, TX: Greenleaf Book Group Press, 2008.

Grant, Jacqueline. *White Women's Christ and Black Women's Jesus*. Atlanta: Scholars Press, 1989.

Green, Joel. *The Gospel of Luke*. New International Commentary on the New Testament. Grand Rapids, MI: Eerdmans, 1997.

Grenz, Stanley J. *The Moral Quest*. Downers Grove, IL: IVP Academic, 2000.

Gross, Fred. *One Step Ahead of Hitler*. Macon, GA: Mercer University Press, 2009.

Gushee, David P. *After Evangelicalism*. Louisville: Westminster John Knox Press, 2020.

Gushee, David P. *Changing Our Mind*, 3rd edition. Canton, MI: Read the Spirit Books, 2017.

Gushee, David P. "Five Reasons Torture Is Always Wrong." https://www.christianitytoday.com/ct/2006/february/23.32.html *Christianity Today*, February 1, 2006.

Gushee, David P. *The Future of Faith in American Politics*. Waco, TX: Baylor University Press, 2008.

Gushee, David P. *Getting Marriage Right*. Grand Rapids: Baker Books, 2004.

Gushee, David P. *The Righteous Gentiles of the Holocaust*, 2nd edition. Minneapolis: Paragon House, 2003.

Gushee, David P. "In the Ruins of White Evangelicalism: Interpreting a Compromised Christian Tradition through the Witness of African-American Literature." *Journal of the American Academy of Religion* 87, 1 (March 2019): 1–17.

Gushee, David P. *The Sacredness of Human Life*. Grand Rapids: Eerdmans Publishing Company, 2013.

Gushee, David P., and Glen H. Stassen. *Kingdom Ethics*, 2nd edition. Grand Rapids: Eerdmans Publishing Company, 2016. (First Edition: Intervarsity Press, 2003.)

Gutierrez, Gustavo. *A Theology of Liberation*. Maryknoll, New York: Orbis Books, [1971] 1973.

Haas, Peter J. *Morality After Auschwitz*. Philadelphia: Fortress Press, 1988.

Harrison, Beverly Wildung. *Justice in the Making*. Louisville: Westminster John Knox Press, 2004.

Harrison, Beverly Wildung. *Our Right to Choose*. Boston: Beacon Press, 1983.

Harvey, Paul. *Howard Thurman and the Disinherited*. Grand Rapids, MI: Eerdmans Publishing Company, 2020.

Hauerwas, Stanley. *A Community of Character*. Notre Dame, IN: University of Notre Dame Press, 1981.

Hauerwas, Stanley, and L. Gregory Jones, editors. *Why Narrative?* Grand Rapids: Eerdmans Publishing Company, 1989.

Hugenberger, Gordon. *Marriage as a Covenant*. Grand Rapids, MI: Baker Books, 1998.

Hughes, Langston. *The Ways of White Folks*. New York: Vintage Classics, [1933] 1990.

Hughes, Langston. *Not Without Laughter*. New York: Scribner Paperback Fiction, [1930] 1995.

Hurston, Zora Neale. *Their Eyes Were Watching God*. New York: HarperPerennial Modern Classics, [1937] 2006.

Jewett, Robert. *Romans*. Hermeneia Commentary. Minneapolis: Fortress Press, 2007.

Johnson, James Turner. *Morality and Contemporary Warfare*. New Haven/ London: Yale University Press, 1999.

Johnson, James Turner. *The Holy War Idea in Western and Islamic Traditions*. University Park, PA: Pennsylvania State University Press, 1997.

Jones, David H. *Moral Responsibility in the Holocaust*. Lanham, MD: Rowman & Littlefield, 1999.

Jones, L. Gregory. *Embodying Forgiveness*. Grand Rapids, MI: Eerdmans Publishing Company, 1995.

Kant, Immanuel. *The Critique of Practical* Reason, revised edition. Translated by Mary Gregor. Cambridge: Cambridge University Press, [1788] 2015.

Kilner, John F., Arlene B. Miller, and Edmund D. Pellegrino, editors. *Dignity and Dying*. Grand Rapids, MI: Eerdmans Publishing Company, 1996.

King, Martin Luther, Jr. "Letter from Birmingham City Jail." In A Testament of Hope, edited by James Melvin Washington. San Francisco: Harper & Row, [1963] 1986.

Klein, Linda Kay. *Pure*. New York: Touchstone, 2019.

Knapp, Jennifer. *Facing the Music*. New York: Howard Books, 2014.

Knowlton, Paul and Aaron Hedges. *A Better Capitalism*. Eugene, OR: Wipf & Stock, 2021.

Kristof, Nicholas D., and Sheryl WuDunn. *Half the Sky*. New York: Vintage, 2010.

Lebacqz, Karen. *Justice in an Unjust World*. Minneapolis: Augsburg Publishing House, 1987.

Lebacqz, Karen. *Professional Ethics*. Nashville: Abingdon Press, 1985.

Lee, Hak Joon. *Christian Ethics: A New Covenant Model*. Grand Rapids, MI: Eerdmans Publishing Company, 2021.

Lee, Justin. *Torn*. New York: Jericho Books, 2012.

Lindbeck, George A. *The Nature of Doctrine*. Philadelphia: Westminster Press, 1984.

Littell, Franklin H. and Hubert G. Locke, editors. *The German Church Struggle and the Holocaust.* San Francisco: Mellen Research University Press, 1990.

Luther, Martin. *On the Jews and Their Lies.* In Luther's Works, Volume 47. Edited by Franklin Sherman. Philadelphia: Fortress Press, [1543] 1971.

Maass, Peter. *Love Thy Neighbor: A Story of War.* New York: Alfred A. Knopf, 1996.

MacIntyre, Alasdair. *After Virtue.* Notre Dame, IN: University of Notre Dame Press, 1981.

Mackie, J.L. *Ethics: Inventing Right and Wrong.* New York: Penguin Books, 1977.

McClendon, James Wm., and James M. Smith. *Defusing Religious Relativism*, revised edition. Valley Forge, PA: Trinity Press International, 1994.

Megivern, James J. *The Death Penalty.* New York: Paulist Press, 1997.

Miller, Nicholas. *The Religious Roots of the First Amendment.* Oxford: Oxford University Press, 2012.

Morrison, Toni. *Beloved.* New York: Vintage, [1987] 2004.

Mott, Stephen Charles. *Biblical Ethics and Social Change*, 2nd edition. Oxford: Oxford University Press, 2011.

National Conference of Catholic Bishops. *The Challenge of Peace.* Washington: United States Catholic Conference, 1983.

Niebuhr, H. Richard. "The Responsibility of the Church for Society. In *The Gospel, the Church, and the World*, edited by Kenneth Scott Latourette. New York: Harper, 1946: 111–133.

Niebuhr, H. Richard. *The Responsible Self.* New York: Harper & Row, 1963.

Niebuhr, Reinhold. *An Interpretation of Christian Ethics.* New York: Harper & Brothers, 1935.

Niebuhr, Reinhold. *Moral Man and Immoral Society.* New York: Charles Scribner's Sons, 1932.

Nietzsche, Friedrich. *Human, All Too Human.* Lincoln, NE: University of Nebraska Press, [1878] 1996.

Nietzsche, Friedrich. *Twilight of the Idols.* New York: Penguin Books, [1889] 1985.

Northcott, Michael S. *The Environment and Christian Ethics*. Cambridge: Cambridge University Press, 1996.

Noyce, Gaylord. *Pastoral Ethics*. Nashville: Abingdon Press, 1988.

Nygren, Anders. *Agape and Eros*. London: SPCK, [1932] 1954.

O'Donovan, Oliver. *The Desire of the Nations*. Cambridge: Cambridge University Press, 1996.

"Origen Contra Celsus." In *Ante-Nicene Fathers*, Volume 4, edited by Alexander Roberts and James Donaldson. Peabody, MA: Hendrickson Publishers, 2004: 395–669.

Outka, Gene. *Agape: An Ethical Analysis*. New Haven: Yale University Press, 1972.

Parham, Robert. *Loving Neighbors Across Time*. Atlanta: New Hope Publishing, 1992.

Peters, Ted. *God: The World's Future*. Minneapolis: Fortress Press, 1992.

Phillips, Roderick. *Untying the Knot*. Cambridge: Cambridge University Press, 1991.

Pontifical Council for Justice and Peace. *Compendium of the Social Doctrine of the Church*. Washington: United States Council of Catholic Bishops, 2004.

Pope John Paul II. *The Gospel of Life (Evangelium Vitae)*. New York: Times Books, 1995.

Rasmussen, Larry L. *Earth Community, Earth Ethics*. Maryknoll, NY: Orbis Books, 1996.

Rasmussen, Larry L. *Earth-Honoring Faith*. Oxford: Oxford University Press, 2013.

Rauschenbusch, Walter. *Christianity and the Social Crisis. In Walter Rauschenbusch: Published Works and Selected Writings*, Vol. 1, edited by William H. Brackney. Macon, GA: Mercer University Press, [1907] 2018.

Ruether, Rosemary Radford. *Faith and Fratricide*. Minneapolis: Seabury Press, 1974.

Shriver, Donald W., Jr. *An Ethic for Enemies*. New York and Oxford: Oxford University Press, 1995.

Sider, Ronald J. *Just Politics*, 2nd edition. Grand Rapids, MI: Brazos, 2012.

Sider, Ronald J. *Rich Christians in an Age of Hunger*, 4th edition. Dallas: Word Publishing, 1997.

Skillen, James W. *Recharging the American Experiment*. Grand Rapids, MI: Baker Books, 1994.

Snyder, Howard A., with Joel Scandrett. *Salvation Means Creation Healed*. Eugene, OR: Cascade Books, 2011.

Stassen, Glen H., editor. *Just Peacemaking*. Cleveland: Pilgrim Press, 2008.

Steffen, Lloyd. *Holy War, Just War*. Lanham, MD: Rowman & Littlefield, 2007.

Sullivan-Dunbar, Sandra. *Human Dependency and Christian Ethics*. Cambridge: Cambridge University Press, 2017.

Tec, Nechama. *When Light Pierced the Darkness*. New York: Oxford University Press, 1987.

Thurman, Howard. *Jesus and the Disinherited*. Boston: Beacon Press, [1949] 1976.

Townes, Emilie. *Womanist Justice, Womanist Hope*. Atlanta: Scholars Press, 1993.

Trull, Joe E, and James E. Carter. *Ministerial Ethics*, 2nd edition. Grand Rapids, MI: Baker Academic, 2004.

Vacek, Edward Collins, S.J. *Love, Human and Divine*. Washington: Georgetown University Press, 1994.

Walker, Alice. *The Color Purple*. New York: Harcourt, [1982] 2003.

Waller, James. *Becoming Evil*, 2nd edition. New York: Oxford University Press, 2007.

Wallerstein, Judith, Julia M. Lewis, and Sandra Blakeslee. *The Unexpected Legacy of Divorce*. New York: Hyperion, 2000.

Walzer, Michael. *In God's Shadow*. New Haven: Yale University Press, 2012.

Walzer, Michael. *Exodus and Revolution*. New York: Basic Books, 1984

Weems, Renita. *Just a Sister Away*. Publishing/Editing Network, 1988.

Weikart, Richard. *Hitler's Ethic*. New York: Palgrave Macmillan, 2009.

Wells, Samuel. *Improvisation*. Grand Rapids, MI: Brazos, 2004.

Wennberg, Robert. *God, Human, and Animals*. Grand Rapids, MI: Eerdmans Publishing Company, 2003.

West, Dorothy. *The Wedding*. New York: Doubleday, 1995.

Wheeler, Sondra. *The Minister as Moral Theologian*. Grand Rapids, MI: Baker Academic, 2017.

Wheeler, Sondra. *What We Were Made For*. San Francisco: Jossey-Bass, 2007.

White, Lynn. "The Historical Roots of Our Ecological Crisis." *Science* 155 (1967): 1203–1207.

Whitehead, Barbara Dafoe. *The Divorce Culture*. New York: Alfred A. Knopf, 1997.

Wiest, Walter E., and Elwyn A. Smith. *Ethics in Ministry*. Minneapolis: Fortress Press, 1990.

Wilcox, W. Bradford. *Soft Patriarchs, New Men*. Chicago: University of Chicago Press, 2004.

Wilkinson, Loren. *Earthkeeping in the '90s*. Grand Rapids, MI: Eerdmans Publishing Company, 1991.

Wirzba, Norman. *Food and Faith*, 2nd edition. Cambridge: Cambridge University Press, 2019.

Wogaman, J. Philip. *Christian Ethics: A Historical Introduction*. Louisville: Westminster John Knox Press, 1993.

Wogaman, J. Philip and Douglas M. Strong, editors. *Readings in Christian Ethics*. Louisville: Westminster John Knox, 1996.

Wolterstorff, Nicholas. *Justice: Rights and Wrongs*. Princeton and Oxford: Princeton University Press, 2008.

Wright, N.T. *Jesus and the Victory of God*. Minneapolis: Fortress Press, 1996.

Wright, Richard. *Native Son*. New York: HarperPerennial Modern Classics, [1940] 2005.

Yoder, John Howard. *Nevertheless*. Scottdale, PA: Herald Press, 1971.

Yoder, John Howard. *The Politics of Jesus*. Grand Rapids, MI: Eerdmans Publishing Company, 1972.

Zimmermann, Jens. *Dietrich Bonhoeffer's Christian Humanism*. Oxford: Oxford University Press, 2019.

Also by David P. Gushee

Kingdom Ethics, Second Edition:
Following Jesus in Contemporary Context

David Gushee and Glen Stassen's *Kingdom Ethics* is
the leading Christian introductory ethics textbook
for the 21st century. Solidly rooted in Scripture—
and uniquely focusing on Jesus's teachings in the
Sermon on the Mount—the book has offered
students, pastors, and other readers a comprehensive
and challenging framework for Christian ethical
thought.

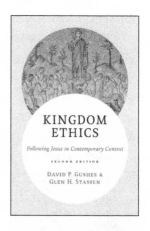

Changing Our Mind: Definitive Third Edition of the
Landmark Call for Inclusion of LGBTQ Christians
with Response to Critics

Changing Our Mind has helped thousands of families and congregations carefully and compassionately
rethink traditional religious teachings about full
LGBTQ inclusion. Dr. Gushee offers a powerful,
inspiring message of hope and healing by helping
Christians to return to Bible study, prayer, and
reflection in a way that creates a vision for a more
inclusive church.

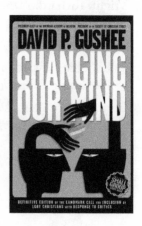

About the Author

Dr. David P. Gushee (PhD, Union Theological Seminary, New York) is Distinguished University Professor of Christian Ethics at Mercer University, Chair of Christian Social Ethics Vrije Universiteit Amsterdam, and Senior Research Fellow, International Baptist Theological Study Centre.

Gushee is the elected Past-President of both the American Academy of Religion and Society of Christian Ethics, signaling his role as one of America's leading Christian ethicists. He is the author, co-author, editor, or co-editor of 25 books and approximately 175 book chapters, journal articles, and reviews. His most recognized works include Righteous Gentiles of the Holocaust, Kingdom Ethics, and The Sacredness of Human Life. Also, with his Changing Our Mind and After Evangelicalism, he charts a theological and ethical course for post-evangelical Christians, a course he more personally relates in his memoir, Still Christian.

Over a full 28-year career, he's been a devoted teacher as Professor Gushee to college students, seminarians, and PhD students. He's also led activist efforts on climate, torture, and LGBTQ inclusion, and is a keynote speaker at churches, forums, and universities.

For the general media, Dr. Gushee has written hundreds of opinion pieces and given interviews to major outlets and podcasts. Along with his friend Jeremy Hall, he also co-hosts the podcast "Kingdom Ethics."

Dr. Gushee and his wife Jeanie live in Atlanta, and you can connect with him and subscribe to his newsletter at davidpgushee.com or follow @dpgushee on social media.

CPSIA information can be obtained
at www.ICGtesting.com
Printed in the USA
BVHW031227220222
629770BV00001B/75

9 781641 801270